PREHISTORY
IN THE PEAK

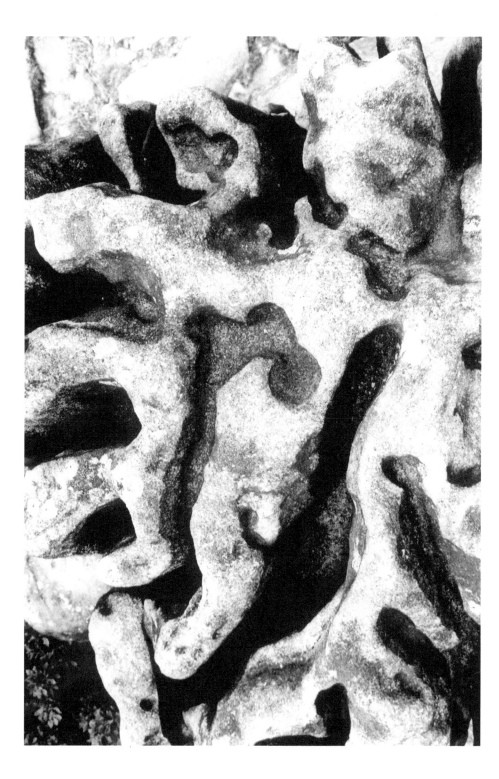

PREHISTORY
IN THE PEAK

MARK EDMONDS & TIM SEABORNE

The
History
Press

First published in 2001 by Tempus Publishing
Reprinted 2002, 2005

Reprinted in 2010 by
The History Press
The Mill, Brimscombe Port
Stroud, Gloucestershire GL5 2QG
www.thehistorypress.co.uk

British Library Cataloguing in Publication Data.
A catalogue record for this book is available from the British Library.

ISBN 978 0 7524 1483 6

Typesetting and origination by Tempus Publishing.
Printed and bound in Great Britain.

Contents

1 Walking in

Rivelin

. . . And now I am come to this wonderful place, the Peak, where you will expect I should do as some others have (I think foolishly) done before me, viz, tell you strange long stories of wonders as (I must say) they are most weakly called. Now to have a man so great as Mr Hobbes and after him Mr Cotton, celebrate the trifles here, the first in a fine latin poem, the last in English verse, as if they were the most exalted wonders in the world: I cannot but, after wondering at their making wonders of them, desire you, my friend, to travel with me through this howling wilderness in your imagination, and you shall soon find all that is wonderful about it . . .
Daniel Defoe 1725

Mist and fog are common in the Peak. Even those who know their way can find themselves at odds with their surroundings, uncertain as to terrain, the path ahead or the path behind. It is easy to get lost, to take false trails or come full circle. It is like that in the study of prehistory. There are few landmarks and only the occasional glimpse of paths worth taking. Terra incognita.

This book is a journey along some of those paths. An attempt to explore how people's lives unfolded over some 10,000 years in what we now call the Peak District. It moves between prominent landmarks, monuments that can still be seen today. It also fastens onto 'small things forgotten'; those more ephemeral traces that sometimes catch the eye on the trail. In a sense, it is about learning how to look.

The region has a chequered history to match the varied topography. On both the limestone and the grits — the White Peak and the Dark — there is ground where prehistory still stands above the surface. Barrows, stone circles and far older tombs. There are also building platforms and fields, plots where people turned the earth, and cliffs in deep valleys where they quarried for stone. In all, a wide range of features over a broad span of time. In other areas, history from the Medieval period onwards has often been written 'on the ground' to the detriment of far older traces. Though destruction has not been total, much has been lost.

The situation could be worse. In fact, we know a good deal, most of it thanks to the sustained and dedicated efforts of a relatively small number of people. Antiquarians like Hayman Rooke, Samuel Pegge and Thomas Bateman, excavated and recorded what they saw, albeit through the filter of their times and with varying degrees of licence. As far back as 1788, Rooke was driven to write; 'I must beg leave to observe, that no place affords a more ample field for the antiquary's investigation than the uncultivated parts of the Peak. There is hardly a crag, hill or an assemblage of rocks, where the remains of British or Roman antiquities cannot be found.' Later generations have taken Rooke at his word. There are few recognised prehistoric monuments that do not bear the scars of prior investigation. Most were dug in the nineteenth century and a good deal of what gets done today is the excavation of Victorian archives.

In the last century or so, work has continued on several fronts. Individuals returning again and again to dig monuments on the same stretch of moor; people working more extensively, but concentrating on specific classes of site. More recently, the growth of archaeology as part of the planning process has led to an explosion of 'developer-funded' work, all of it adding more detail. As time has passed, we have been able to take these different elements and combine them in a broader picture. The image is still a sketch. But it is a start, and is only possible because more recent work has often been broad and inclusive in its scope: survey, excavation and source criticism; the mapping of entire landscapes and the analysis of ancient pollen and sediment.

There is another factor that works to our advantage. The survival of a good many prehistoric monuments is accidental. Barrows or stone circles that lie outwith the main areas of Medieval and post-Medieval agriculture have had the good fortune to escape the ravages of the plough. Those on cultivated 'intake' land have usually fared rather worse. Yet there are also sites where survival seems more considered, even deliberate. In certain places it is clear that historic communities fostered or rediscovered older monuments, assigning them a new significance over time. This has sometimes left them 'high and dry' — islands of prehistory in a sea of arable or improved pasture. The past in the past, and what it may have meant, is another of the paths we will try to follow.

Paths have been established for some time. Antiquarian research on the 'wonders of the Peak' was a valued pursuit for gentlemen from the eighteenth century onwards, those with the time and income required to cultivate and indulge their passion for antiquities. Earlier on, that passion was a reflection of taste and an instrument of competition amongst aristocrats and gentry. It mattered to be able to discourse about the contents of a cabinet of curiosities, just as it was important that gardens were replete with the right classical statuary, or that a park portrayed nature in a pleasing manner. To be knowledgeable on such matters bestowed a certain standing within polite society. And it helped, of course, if one had the finances required to establish fine collections. Many of today's institutions and disciplines are built on these foundations.

By the nineteenth century, the situation was changing. Interests began to cohere around common principles and questions, and work became more focused. Old cabinets were opened and their contents divided up along disciplinary lines. For the school teachers, clerics and gentry who joined learned societies and contributed to early journals, curios became categories of object and classes of site. Even then, agendas were varied. The details of local history, how the past was written on familiar ground, was paramount for some; a lifelong pursuit. For others, it was how that evidence added fuel to the fire of broader debates about evolution and history. And for others still, and even now, antiquities were simply valued because, like books, they 'furnished a room'.

Our perspectives have shifted many times since Thomas Bateman published his Vestiges of the Antiquities of Derbyshire in 1848. In the intervening period, archaeology's object has been many things: tracing the movement and extent of cultures; detailing past economies; charting social evolution. There has been talk of ideology and of cosmologies, of power and social identity. And alongside these have been interests taking different paths, albeit ones that sometimes overlap. A fascination with sacred geographies, with alignments traceable in monuments, and with the relation of sites to the shape and character of the land. There remains a tension between these different interests. But at a time when a sense of past humanity is often difficult to trace in the flow of grand and abstract academic narrative, that tension is valuable.

A howling wilderness?

This brings us to a problem of perception. What does it mean to write a prehistory of the Peak District? Is the region a given? Where do we draw the line? The questions are basic. But they are often difficult to answer because at heart they are concerned with defining an entity which lacks clear boundaries. The Peak today is many things. A home to thousands; a place of interest and escape for millions. Several counties overlap its boundaries, and daily life carries many people in and out of the region. The tangle of administration that characterises current planning is an effective illustration of how places can be regarded in several ways at the same time.

Millers Dale

The Peak, or a large part of it, is a National Park. Established in 1951, it was the first to be created in Britain. The title and the legislative principle were borrowed from across the Atlantic, where the origin myths of the United States had fostered a fascination with nature and wilderness for some time. Initially, the area was selected and designated as an AONB — an area of outstanding natural beauty. More recently, that definition has been expanded to encompass what is called 'the historic environment'.

The Peak is also historic, not just because it is rich in remains, but also because it is mentioned by name in sources that stretch back over many centuries. There are even early Medieval references to a distinct group of people — the Pecsaete — identity tied close to the land. Since then, the region has been reconfigured many times. Large tracts held as monastic estates and farmed from granges. Manors with their seigneurial lords. The social and political realities of the time mapped out in the order of settlement, landholding and land use. Change worked through on the ground as well as in the courts.

Nature first and history second. What does this tell us? Perhaps that both terms are rather difficult to tie down. For many visiting the Peak today, one of the attractions, as it has been for a century and more, is the chance of escape from an urban environment. Walking along the edges of the East Moors, across Bleaklow or Kinder, many find a comfort in the idea that they have put a space between themselves and society, set apart in a 'natural' landscape. For others, it is the rural that is the attraction; the seemingly small scale of living and the apparent constancy, a contrast to the breakneck pace of urban development. Both views are from a particular vantage. In fact, it would be hard to find

Bleaklow

any corner of the Peak owing nothing to the complex historical relationship between people and land. Wilderness it is not. By the same token, the constancy we identify today is itself historical. You can't have a countryside without towns to oppose it to. In any case, things were very different only a century or two ago, when Enclosure and the Agricultural and Industrial Revolutions transformed the lives of many communities across the area. The loss of commons, the growth of estates and of settlement around new industries; the demands of towns and the cutting of new roads. Though a sentimental nostalgia often colours our impressions, the Peak has changed.

It is a strange time to be making this argument against a background of the recent collapse of sheep prices. Beyond transforming the lives of many hill farmers, shifts in grazing levels have meant that long open moorlands and dalesides have started to change in their appearance. Without the steady bite of stock, land has begun to acquire scrub, and birches are sprouting where they have not been seen for years. This has prompted many agencies to talk of landscape value, and to contemplate subsidies for farmers that will allow the traditional appearance of the land to be maintained. That the money is needed is beyond question. But it is a curious situation that we find ourselves in, when people are paid to engage in food production, not because that food is allowed to satisfy a basic need, but because it fosters an aesthetic — a value given to a way of seeing.

There have been other ways of seeing. Visiting on his tour of the country in the 1720s, Daniel Defoe was not impressed with the Peak. Though he acknowledged that many of the dales were fruitful, he regarded much of the area as 'the most desolate, wild and abandoned country in all England'. Like those who travelled much further afield, he was fascinated by the indigenous population, by their curious customs and by the conditions in which lead miners worked. He recorded with wide-eyed amazement the woman who, not for want of manners, lived with her family in a cave. His evaluation was based on several things. On the one hand, there was his disappointment at the 'Wonders of the Peak' recorded in the seventeenth century by Hobbes and Cotton; all landscape features save for Chatsworth House. On the other, there was his distaste for land that seemed unimproved by the standards of his day. Like Celia Fiennes before him, a seventeenth-century explorer who had trouble with her 'bearers', Defoe had few complimentary things to say.

Defoe's opinions were not shared by all. At around the same time, there are descriptions of '. . . such stupendous prospects that one could hardly believe they were anywhere to be found but in a picture . . .'. The parallel is a telling one, for this was also a time of great demand for landscape portraits — depictions of scenery in idealised forms. And in the century after his visit, values changed. Fashion amongst the gentry, the growth of towns and industry, each encouraged a change of perspective. Areas like the Peak came to be valued positively and precisely because they possessed the qualities that Defoe had found so distasteful. The description of the Peak as a 'Green Lung' could not have been made before this time. Engravings and paintings of striking natural features became more common, as did discourse on what forces had shaped the land. Archaeology too gained in scope and audience at this time, a development not unrelated. On occasion, the aesthetics of polite society led some to create 'Nature' in their parks — tors, serpentine rivers and rolling hills; even cliffs. Thousands of days of labour. Idealised images produced at a one-to-one scale and framed by careful planting.

By the nineteenth century these values led people like John Ruskin to suggest that the contemplation of nature, not to mention the clean air, were vital to the continued health and 'improvement' of urban workers. Rail opened up the Peak to forays from nearby towns, raising arguments that can still be heard today about access, change and senses of place.

This history of shifting values has a legacy that we acknowledge in the ways we think about the Peak today, even in our attitudes towards conservation. If it did not, the Peak would not be one of the most frequently visited areas in the world. It also tells us that the perception of anything, even nature, is bound to the social and political; a product of particular historical conditions. It follows from this that if landscapes are perceived from a certain point of view, they are also contested. Different people see things differently, and perceptions of landscape can be a field for argument.

The more recent history of the Peak is a testament to clashes of perspective. In the early twentieth century, one of the outcomes of Victorian attitudes towards the countryside and nature was an explosion of interest in the region. There were walkers associations and cycling groups; factory trips and workers sports clubs. Thousands pouring out of Manchester, Derby, Birmingham and Sheffield each weekend to break from the working routine. One of the most well known expressions of these developments was the Clarion Ramblers' journals. Begun in 1900, and designed to fit the rambler's pocket, the pages are stuffed with details of walks, with poetry and political commentary. Each cover bears the motto: 'A Rambler made is a man improved'. This was just

one expression amongst many. Details on where to walk each weekend were sometimes scratched in chalk outside factory gates.

These interests in the Peak provoked arguments over access. A high percentage of the region, particularly the more dramatic ranges, was still in the hands of large estates. It was these more remote 'wildscapes' that attracted the interest of walkers the most. Managed extensively as grousemoor, there were major restrictions in these areas on people's 'right to roam'. Journals and newsletters at the time paint a vivid portrait of the conditions encountered. There are references to assault and intimidation by gamekeepers, and to the loss of paths. There is talk of 'wooden liars'; signs that told of prosecution for trespass, and letters that celebrate their tearing down. There are also some of the first complaints about litter, the comments themselves a concern about the volume of traffic on popular trails. Tips are also offered on how to get around things. If you see a gamekeeper coming in time, turn 180 degrees. Then, when you are met, you can be turned around and set on the way you had intended.

These tensions expressed themselves in the Mass Trespass of 1932. We could say culminated, but that would imply that the issue was closed. A large assembly of ramblers, drawn from a variety of backgrounds, met at Hayfield and walked towards Kinder. Clashes with gamekeepers were inevitable, the scale of the confrontation varied depending on who you read. Several 'trespassers' were imprisoned. As a result of their efforts, access became an issue, one which demanded the attention of politicians. Though much remains private, legislation since then has created a patchwork of open access areas. The freedom of movement that people have today is a consequence of this struggle. Not that it is over, nor others that run alongside it. There are tensions, many difficult to resolve, between tourists and farmers, landowners and tenants, even archaeologists and ecologists. And more basic distinctions still. The Peak may be one of the most frequently visited parks in the world, but the catchment of people it attracts is still restricted; not by any means a full cross-section of a multicultural society. There may be no single reason for this bias. But where popular images of the 'countryside' foster a conservative and exclusive sense of national identity, it is hardly surprising that perception often breaks along lines of ethnicity.

Quarrying brings these tensions out like nothing else. The grits and limestone of various grades, the lead and the coal have made the Peak a honeypot for quarrying and mining. It has been so for thousands of years. The hallmarks of this earlier interest

are protected by law. Yet new bites, or those working out old agreements, are rightly contested. Some see them as sources of pollution, development scratching across their cosy image of a stable and unchanging land. Others see quarries as sources of employment in an area where work is scarce, where people with relatively little live next door to millionaires. There are also those who recognise them as places of beauty; 'crags' for climbing or simply for contemplation. Contingent lines drawn between the icons of historic labour and the eyesores of modern working. They are also an outcome of politics. The choice we make between local interests, aesthetics and the basis of our demand for stone. Demand is never absolute.

It is not just quarrying that sends up clouds of confusion. Even areas that we see as marginal or uncontentious can change when we shift our vantage. Take Big Moor, near Baslow. How do you describe it? Heather moorland certainly, the cover of the land a product of active management. Left alone, much of it would be woodland in a handful of years. It is not nature but a choice we have made. The moor is also ground to walk across on the way to White Edge or Curbar, a place above the intakes where fog is thick and frequent. It is also grazing land; sheep and sometimes cattle keeping the coarse grass down. At the same time it is a Scheduled Ancient Monument and a Site of Special Scientific Interest. There are coal mines and pack horse routes, the impact craters and bullet holes of wartime training. There are also many prehistoric features and a rich abundance of flora and fauna. Archaeology and ecology are now protected by law, the moor a Sanctuary Area where people are encouraged to walk only along certain lines. The

moor is managed by the National Park and contains reservoirs regulated by those who claim authority over the water. Far from being marginal or 'out of the way', this piece of ground has had and continues to have many identities, not all of them easily reconciled.

A sense of direction

So how should we describe the Peak? Where do we start? There is the land itself. But the land is never by itself. It was first mapped with a modern 'cartographic' eye by Burdett; the map published at a price of four guineas in 1767. But these maps deal largely with the surface and are always partial. What lies beneath?

Geological survey reveals a long and fascinating sequence. Much of the Peak is the result of processes established in the Carboniferous era, around three hundred million years ago. At that time, the area was part of a shallow tropical sea. The slow, steady and persistent sedimentation of marine creatures on the bottom created the limestone. Angular hills like Thorpe Cloud or Chrome Hill in the south and west are parts of the coral reefs that formed in this sea, left high and dry by pressure and time.

Marine conditions changed. Tides and drainage shifted and other sediments were laid down; the mudstones and shales and the sandstones we now recognise as grit. One imposed upon another. Varied in their resistance to erosion, these strata have been twisted, buckled and weathered; terraces and edges on the grits largely a product of faulting and erosion. The underlying limestone has also been exposed, erosion and uplift combining to create the central plateau. In between the two are numerous small fissures, dales and valleys, most notably the Derwent and the Wye. Often characterised by softer shales, these areas have eroded much more rapidly than the surrounding rock.

. . . The waller bounces the stone in his hand; feels its weight and shape. Too small. He folds the heavy glove around it; sees the coil of a fossil. The white stone is the heart of the Peak; the glove the grit upon it . . .

These varied conditions give the Peak its character. Steep sided dales, upland basins and long ridges on the limestone. The East Moors, the Dark Peak in the north and the Staffordshire Moors to the west. A range of landforms, soils and drainage patterns which have been reworked ever since. Climate and erosion; glaciation; the actions of people. And because they are so varied, the conditions in the Peak have always offered a series of different potentials for where people lived and how they moved.

How did prehistoric communities make sense of their worlds? How did they think about themselves, their ties to others, and to the land? We can start by acknowledging that social institutions are not entirely abstract concepts. They are bound up in the material traditions or practices that make up life. We can see this around us today. Our senses of ourselves and our relation to others is intimately tied to the character of our day-to-day lives. As men and women, as children or adults, as members of different families, classes and cultural traditions. Things are never entirely determined. But the places in which we live and work, the pattern of our associations with others, even the ways we hold and adorn our bodies, are bound up in concepts of identity, community and authority. Often tacit, these values are sometimes brought into sharper focus. Crossing important thresholds in our lives; participating in formal rituals; breaking with convention in some way. Spoken or unspoken, attitudes often have a material expression. Dealing as it does with the material conditions of the past, archaeology offers at least some basis for asking how the social worlds of prehistory were ordered and reproduced. In charting the changing character of prehistoric landscapes, we can begin to ask how they were inhabited and how they helped shape the social institutions that people recognised. We can ask how the land itself was implicated in history.

What has been said so far is no more than preamble; a walking in. Our purpose here has been to suggest, like others before us, that landscapes are deceptive. They may seem stable and self evident, but this is seldom the case. They are constituted through the interests of different communities and this makes their use and perception a form of politics. And they change. That was true of the past just as it is true of the present.

2 After the ice
16000–6000 BC

Rushup

Bleaklow; breathless after the climb from Longdendale. Legs extend and lose their tightness as the ground levels out. Singular on the rise, the path divides across the dark country. Trails branch off in groughs between withered hags and under vestigial drifts of snow. Freeze and thaw have scattered crystals across the white. Hare's tail and cotton grass rattle in the wind, their usual whisper amplified by beads of ice.

Time to pause; to roll a cigarette between numb and unresponsive fingers. To look around. Black Hill; Featherbed Moss; Coldharbour Moor and Kinder to the south. Then on, over Alport to Howden and Langsett; across Britland Edge and Heyden to complete the circle. The highest ground stands black against the horizon. Paths radiate out from the pause, each one a trail blazed through millennia of peat. South towards Shelf Moss and Hern Clough, west towards Alport Head and the Bleaklow stones; the sculpted tors of the Trident and the Anvil.

Times overlap here. Time alone; the duration of a journey; a return after three seasons. The eye carries you one or maybe two days walk at most; across recent access land and older private estates, down valley sides and around reservoirs. Looking down, you travel further. Time stretches over millennia, prehistory held in the peat's sodden blanket. There are branches of birch and oak, bark still traceable on soft and darkened surfaces. Some are centuries old, woodland around Swains Greave as late as the seventeenth century. Others are older and more extensive forest, growth rings and radiocarbon pushing the line back to the Mesolithic. Ten thousand years in ten feet of peat.

Beginnings

When walking, it is sometimes best to do the hard part of the journey first; the steepest rise and the heaviest going. So it is here. There have probably been people in the Peak for the last half-a-million years or so, populations retreating and advancing in a slow dance with the ice sheets across several Ice Ages and warmer Interglacials. Yet for much of that time we have no evidence; only fragments preserved in exceptional circumstances. The earliest and longest phases of prehistory are the most difficult of all to explore.

There are few paths into what we call the Palaeolithic and those that there are do not take us very far. Most of what we know concerns only the latest phase, the Upper Palaeolithic, and the period of time from the last glacial maximum around sixteen thousand years ago. Our problems here are largely ones of preservation. Though we sometimes like to see nature as a constant, a contrast to the seemingly breakneck pace of human time, the land has actually changed out of all recognition. It is changing still. It is difficult for us to imagine just how different the Peak once was, and how much it has shifted shape and cover, even over the last sixteen thousand years. Permafrost and stone; rivers enraged by meltwater; broken rock and tundra; pine and birch then oak and other broader leaves. Unfolding over a span that represents more than seven hundred human generations, those sixteen thousand years have erased all but the most recent footprints.

The best evidence we have for the Palaeolithic comes from caves that are common on the limestone; gaping maws and smaller hidden passages into the earth. Places like Fox Hole on High Wheeldon, Thor's Fissure, Old Woman's House, Elder Bush and Ossum's caves, many in the Manifold Valley. The history of excavations in many Peak District caves is sadly as poorly archived as it is long. However, enough is known to demonstrate that some saw a variety of uses in the millennia that followed the last glacial maximum.

Plato once imagined how difficult it would be to understand the world if one's life and one's experience were tethered entirely to the recesses of a cave. What would one make of shadows and noises, the snatched glimpses of life as it unfolded out in the light? In some bizarre inversion of his problem, we base most of what we know about the Palaeolithic world from what survives within. Fragments of bison, reindeer, bear and people; bone points and tools of flint. Long, patinated blades with the chattered scars of careful trimming. This brings with it many problems. We only see what made its way inside and must allow that there was more than one path to a cave. Some people came as occupants, finding shelter in larger and more habitable recesses. A season, maybe sometimes longer. For others, shelter was short-lived; time spent out of the wind and the rain, a pause and a meal by the fire before moving on. A blade or two left behind, edges worn from heavy use; a cache of dried meat to be eaten later. Others perhaps withdrew into the earth to commune with spirits and still more may have made their way to lairs as prey; fed to young hyaenas or wolverines.

At Creswell Crags, a few days' walk to the south-east, the picture is a little clearer. Here a dramatic Magnesian Limestone gorge forms a natural path of access between two more low-lying areas, a trail that was probably used by both migrating animals and the people who followed them. The near vertical cliffs are cut on either side by a series of caves that contain some of the richest Palaeolithic deposits in Britain. Mother Grundy's

Thor's cave

Parlour, Church Hole, Robin Hood's Cave and Pinhole. The sequences here are long and complex; we do not know quite how far back they go.

Nineteenth-century and later excavations have brought bone to light at Creswell which takes us back to tundra and steppe. Herds of bison, reindeer and wild horse following their tongues across hard ground and along seasonal grazing trails. There are also mammoth and woolly rhino, hyena, arctic fox and hare. Some hunted, some scavenged, some present because the caves were also their lairs. Cut marks on many arctic hare bones suggest an interest in fur as well as meat, and in Robin Hood's Cave a piece of rib was carved with an image of a horse's head. Wild horses seem to have been consistent prey. In addition to bone, there are pieces of worked antler and long blades of flint, many heavily worn.

Much of the work at Creswell remains unpublished. Yet what there is suggests that the crags were a well-known place on the trail for many thousands of years. Used by people at certain times, at others by animals; places to live and places of shelter during the seasonal dance with game. How life was ordered beyond these hollows is difficult to say; erosion and development have had a considerable impact on our picture. In the tundra and steppe-like conditions of the time, communities may have been highly mobile, moving along trails created by migrating herds. There would have been camps along ridges and near water, paths that wound through valleys where, in a few places, stands of birch or pine began to set a shadow on the ground. The land was changing, and as millennia passed, these woodlands spread over much of the land, changing the soils and the character of life as they went.

The seasonal cycle set a pattern to movement and to presence in different settings and there are hints that the ranges over which people moved may have been extensive. The blades found in several caves are from sources beyond the region and though some were obtained through trading, people also embedded the procurement of stone from river gravels, chalk and clay within broader cycles of movement. Where choices were made, there is a clear preference for better quality, more fine-grained flint, material well suited to the making of long blades. That these often occur on their own suggests that they were highly curated; a few carried on the trail and used extensively before finally being deposited or discarded. Close parallels with implements as far away as Kent's Cavern in Devon may indicate that seasonal ranges across cold and largely open country may have been in the region of a hundred miles or more across. Some probably went east as well; it was not until about eight-and-a-half thousand years ago that the 'land bridge' between what we term the British Isles and the Continent was finally broken. Until that happened, communities ranged freely back and forth. This encouraged an ebb and flow of populations in the area now recognised as Britain, expansion and contraction in step with cycles of warmer and colder conditions.

The fragments that we have to work with often encourage a very minimal view of life at the time. We talk of gathering and hunting and dwell upon the relative merits of different strategies for securing game. It is easy to conjure an image of people living a 'poor, bare and forked' existence. What often gets missed in these accounts is humanity; the relation of people to the land and to each other. It is likely that the paths of different groups overlapped, particularly where movement was in step with animal migration or the seasonal abundance of resources in particular places. A time to gather salmon or to harvest other food was a time to meet others. These moments, some of them cyclical, set a tempo for interaction and created networks that drew people, materials and ideas back and forth across vast areas. Geography was never just physical; it was always social.

. . . There. Where the path has made a fresh cut in the side of the hag. Amongst the sand and weathered peat, a few small blades of stone. A camp on the high ground where the forest once gave way to more open country. A pause on a different trail. Held between eye and light, the flint becomes translucent, a thin section of feathered filaments. The signature of Cretaceous time, set down in the chalk of hills four days to the east . . .

It is this complexity to life that we often miss when we talk simply of gathering or hunting. The archetype gives little sense of the ways that people may have thought about the broader world. It even misses how routine tasks are always embedded socially, creating the frame through which people come to know the world and their place within it. What we do know is that communities whose lives involve routine movement seldom perceive the landscape as an object to be parcelled up or divided into discrete entities. Instead, they often emphasise concepts of place and pathway which may overlap or cut across one another. The ties that bind people to these places often involve the evocation of a sense of tenure to be renewed rather than territory to be held. And this tenure is often grounded in a sense of ancestry, sustained through origin myths and identified with the physical evidence of the past encountered in the course of practical experience. Social boundaries of various forms can be recognised and respected. At times they can be actively contested.

Hanging stone

But their horizons can retain a fluidity as communities combine, divide and relocate in tempo with seasonal cycles and as one generation gives way to another.

Under these conditions, the turning of the year involves the periodic renewal of ties to place, and through this, a sense of belonging to country that is often a hallmark of social identity. Being a member of a particular community or broader group is bound up with attachments to place, attachments that are often understood in spiritual as much as practical terms. Ancestral powers and histories are sometimes vested in trees or stones and spirits of the dead may be seen in their forms. It is often the renewal of the relationship between the living and these forces that is seen as fundamental. To break the cycle of respect and observance is to break with the land itself. Even rivers or ridge tops can occupy positions in myth, these values being drawn upon where features serve as boundaries or places for spiritual communication. Prominent features in origin stories, and often shrouded with proscription and taboo, materials and places are drawn upon as people renew their connections with the land and as they cross important thresholds in their lives. Rites of passage often involve separation from the community at large and visits to sacred sites can be pivotal moments in the transition from one state of being to another. Like the right to participate in these events, knowledge of certain places might be acquired as one moved from adolescence to adulthood or from one kin group to another. Some stories may have only been heard by the elders or by ritual specialists; the telling and hearing of others may have been the prerogative of particular sections of the community.

Just how later Palaeolithic communities in the Peak attached themselves to particular places is unclear; we have so little to go on. Caves were certainly important, used repeatedly for practical or more sacred purposes, perhaps both. Where people moved in step with the migrations of wild horse or reindeer, hoof and footprint one behind another, it may well be that certain animals also had a significance that went beyond the practical. A rich source of metaphor and a model of progression in life, some herds may have developed a 'special relationship' with people, one that acknowledged the close ties in their fortunes. Some herds may have even been selectively managed. Beyond this, it is possible that the classification of animals was tied to concepts of totemism, some taking on an iconic significance for particular groups. The Elk, a solitary wanderer who never lost the trail; the Bear who walked and lived as people did. What made some animals worthy of respect or fear was the spirit that they carried or the soul they embodied.

After the Ice

Current evidence suggests that the last Ice Age came to a close around ten thousand years ago. In the Peak, the permafrost thawed, releasing the water that had shaped soil and stone into periglacial swirls and stripes. Things had always been changing, but from this time on, the pace quickened. Rapid increases in temperature over perhaps a few decades encouraged the proliferation of woodland across much of the region. Open country still remained, particularly on the highest ground, but much of the land was increasingly covered by varied spreads of birch, pine or mixed deciduous trees. Valleys soon darkened and old trails across once open ground became lost. Forests even flourished on much of what appear to us now as the bleak wastes of the Dark Peak.

Froggatt

These changes were inhabited by people who even at this early stage may have influenced developments. Rising temperatures and the spread of varied forests fostered changes in animal behaviour and in the dominance of particular species. With time, the large-scale migration of horses, bison or reindeer gave way to new and more localised patterns of movement in which red deer, roe deer, aurochs, wild pig and elk were prominent. Though some of the old paths and names may have remained, others were recalled only in myths of origin as new patterns of movement and activity were hung upon the seasonal cycle. It is against this changing background that archaeologists talk of a new period, the Mesolithic, which runs from *c*.9000 to *c*.4000 BC and is divided into earlier and later phases around 6500 BC. Mesolithic material is present in caves, including some of those at Creswell, and the deposits here caution us from seeing the period division as some form of complete and radical break with the past. That said, things were changing; trends reflected in stone and ancient pollen.

. . . Open ground, above the forest margin. Three are sat repairing tools they used that day and talking of the next. Below, the fringe of trees and the path that leads down onto darker slopes. Above, the stone teeth where they had squatted on the long wait for game . . .

With one or two exceptions, evidence for the Mesolithic in the Peak takes the form of scatters of worked stone; dark cherts from outcrops on the limestone and flint from further afield. Blades and flakes, or the cores of parent stone from which they were struck, recognised now by the ridges and scars created during working. Brought to the surface by the plough, by development and erosion, these scatters vary in their scale and composition. Where excavated, few produce evidence of substantial dwellings or other structures.

Some scatters are small indeed. Often found by chance, they can be no more than a few metres in diameter, comprising small cores, endscrapers and narrow blades. A presence in particular places can even be marked by no more than one or two tools. Often these are the microliths that were made at this time; small blades of flint or chert trimmed to produce 'geometric' shapes for use in composite tools. These often occur as the dominant elements in more elevated settings; near ridge tops and the higher sides of valleys. Rather more rare as chance finds are flaked 'tranchet' axes; so called because of a deliberate, lateral blow administered to the end of the axe to produce a sharp cutting edge. Only a few have been identified in the Peak so far, among them one from Stoney Low near Ashover and another in a rock fissure in Lathkill Dale. Both are made of cherts that were probably local to the region.

Thousands have passed over this material, feet pressing eroded blades unnoticed into the matrix of paths. For each time someone looks down and pauses to pick up a core on the trail, there are countless more where worked stone has gone unrecognised. Herdsmen from a thousand years ago. Peat cutters back from higher ground. Mourners carrying their dead along wake walks to be laid to rest in the mother church. These 'one-off' finds reflect many things. Chance losses; the disappearance of an arrow into tangled understorey or an axe fallen from a bag. Some may also be deliberate deposits; caches left for future use or offerings of stone made to the spirit of a place. That people sometimes deposited material with some deliberation is suggested by a hoard of microliths found on Beeley Moor; around eighty small trimmed blades of grey-white flint cached together in a small pit.

Not all chance finds are isolated. There are scatters in many areas comprising handfuls of tools or waste flakes; evidence for use as well as the working of stone. Places like Ault Hucknall, Flask Edge, Pikehall and Brassington. Found on natural access routes or ridge-tops, in open settings or above small streams and basins, these often reflect the sporadic use of particular locations. Small camps established for part of a season, or places through which people passed. Camps for hunters, for those collecting honey, pausing near sacred ground or travelling on to meet with others. Moments on the path.

Other scatters are different again. Some take the form of more extensive spreads, their distribution an accumulation of human time. A variety of tasks and a sense of duration. Sometimes the waste itself will indicate specific acts: the working of axes, the careful coaxing of cores, the making of microliths or the sharpening of scrapers. Undertaken on the margins of a winter settlement, near the fire of a camp or as people sat talking, the ring of hammer on stone echoed across many places. Sites like these are found in many parts of the region; in the Dark Peak, on the limestone, on the margins of larger valleys like the Derwent and along the gritstone edges.

Other scatters are larger still. At places like Unstone on the coal measures, or Shacklow and Demon's Dale on the limestone, work has revealed even greater densities and ranges of material. In a few cases, excavation reveals clusters of stake holes and hearths; scorched earth still surviving as a reddening of the underlying soil. These 'sites' are not easy to interpret. Their scale could be a product of people coming together, perhaps in step with the seasonal abundance of particular plants or animals or with the use of other resources. It might also reflect the passing of a different form of time. There were the hard and densely forested grounds of winter, the more open country of late summer; the springs and sources once used by long dead kin. These were places to which people returned; each year or generation of activity adding to the sense of attachment that they held. Old hammers could be taken up again. Here was a place where the earth had been broken, where nodules found beneath the surface were tested by tapping and the removal of one or two flakes. Here was a larger spread of tools and waste, and of burnt stone scattered in an old clearing. Who had spent time here? What did this scatter say about the nature and duration of their stay? Perhaps the roots of some scatters stretched beyond the genealogies of specific communities and into a wider and more 'timeless' ancestral past.

. . . Returning in the spring, the young learn how to find their way around the task. With time, their hands and eyes grow accustomed; their ears more attuned to the sound of good stone and good work. Moving along the valley, they learn how to read pebbles as signs of a source upstream. And all the while, there are stories of the past, gestures made towards the archaeology of old clearings . . .

Different places, different times; varied tasks, varied communities. That was how it was. This complexity is suggested by stone itself. Flint does not originate within the region, and thus must have been brought in by people. Translucent flint from the boulder clays and river gravels of the Trent and Cheshire Plain, ranging in colour from yellow, honeyed tones to darker browns. Although difficult to source precisely, these materials suggest communication and movement between the Peak and areas to the south and west. Also present is a more mottled flint that probably comes directly or indirectly from the Yorkshire and Lincolnshire Wolds. There are also local cherts, particularly the darker and finer stone that outcrops in a number of White Peak valleys, notably in the area around Ashford. These saw more common use from the later Mesolithic onwards. The simple presence of these different materials hints at the ebb and flow of people in and out of the region. Procurement trips and webs of exchange cut across the boundaries and ranges of different kin groups.

How did people get hold of stone? Material could be acquired by chance, from a riverbank or from a tree throw. It could also be won through the use of local sources, through transaction, or by visits to more distant places. Sometimes sustained over centuries, these varied traditions had important consequences for how people understood themselves and their relations with others. Growing up in a particular community involved learning the seasonal pattern of the land and its history. As an aspect of this knowledge, and no doubt cut through with myth, were themes related to the winning and working of stone. Where were long used sources? Who could work there and who could not, and when was it appropriate to work? In maintaining these traditions, communities maintained their attachment to the landscape itself and passed that connection down across generations. Learning to look and learning to work also meant learning about one's place in the wider community.

The character of stoneworking is also a suggestion of movement. A transience to some places and more repetitive or sustained connections with others. One of the hallmarks of working at this time was the systematic flaking of good quality stone to produce regular blade and flake cores. These, in their turn, were worked with care and anticipation to produce regular, parallel-sided pieces. Blades could be used as they were, or snapped and retouched into a rich variety of microliths capable of being hafted in various ways. Tools for shredding and cutting, or armatures for projectiles used in fighting and the hunt.

These may be the hallmarks of an attitude towards stone that went hand in hand with cycles of movement over seasons, years and generations. Where people were on the move, it may have been important to be frugal with stone, to show it respect by careful working. The portability of toolkits was of some importance on the trail. Material ready to hand whenever it was needed; many blades held dormant in a lump of stone no bigger than a child's fist. Blades and microliths were flexible too, capable of being used in a variety of different ways. Over time, the manner in which these elements were made seems to have changed. Blades became a little smaller and microliths yet more geometric, a trend reflected in the names we give to later examples: rods, points and scalene triangles. Raw material patterns also changed, flint from some distant sources becoming a little less common and local stone more frequent. Some have taken this as evidence for a gradual diminution in the scale of the ranges over which people moved.

Working stone meant other things as well. Where skill was something to be observed and learned, the mimicry of gestures and active instruction provided a rough index of where one stood in the companies one kept. We do not know whether working was inscribed with particular divisions of labour, but age and experience would have counted for a good deal. Diminutive and simple though they seem to us, microliths and other blades were the products of structured patterns of working. It took time for these to become habits, and the choices people made reflected on where and from whom they had learned. Attention to platforms; the trimming and preparation of edges; the careful placement of the blow. There was satisfaction to be had from bringing the hammer down exactly where it was needed; hearing the ring of the blade as it came away; inspecting the thin, parallel ridges that were left on the core. Nods of respect when this was repeated in company. Though there is much that is difficult for us to grasp, it is likely that skill in stoneworking, like skill in the use of stone in different tasks, contributed to the ways in which people saw themselves and how they, in turn, were regarded. A child struggling to handle a simple task, a woman with years of working behind her, another for whom long blades leapt from the core at the slightest touch. One whose hands or eyes had failed, content now to comment on the work of others and to pass on instruction.

. . . A space near the lodge where people tread carefully; a pile of waste from making the cores that will be carried in the coming season. Fragments of dark stone from further up the valley lie amongst spills of flint with weathered skins from chalk hills to the east. Some are cracked and crazed from hours in the fire. And amongst the waste a scraper, twice resharpened and discarded, thick with fat from a hide . . .

Recognition may have worked at broader scales as well. Where we see flint or chert, people at the time may have recognised many different materials, dividing stone up along social and even spiritual lines. Simply working certain types of stone was sometimes an acknowledgement of the ties that bound you into broader networks of exchange, or into webs of kinship and affiliation that stretched many days to the south or east. And there were also the sources themselves. Flint in chalk hills and clay cliffs to the east, nodules in the valley gravels to the south, blocks of chert in the limestone at the heart of the region. Sources that were visited and worked repeatedly. The consistent appearance of a shiny black chert in later Mesolithic assemblages from across the region suggests continuity in traditions of procurement that stretched over many generations.

How were these sources used? When people travelled across to the east coast, winter storms would bring fresh nodules to light. In certain seasons, smoke from the fires of a number of camps may have risen above the cliffs. Clambering across the sticky face of the boulder clay, levering stone with antler and wood. Picking over nodules on the beach, tapping to see which ones rang true. The possibility of meeting with others not seen for some time. Similar encounters may have taken place around sources on the Wolds. The journey and the work brought people into routine contact with others. Trails crossed and food shared at a scale that broke with the everyday. A movement of news and new ideas; obligations and people.

From the later Mesolithic at least, it is likely that limestone valleys rich in workable chert saw use by different groups, communities nonetheless bound by broader ties. Under these conditions, a visit may have required consent and negotiation, a sharing of the venture and the coming together of people. Camps by the rivers edge; disappearance through the trees to cliffs and overhangs; firing, hammering, shouting. The sound of different voices and the rhythmic reports of flaking. Echoes bouncing from one side of the valley to the other.

We see stone knapping as a practical activity; a task. For people at the time, it was also a social fact; an ability to recognise different hands in working and an obligation to labour with others when the time was right. Sources were also a potential source of tension, friction arising where traditional rights of access were disregarded. Sources themselves were a testament to the endurance of that obligation. Those visiting Lathkill or the Wye in the spring would have seen the tell-tale traces of earlier visits. Some they remembered as they reacquainted themselves with mauls for quarrying and stood before the dark bands in the white stone. Some had always been there; the remnants of working by spirits.

What did people see when they looked at the filaments in a thin flint flake or as they stood at the base of a limestone cliff? A gift from the ancestral past; the bones, teeth or feathers of spirits; the scars of earlier generations of working. Perhaps all of these and more besides. Though it is difficult for us to grasp, it may well be that working itself was an act of respect. It renewed ties with the land, and through labour it fostered bonds between scattered communities. Perhaps that bond was also renewed in the sharing of news and stories, and in the passing on of knowledge about the stone itself.

The scatters we identify reflect patterns of living that revolved around many themes. Found today in a ploughed field or on the edge of acid moorlands, it is difficult to picture the setting and the circumstances of the acts that made them. This is partly because of the history of investigation. Evidence from caves and rock shelters is for the most part poorly understood, and there have been few well-recorded excavations of either earlier or later Mesolithic open sites. One class of evidence helps us with part of this problem. Preserved in sediments that built up over millennia, in peats and on a few well-recorded sites, pollen grains from different plants demonstrate that many scatters were created in woodland settings.

The proliferation of woodlands during the Mesolithic did more than simply change the scenery that people saw as they moved. It reworked much of the way in which they lived, and because forests are themselves dynamic, things were always changing. Extensive mixed deciduous tracts, birch scrub and reed swamp margins were the setting and the medium for much of life. What we might now call wildwoods were forests with long histories of use and reuse. Places for food, for living and perhaps even places of spiritual danger, forests carried the marks of a human and ancestral presence. They were the familiar frame in which many people's lives unfolded.

. . . Forests shift. They change behind our backs and look different depending on our vantage. In the Medieval world, there were many different views. There was wood pasture and the dark ground where pigs foraged, where peasants lopped pollards in the spring, took windfalls and other resources. Some tracts were also held as Royal hunting grounds or the Lord's demesne, a clash of perceptions that could bring tensions to the surface. The Forest was also a place of danger and of chaotic forces. Like the heath, it was sometimes liminal ground, a space between. For the Cistercian brothers on granges in the Peak, it was all of these and wilderness; a place away from mammon and close to God . . .

Communities moved in and out of step with the rhythms of woodlands. Where storms, lightning or disease created clearings, these might see occupation; land opened up for people by beneficent forces. Perhaps the ground opened up in this way reflected the help of the ancestors in guiding settlement amongst the living. Other places, like higher ridges or gritstone edges, were relatively free of trees, and camps may have been strung out along margins. As the seasons turned, the forest provided varied crops: firewood, bark and honey, crab apples, nuts and other fruit. Open canopied and light in places, dense and dark in others, forests were bisected by many trails; some made by people, some by other animals.

Evidence from a number of pollen cores suggests that the close relationship between forests and people was made all the more intimate by manipulation and management. Changes in the frequency of species and the presence of charcoal suggest that cover was sometimes opened up and clearings maintained. It is difficult to be certain when using this evidence; forests are often altered by wildfires or changes of fortune which have their own momentum. However, the patterns that we see make it likely that communities intervened in those cycles, bringing changes that were once again as social as they were practical. Cut close to the earth or relieved of their boughs, many trees generate new shoots and an abundance of leaves that are easily reached and often favoured by browsing animals. Where practised, the firing of woodland or scrub encourages similar patterns of regeneration. Renewed over time, these clearings were places to which both animals and people would return, where prey might be anticipated and old camps re-established in certain seasons. Scattered along traditional routes, they could be places of chance acquaintance — where members of one kin group might meet others, where stories might be told, news passed and materials traded.

Clearance, of course, serves other purposes. The opening up of the canopy or the consolidation of older clearings is a common precursor to settlement, the clearing of ground being one of the ways in which people may make a commitment to place. In a country where unchecked woodland regeneration can have a significant impact in a handful of years, that commitment would need to be made and made again. We should not underestimate the importance that routine clearance may have held, and might allow that woodland management was also a form of respect shown to country.

With woodland management comes the creation of resources. Valuable tools and hafts were cultivated over a handful of years and structural timber harvested from one generation to the next. Coppicing generated browse for animals. It also fostered the growth of underwood for tool hafts or the flexible rods to be woven into the fabric of buildings, baskets and hurdles. Not only that, cleared ground created the space in which to experiment with indigenous and imported cereal crops, a practice that probably began in the later part of the Mesolithic. Some tasks were undertaken alone; others in larger and more varied companies. A visit to an old hunting stand, the sharing of labour in a clearing, close cooperation in harvesting the fruits of the forest.

The tasks bound up in woodland management also encouraged a recognition of time that went beyond the short term and immediate. Different materials grew at different rhythms and needed different frequencies of attention. Coppice stools and pollards are often cut in the winter after the sap has fallen. Understorey is best cleared out when dry. Tasks such as these may have been tied with seasons and into longer term cycles of movement and residence. Ring barking demanded an acknowledgement of yet longer cycles, a form of clearance that stretched over ten or fifteen years.

This variety was important for the significance that people attached to particular places. On a day-to-day basis and in the course of the annual cycle, the condition of forests provided evidence of activities conducted in the recent past. A small group moving on a hunting trip would have recognised the subtle changes in the state of the ground that spoke of human action and the relative time scales involved. Returning to a clearing meant an encounter with the past. In landscapes composed of small, dispersed communities, these readings were a source of information and a sense of history.

The temporality of woodlands could also be acknowledged over longer timescales. With the passing of generations, the state of forests was a testament to the roots that linked people to the land. Located in oral tradition, the places where long-dead kin once lived and worked could be recognised and remembered; new settlements were grafted onto the roots of the old. Long forgotten but still acknowledged were other places where people traced the actions of spirits. These were the traces of an ancestral hunting camp or a settlement where the old ones lived. Nearby was the river along which people had first arrived, their bones returned to its currents on death. Tending and reworking the land offered quiet confirmation of the histories that bound people to particular places.

. . . Keep to the trail; tread in the footprints of those who walk in front. Remember them when you return to the lodge by the river, to the crags where their bones are scattered. Show respect. The Forest watches . . .

Evidence for the manipulation of woodlands becomes more common from the centuries around 6500 BC onwards, a time when other aspects of life were changing in various ways. Along with shifts in the use of different raw materials and ways of working stone, these changes in the pollen record have encouraged speculation on the nature of 'driving forces'. Some take the long view, citing the loss of the land bridge, the disappearance of migrating herds and the need for new hunting strategies in the more dense and varied woodland conditions of the time. Others fall back upon a favourite 'prime mover' — population pressure, suggesting that an infilling of the landscape limited the scale of movement and people's options. Many of these factors are important but it may be unhelpful to single out any one as dominant. Moreover, population pressure is never something that is assessed independently — a point where the physical carrying capacity of land is reached. It is always a matter of perception and this changes historically.

Though they are difficult to understand, the changes that we glimpse were as much a consequence of the playing out of relations between people as they were responses to other 'external' factors. This is easy to assert but difficult to explore, not least because of problems of perception. Ever since the nineteenth century, when antiquarians sought to emulate Darwin and Lyall, it has been common to discuss the movement of the past in terms of the evolution of social complexity. Tied to prevailing notions of progress as technologically driven, social evolutionary models were quick to equate distance in space with succession in time. Put simply, it was common to assume that the further one went

Kinder

from the West, the more 'primitive' people became, a valuation based on the apparent simplicity of the tools they used and a lack of institutionalised political hierarchies.

Most now rightly distance themselves from these views, recognising in them a legacy of colonial and other morally bankrupt political agendas. And yet, when we talk of hunter-gatherers, we still usually conjure images of largely egalitarian and undifferentiated institutions. This remains caricature. In fact, history and anthropology demonstrate that hunting and gathering societies are some of the most complex social formations to be found at any place or time. They may sometimes lack the hierarchies fastened upon by nineteenth-century and later theorists. But they make up for these with more contingent distinctions of authority and with extensive and complex webs of kinship and affiliation. These work at many scales, from the individual born into a close kin group, through age and gender grading, and on to lineages, clans and still broader federations. These webs of social and political relations are continually reworked in the flow of practical cycles.

We may never be able to reconstruct the particular structures of kinship or association that Mesolithic communities in the Peak took for granted. Yet it is likely that those understandings were hung upon familiar landmarks; places with practical, historic and spiritual associations. Within these were more local senses of identity and authority. Spaces between the young and the old, men and women, the elders and their juniors. And as each generation passed, relations changed. Tensions within lines, argument between age grades or over access, social competition. All played their part.

. . . On High Neb, two days from the lodge. The open trail along the edge till the brook pulls the path off to the north. The going is easy at first; woodlands thin and the trail clear. Then the ground drops towards deeper valleys and trees crowd in upon the path. Light fades. People walk softly, listening to the voices of the forest. It will be another day before the others are met at the river's edge. A time to share food and company before returning to the trail. The welcome should be strong. There has been plenty of game and bags are heavy with the good stone . . .

3 In an antique land
6000-3000 BC

Museum Accession No. 1997/216: c.15,000 flints, mostly Mesolithic, some Neolithic — microliths, cores, leaf-shaped arrowheads etc. Collected by Mrs B... and donated by her daughter. See boxes for details of provenance.

She caught the passion from her father, but unlike him, did not range all that far. Each spring she returned to the same dark hill behind the farm, where the winter winds had taken yet another bite into the peat. Each spring she gave the new exposures a number or letter, worked stone collected according to her plan. Twenty-seven years.

She had been curious at first, puzzled as to how all that stone got under the peat and why they had chosen to live so high. She had her favourites too; the slender blades and the arrowheads that looked like young willow leaves. Then, as she learned about deep time, the fascination grew, the possibility of glimpsing how people had lived before the hill was lost beneath a mantle of bog. She liked to think they were her ancestors; that she was part of the line. After that, it was habit. Evenings in March and April spent washing each piece; sorting by area and caching it all in boxes beneath her bed.

Her daughter's excavations were more personal. An old promise to see that it all went to the museum. For her it was the boxes. A new pair of shoes each year; the radio she had given when she first left home. Bendicks chocolate mints; a treat for Christmas that was still being eaten when the flints were washed. Bronnley soap; they always kept it in the shop for her. Basildon Bond; the boxes the colour of the letters she'd received each week without fail. She'd kept them all; her own archive.

And annotated matchboxes. Dozens of them. Bryant and May; Swan Vestas, designs changing only slightly over the years. Her handwriting on each one still familiar. She had never wanted central heating; insisted it was bad for the chest. Each box a memory of the morning ritual by the grate.

Transitions

One of the constants in the study of prehistory has been our division of the linear flow of time into a series of discrete and successive periods. Another legacy of nineteenth-century thought, these periods are usually divided one from another by changes in material culture; in particular, by what scholars saw as crucial changes in technology. Within this schema, the old and new ages of Stone gave way to successive ages of Bronze and Iron, each one characterised by a 'great leap forward' in productive technology. Built on principles of stratigraphy, on analogy, and more recently on radiocarbon dates, these divisions have become deeply embedded in the archaeological imagination. More often than not, we take them for granted, accepting them as dramatic thresholds across which prehistoric society was somehow transformed.

There are many good reasons for questioning this assumption. Looked at closely, the transition between any two periods often loses its clarity and becomes a more complex historical amalgam of both continuity and change. Nowhere is this clearer than in the fifth and fourth millennia, and on the threshold between what we call the Mesolithic and the Neolithic. This transition has loomed particularly large in the literature and has often been caricatured. On the one hand we have the Mesolithic, a time of gathering and hunting, when people lived largely within the cycles of nature. On the other, we have the Neolithic, conventionally associated with domesticated plants and animals, the manufacturing of pottery and polished stone tools, and the first appearance of built monuments.

Having established this opposition, archaeologists over the last century or so have sought to explain the change from one state to another in a variety of ways. For many years, changes in the economy, in material traditions and even monument building itself were taken as evidence for a sudden and significant influx of people. Colonists migrating from across the channel, bringing with them new resources and ideas and driving out or assimilating the indigenous forager population. These new 'cultures' effectively broke with the past, cleared the land, settled down and established a pattern of life which revolved around mixed agriculture.

We now recognise that the situation is not quite so clear cut. Current arguments tend to favour the idea that many of the developments we see at this time were the result of largely indigenous processes. To be sure, there was an ebb and flow of people across the channel, just as there probably always had been since the land bridge was lost. The sea was not then the cultural barrier that it has more recently become. It was through networks of contact that went back and forth across the water that resources, people and ideas were carried into different settings. The same pattern was repeated further inland over the course of the later fifth and earlier fourth millennia.

The Neolithic was not a tight package — a new way of living or thinking that completely broke with the past. This has been difficult for us to accept because the transition has often been regarded as one of the major watersheds of human history. It is to farming and an assumed shift to sedentary patterns of life that we have often looked when searching for the roots of contemporary attitudes. In fact, many older understandings and practical traditions persisted across the divide, innovations only taken up where they served particular local interests. For communities of the time, the transition as archaeologists understand it did not exist.

In the Peak of the sixth and fifth millennia, it is likely that people were bound together in extensive networks of kinship and alliance. Small groups who nonetheless recognised themselves as parts of broader social worlds. These networks found expression in the ways that certain paths overlapped, in the names given to prominent features, and in the origin myths that were mapped across the land. They were also expressed through trade and exchange; the keeping of partners and the giving of gifts. Rooted perhaps in an ethos of sharing that was common on the trail, gifts bound people together in varied combinations, sometimes establishing principles of debt and obligation. With time these social geographies were themselves reworked.

This situation began to change in the fifth millennium, but only insofar as the continual interplay of social relations took up new resources. In the Peak, we get little sense of the arrival of a tight 'package' of new materials and ideas. Changes unfolded in a piecemeal fashion. This happened over generations, not overnight, which makes our path more difficult to follow.

. . . A path along the side of Linch clough, a sharp line down towards the limits of intake. Steps to decelerate the sledges that people drew behind them, each loaded with a crop of peat. Medieval Turbary exercised for centuries; access to fuel and grazing a customary and moral right. But with large estates the line was broken, access denied. The path remains . . .

Ways of working, ways of life

Just how different parts of the Peak were inhabited in the earlier Neolithic is difficult to determine. Evidence is thin on the ground and seldom easy to translate. However, there is little to suggest a radical or substantive break with the past.

Just as they had been for many generations, the landscapes of the region were populated by scattered and fragmented groups. Often these were perhaps no more than extended families. Small communities, defined by close kinship, who traced themselves and their ties to others through concepts of ancestry, descent and renown. These communities probably understood themselves in relation to concepts of lineage or even clan membership; more basic distinctions drawn between age and gender grades, each changing over the course of a lifetime.

With such diverse topographies and ecologies, we should not assume that all areas were necessarily occupied in the same ways. And things changed. There was a dynamism in the relation of people to land, a flow that saw particular places change in character and significance from season to season and from one generation to the next. If landscape at this time was a patchwork, it was one in which elements and details were constantly being added and reworked. Many threads in the pattern of life could probably be traced back into the distant past, hung upon familiar landmarks and along paths that had 'always been there'. But there were also new currents in the flow — domesticated plants and animals, the working of stone and clay in novel ways and the building of what we recognise as the first monuments.

Once again, we catch glimpses of life at this time in the evidence of pollen and stone. Pollen sequences for the period suggest that the region saw only limited woodland clearance, and as before, a good measure of variation in the nature of cover. On parts of the limestone plateau, where limited clearance has been recognised from as early as the fifth millennium, there remained a variety to the conditions that people experienced. Open ground near prominent outcrops and along the spines of major ridges; extensive and varied woodlands running down into upland basins and across perched shelves. Open woodlands of Birch, Hazel and Ash; darker tracts where Lime and Oak predominated. Cereal pollen, present in some areas as early as the fifth millennium, features in a number of sequences. Some of the higher clearings had been established for some time, products of millennia of grazing by deer and, on occasion, maintenance by people. Often highlighted in these settings, prominent dolomitic outcrops — tors, towering crags and pillars — may have long been recognised as practical and symbolic landmarks, reference points in geographies of myth.

Lower down, clearings, grassland and woodland margins shifted in and out of focus as people and animals tacked back and forth. Darker still were the forests that remained a commonplace in the larger valleys bounding the plateau on all sides. Even here though, we should not assume a uniform picture. Some of the steep sided valleys and gorges were still intractable, barriers to movement rather than paths of least resistance. But others, particularly those that were wider, may well have seen more varied and open conditions running along the water's edge. How far these ribbons of more open ground were appropriated and maintained by people is difficult to determine. Paths were still created by other animals following their noses towards good water and browsing.

Equally diverse conditions persisted on the gritstone shelves of the East Moors. Here too, there were extensive woodlands and patches of clearer country with good light soils, fertile and more easily worked than the heavier clays in the lower valleys. Some open ground also lay exposed where peats had formed in low-lying areas; around Ringinglow, Hipper Sick and Leash Fen. It is from these locales that some of our longest pollen sequences are derived. Bissected by rivers, particularly where less resistant shales lie against the grit, these terraces were framed by the sharp, continuous line of the edges themselves. Many would have had an apron of woodlands running below them: ash, birch, thorn and twisted oaks; roots clinging like arthritic fingers to scree and clitter. Wind, animals and a lack of good purchase still kept edges exposed as routes and vantages.

. . . She looked down towards the valley. Her eye dwelt on breaks in the cover, on the smoke that rose above other hearths. She followed the trail that had brought her to the edge before the last new moon. And as she made the journey, she caught sight of the herd being moved down to the water. It would be another month before she was on that trail again. First, she would follow the animals to high pasture and to the house of the old ones . . .

Trees had long since gone from some of the higher reaches of the Dark Peak to the north, their place taken by the blanket peat that is now sectioned by footpaths. Climatic shifts and several millennia of management stretching back into the Mesolithic had fostered more open tracts that gradually turned to bog. But even here, pollen and charcoal recovered from beneath tall hags sometimes hints at a diversity at odds with the extensive open peatlands of today. Some areas at least saw the persistence into the fourth millennium of woods, grassland and patches of scrub on favourable slopes and catchments. Some of these patches were to persist for even longer.

Within these conditions, much of life was still conducted in clearings and along forest margins. Dwellings and tasks were still linked by paths that threaded along ridges and through forests that remained alive with an abundance of creatures. For many, livestock and limited cultivation made a significant contribution to the rhythm and content of daily and annual rounds. For others, the pattern of the year owed more to the character and availability of other species. There is every reason to suppose that gathering and hunting remained important — a compliment rather than alternative to the husbandry of crops and stock.

Stone provides another piece of the puzzle, though not perhaps one that resolves the picture as clearly as we might like. Simply recognising stoneworking assemblages from the fifth and earlier fourth millennia, let alone differentiating them, is by no means easy. Much of our evidence is again in the form of surface scatters, so known distributions are heavily influenced by more recent histories of land use. Many scatters are also palimpsests — the accumulated residues of different episodes of activity across several thousand years. This is less of a problem in parts of the Dark Peak, where the peat that masks scatters of flint and chert was already established before the fifth millennium. Here we may still be dealing with accumulated episodes of activity in a specific place. But these often date to before what we recognise as the Neolithic, though there are later exceptions even here. In other areas, on the raised basins and shelves of the limestone, or on the terraces of the Eastern Moors, it is not uncommon to find Mesolithic material cheek by jowl with tools and waste from the Neolithic and the Bronze Age. This is less marked along the flanks of the Derwent Valley, though substantive multi-period scatters have been found.

Our inability to differentiate easily between Later Mesolithic and Earlier Neolithic assemblages also stems from continuities in the character of stoneworking. Tasks varied from place to place, but often we see a common and continued emphasis on the working of cores to produce narrow flakes and blades. This happened alongside the appearance of new and/or modified forms of working, in particular the bifacial flaking and delicate, invasive retouch characteristically used in the fashioning of axes, leaf-shaped arrowheads and knives. But the key issue here is that older and more basic ways of working persisted, as did the routine use of simple tools such as endscrapers and knives made on narrow, regular, pieces of flint and chert. Many of these pieces reflect attention, anticipation and a structure to working, as if people were still concerned to make the most of particular pieces of stone. Cores with single or opposed platforms continued to be worked, often to exhaustion; platforms were maintained with care, or repaired when things went wrong. No doubt people at the time would have recognised a richer variety in these ways of working than we can trace today. Differences in the way an edge was held or turned, in the colour of stone or in the details of a form; 'gleaning the unsaid off the palpable'.

In effect, many assemblages still reflect the careful use of raw materials to produce portable and flexible tools. It still mattered to be frugal with stone; to show it respect. Learning to work was still a mark of progression in life and a way of showing respect to tradition. This may have been important where tasks carried people around, and residence could still vary from one season to another. Many continued to carry stone with them wherever they went: a hammer and core against an anticipated task; an unfinished tool to pass the time. It had always been that way. Microliths themselves may have continued to be fashioned and used throughout the fifth millennium. They are certainly rare in later contexts, and where they do occur are often regarded as residual. But in an area and period where few things are tied down tightly by  radiocarbon dating, it may be better to keep an open mind. Whatever the answer may be, the disappearance of these diminutive components may not have necessarily signalled a radical break with the past in subsistence terms. Perhaps this way of using stone fell away as new techniques took on the role it had played in sustaining people's sense of their place in the community.

Continuities in the ways that hammers were brought down on stone were also matched in traditions of procurement. There are hints that sources with long histories of use continued to be important. Translucent flint from the Trent and the Cheshire Plain, local cherts and mottled flint from the Yorkshire and Lincolnshire Wolds. These materials occur in both later Mesolithic and earlier Neolithic assemblages.

. . . The white stone, mottled like burnt bone, makes knuckles round the chert. It keeps the dark meat fast until the spirits of the place are persuaded to give up their own. There are gifts to be made; sweat and fire and words spoken in secret. Only then . . .

As before, these materials were probably obtained in a number of ways: through trading partners, sharing within certain communities and by direct access to at least some of the sources. Scattered and varied exposures in old glacial head deposits, gravels in the south and outcropping chert in the heart of the region. In the latter case, visiting an outcrop often involved travelling to a place that had already been worked for generations. We can only guess at the stories and significance worked into these places by this time. Analogies with quarries and mines elsewhere in Britain would suggest a periodic or event-like quality to exploitation, perhaps embedded in seasonal rounds of stock husbandry or other tasks. That may have also been the case here. However, many of these more distant sources were used primarily and sometimes almost exclusively for the production of axes, something which is not apparent in the inventories of chert artefacts from the Peak. Very few axes were made from this material, not least because the common forms and sizes of chert tablets and nodules did not really lend themselves to the task.

Just how frequently certain chert seams were visited, and whether those visits were regarded in the same way as mining for flint on the southern chalk or quarrying for stone in the mountains of the west, remains to be seen. What may have been important in the Peak was that particular source areas for chert — narrow valleys like those at Sheldon — had histories and perhaps even spiritual associations that extended far into the past. Then, as before, making the journey and working the stone in customary ways may have been both a practical act, and a medium through which people renewed their ties to the land and to the ancestral past. Scrambling down narrow dales into Lathkill, or up from paths that ran along the river, people who came to prise the dark stone from the white encountered old camps and old scatters. Some they would remember. Others had always been there.

These sources probably continued to be visited by a range of people, a pattern that brought with it a requirement to address customary rights of access and broader social ties. Where visits were scheduled, people could still anticipate meeting others as well as finding stone. A chance to exchange news, materials and ideas, to renew more disparate connections. Stone from these sources may have also moved from hand to hand through various forms of exchange, itself part of the process by which relations between people were renewed over time.

What can we learn from the distribution of worked stone? Often the answer is not very much. In a world where many tasks could be performed with a basic range of tools, it is not always easy to be specific about the activities that occurred in a particular place, let alone when. Often, it is only the presence of pottery, such as Grimston Ware, that signals earlier Neolithic activity. That said, there are occasions when the location, content and scale of assemblages catches something of the character of landscape occupation at the time. What is clear is that the communities that we call Neolithic often moved through many landscapes in similar ways to their forbears, occupying the same places and following established paths.

Material is still found in an array of settings. Clusters have been found around springs, at places like Slipper Low above Aldwark and around the valley of Roystone Grange. Springs may have been significant as both a water supply and as points of reference. Earlier Neolithic material, often arrowheads, can also be traced in the scatters that run between the Cowper Stone, High Neb and Crow Chin along Stanage Edge. The sound of chert-working continued to echo from sites on the shelves overlooking sources in Lathkill Dale and parts of the Wye Valley, and tasks still carried people onto Bradwell Moor to the north, or Beeley, Gibbett and Totley Moors to the east. Concentrations also occur near ridge tops, in upland basins and along watersheds on the limestone, a pattern seen around Moneystones, on Gratton Moor and Elton Common. The accumulated residues of episodes of activity over long periods of time have also been identified by survey at Mount Pleasant, and around Aleck Low. Excavation in these areas has produced few signs of substantial structures. Where evidence survives, it tends to be hollows and shallow features that suggest more ephemeral dwellings and perhaps a periodic quality to the use of these places. Similar patterns have been recorded in the fields a little to the north-east, around Gib Hill, a Neolithic and later burial mound south of Monyash. Here again, later Mesolithic and earlier Neolithic stonework occurs in clusters within scatters that contain a good deal of later material.

These broad patterns suggest that watersheds and ridges served as important axes and break points, activities focused on catchments and on shelves and raised basins. In many areas, there is a sense that scatters get smaller the higher you are, and less visible the lower you dip into the deeper valleys. However, it is not always clear whether this is a genuine pattern or an artefact of recovery. As we shall see, it could be that the lower reaches of at least some valleys contain evidence that we seldom get a chance to explore.

Sometimes we are lucky. A number of excavations of later barrows have produced evidence for earlier activity. More often than not, this takes the form of worked stone, occasional axe fragments and sometimes sherds of Grimston or later pottery. This was the case at Wardlow Pasture in the south of the region, where work recovered a range of artefacts but no structural evidence beneath an Early Bronze Age mound. Some of this material may have been gathered up from the surrounding area during the construction of the barrow. At Liff's Low, Hartington, excavations beneath the mound of a later barrow revealed a slightly different range of evidence for prior activity. Here there was a pit containing charcoal dated to between 3990-3640 BC, a hearth, some forty or so stakeholes set at various angles in the underlying soils, and a small scatter of broken stone. These traces do not suggest substantial structures, still less a protracted quality to dwelling. Camps perhaps for herders or collectors established in the late summer, or hunting stands established in the lee of the rise behind the site. Perhaps these were still remembered and referenced in the building of the later barrow. Clusters of material were also recovered during excavations at Hognaston and Wigber Low, both perched above upland basins. At Wigber, however, it is unclear whether the hill served as a place of occupation or primarily as an area in which the dead were exposed to the elements. Like Liff's Low, this is a place to which we shall return.

Another general clue to the distribution of people can be found in the evidence of stone axes. Unlike flint, which is non-local but difficult to provenance, many of the hundreds of stone axes recovered from the Peak come from known sources. By far the most common are examples from the Langdales in central Cumbria (conventionally known as Group VI), and from Graig Lwyd (Group VII) near Penmaenmawr in north Wales. These were not the only sources from which axes were drawn; a few even come from as far away as Tievebulliagh in County Antrim (Group IX).

As with other materials, the interpretation of stone axes raises problems of temporal definition. Axes from these sources were made throughout the Neolithic. Fragments or complete examples have occasionally been found in excavated contexts, such as Lismore Fields, which demonstrate their presence in the Peak in the fourth millennium. However, others come from later sites, such as the Cumbrian axe recovered from a cairn on Big Moor, another from a barrow at Gospel Hillocks, Earl Sterndale. Several have also been found in caves, usually within multi-period deposits. Unfortunately, the vast majority have been recovered as chance finds. Some made their way into collections in the eighteenth and nineteenth centuries, when antiquarians would pay handsomely for well-fashioned pieces. Others have been found in fieldwalking; by people out for a stroll, or anglers catching sight of a cutting edge protruding from the bank. Walking over many parts of the Peak today, you are probably never that far from an axe.

This lack of context places certain limits on interpretation, but general patterns can still be sketched. Axes are found across the region, and are particularly common on the limestone. This may be because there have been far fewer opportunities to look in the Dark Peak or on the East Moors, except where fires have led to the erosion of soils and where feet or water have cut into the ground. Axes take a variety of forms: from large, highly polished examples which show few signs of use, to the majority; with edges worn down and reworked over time. There are certainly some, however, which for reasons of finish or fragility are likely never to have been used in a practical sense at all.

What are these extraordinary artefacts doing in the Peak? Why should we find axes made from these distinctive rocks at such great distances from their sources? Attempts to answer this question have a long pedigree. For a long time, it was assumed that the distribution of these tools, like the mountains of working debris at their sources, attested to a buoyant and organised trading network that spanned much of the country. Such an argument appealed to common sense. After all, this was a time when farming established a new pattern to the land through clearance, a task that demanded good stone for wholesale deforestation. Nowadays, we are not so sure. We now recognise that the lengths of time over which sources were used and products circulated was actually far longer than once thought. For that reason, there is no need to imagine some prehistoric 'Red Star' delivery service carrying vast numbers of axes across the country. Nor do we need to invoke an image of people working as full-time labour up at the sources. If anything, the evidence points to small-scale, episodic working embedded in other routines. We also don't seem to have the evidence for the wholesale clearance that was assumed in early studies. While axes would have certainly been useful, it is not clear that there was the massive upsurge in practical demand posited by early accounts. Moreover, it is common to find axes from these sources occurring in large numbers in areas that were locally rich in raw materials, notably Yorkshire. These broader patterns alert us to the possibility that something other than practical demand may have been caught up in the movement of these blades.

There is no question that the vast majority of axes were used as tools. From lopping, felling and carpentry through to butchery and even fighting, they served a variety of purposes. As an 'extension of the arm', hafted axes probably hung unnoticed on the shoulders of people as they worked, walked with stock or talked in the company of others.

Where flakes leapt from the edge during use, or when blades snapped against knot or stone, patient reworking prolonged the association. It was because of the potential for these close and lengthy associations that axes, amongst other things, acquired biographies. They carried people with them. This may have been because they also served as tokens of identity — their possession and use marking distinctions of age and perhaps gender. Props and cues in the telling of stories, prominent in gatherings and displays.

The recovery of these 'wandering' axes in the Peak reflects the interplay of these categoric links and more specific biographies. Because of their associations and beyond practical need, they were a potent medium for exchanges between communities. Many moved from hand to hand, and some were also passed down over time. And the distance over which these items travelled, probably in a series of small, if protracted steps, added depth to the patina of their biographies. Although it is not impossible, it is unlikely that people routinely travelled to Cumbria or to North Wales to quarry stone directly. Axes were generally polished by the time they left both areas, suggesting work by communities within each region. It was they who left their cattle on high pastures to make the sometimes precarious seasonal climbs to the quarry faces. People in and around the Peak may have heard about these places, in the news and stories that flowed back and forth between communities. But few may have made the climb, and this added to the attraction of these distinctive blades. Derived from a distant source, they spoke of relations to be remembered and other perhaps more malleable associations.

Things change

As in earlier times, residence and movement brought new clearings into being, or colonised areas freed from cover by wind, fire, grazing and erosion. There were probably also many places where episodes of occupation were separated by significant intervals or by changes in the nature of the tasks that were performed. But in the course of the year, people routinely came upon places that were known to them. Old clearings, middens and scatters of stone, tended or forgotten coppice and other traces lying beneath a mantle of scrub. Sometimes these traces spoke of the previous year, or of events from the relatively recent past. In that way, they were important cues and sometimes evidence for the actions of others. But there were also occasions where memories went further, into a past where genealogies blurred and ancestral forces could be traced in old stands, old stone, and perhaps in distinctive crags and springs. In following traditional patterns of movement, people returned to certain spots as much for spiritual as practical reasons, paying respect to the dead and to the spirits of the place.

The overlap in assemblages also reminds us that the tasks that made up people's lives still carried them around the landscape. Occupation could shift on a seasonal basis and might also move every few years or at the time scale of generations. It is this variety that we often miss when we talk simply in terms of settlement or agriculture, assuming a given, singular, pattern to the lives that lie behind these terms. Shifting stock and planting seed corn; visiting kin or trading with others; collecting honey or crab apples, returning sites of historic and ancestral importance. The round stretched across summer and winter pastures, between higher and lower ground and perhaps along watersheds. Land for over wintering; ground where the animals grew fat or where game was good; places visited from time to time and areas in which encounters with others might be expected. Under these conditions, the understandings that communities had of themselves, and of the land around them, still involved a sense of tenure to be renewed through labour and observance.

. . . What time is this place? It is the time of short light and a bite when the sun sleeps beneath the hill. A time to draw in; back to where we always come. Down near the water. Clay heavy on the foot after rain. A time when stories lengthen to fit the evening; woodsmoke and animals about us. A time to watch the fire . . .

This brings us to Lismore Fields. The site lies on the western side of where Buxton now stands, near the Wye and on the clays that lie below the limestone in the south and the gritstone to the north. Once again, pollen and stone demonstrate a varied and protracted relationship between people and this area. During the later part of the Mesolithic, the area bore open woodlands that alternated with patches of grassland and heath. By the sixth millennium, firing, perhaps deliberate, saw the maintenance of at least some limited clearings. A presence over this time is also suggested by some of the stonework on the site. Blades, microliths and other working debris are scattered across the area, resolved in places into clusters of higher density. Small camps; a season or so; people pausing and passing through. Threads that wound into knots of activity.

Given the limited extent of excavations, we do not know if these patterns are repeated nearby. But given broader trends, it is possible that this part of the valley saw repeated small-scale episodes of occupation, the canopy opening and closing through the attendance of people. Taken in isolation, the evidence evokes a sense of close focus. However, it is not impossible that there were occasions where others were set nearby, the abundance of seasonal plants, nuts or game bringing people together and broader ties into focus. Unfortunately, we cannot see beyond the edges of the trenches that were dug.

Cereal pollen appears in the sequence at Lismore during the fifth millennium. There is a pattern of repeated clearance and regeneration, perhaps a signal of localised management. Open, even tended, woodlands were still a dominant setting in the fourth millennium, and it was at this time that a series of rectangular post-built structures were added to the site. These are remarkably rare in Britain and hitherto unknown in the Peak. Two or perhaps three are represented, their presence marked by the post holes, slots and hearths that cut into the underlying earth. Post alignments and other settings have also been identified, though not all can be assigned to this time.

The acidity of the underlying clays is such that little in the way of bone or other organic material has survived. However, pottery is present, as is worked stone. Material from cut features, post holes and pits includes sherds of Grimston Ware, flakes from a Cumbrian axe, and the remnants of flint and quartz working. Just how material came to be incorporated in these features is uncertain. Often material may have been scuffed or trampled, lodged in slots or eroded into post holes after timbers were removed or burnt in situ. Fragments may have been lost as earth turned toward liquid during heavy rains. In some instances though, it is possible that materials were treated in a more deliberate manner, echoing the patterns found in earlier Neolithic pits and cut features in other regions. These sometimes have a structure to them which suggests purposive acts of selection and placing: food remains, charcoal from a hearth, arranged fragments of pottery and, where they survive, the selected bones of animals. In some cases, fragments of people have also been identified. Why people undertook these acts of interment is lost to us, though it is a concern that is well and widely reflected in evidence from the time. It may be that these acts sustained ties with particular places. They held evidence for past relations and events and fixed them in the earth. This was important where seasonal and even generational cycles carried people from one setting to another, though deposits may have also marked more specific events.

How did people live here? Residues on sherds include traces of dairy products and honey, with an even wider range of wild and domesticated plants preserved as fragmentary charred remains. Flax, hazelnut shells, emmer wheat and crab apples; a varied crop. Cereals are well represented. Interpreted as dwellings, the structures demonstrate a significant commitment to the place. The clearance or consolidation of an open area; the selection and felling of timber; working with others on the build. It is unclear if all the structures are contemporary. The more eastern example may have been two separate buildings, built back to back or in close sequence. If the latter was the case, the building of a second structure that tacked on to the position of the first may have helped evoke a sense of continuity between generations. When timbers of this size are cherished, they can certainly stand beyond the lifetime of a person, so however they were used, these buildings were a tie to a scale of time that went beyond the individual. This extended back into the timbers themselves and the years they had taken to mature. Posts glossed and darkened by lanolin, patinated by people moving to and fro, or resting their backs at the end of the day.

Lismore Fields tantalises us. It offers insights into the minutiae of certain tasks but remains silent on other issues. Though cereals are present in some quantity, we do not know whether crops stood nearby at certain times, or in small fields at a distance. The pollen is also equivocal on this point. However, the evidence does suggest a rich variety to the activities that flowed around these buildings. Just how long they were lived in and whether this was all year round cannot be determined, but given the pattern of life at the time, both are possible. There may have been seasons when some left to move the stock or meet with others along the path; others when people drew in, around the harvest or as winter brought the horizon down. We will never catch the details, but can acknowledge that the site was well placed to give access to a variety of settings.

Taking stock

Much in the pattern of the lives that turned through Lismore and places like it was probably in step with traditions so old they were often taken for granted. But things were changing, not least in ties between people, plants and animals. What we call the wild was

still central to much of life. But now, perhaps already for some time, there were other ties to attend to. People had always taken a rich variety of game, from aurochs and deer, through to beaver and waterfowl. They set part of the pattern to the seasons and helped shape how different landscapes were used and understood. Animals were also respected, some with the deference that follows fear, or perhaps because they held important spirits. Wolves, birds of prey, bears. In attending to land, to plants and other resources, harvesting the wild on a routine basis had created complex relationships. These did not simply vanish with the arrival of the first domesticates, nor were they necessarily any less close than those established with new species. Yet in taking stock, communities came to rework old values and open up new potentials.

. . . It took hours to deliver him. Calving went all through the night and on beyond the dawn. He was strong and stubborn even then. His mother moaned as we pulled, her face cloaked to keep her down. And now he is yours. In time, his blood will mingle with your own, a line to grow alongside our children. We will eat well . . .

Stock set part of the rhythm of life. Cattle and sheep grazed on open ground in many parts of the Peak, while pigs turned the earth beneath the trees and around the edges of settlements. Like other creatures, these animals provided a rich array of resources; food to share and materials for clothing, tools and exchange. What made them different was that through accumulation, breeding and selection, they offered new ways of defining relations between people.

An involvement with stock established new concerns, among them the requirement to bring cattle and sheep to seasonal pastures, and probably to keep them close in winter. Movement between valleys and higher ground and perhaps longer journeys. The turning of the year may have seen people moving with stock from the gritstones eastward down the dipslope; from the limestone south towards the Trent Valley or north and west towards higher ground. Perhaps there were times when elders took children off to late summer pastures, explaining the ancestral landmarks they encountered on the way. Task, talk and tradition went hand in hand.

And behind stock lay grazing and watering, access to paths and to woodland fodder when required. All of these concerns involved dealing with others, and it is likely that land used periodically was sometimes the object of competition, clearance itself caught up in the process. The patchwork had loose threads. Husbandry also involved periodic changes in the scale and composition of herds. Small groups could not remain isolated forever, and one of the hallmarks of the new round was the mingling of stock, either singly and under direction, or when herds were brought together. Late summer on the shelf below Stanage may have seen the bull of one line serve the cows of another, with calves born in the lower valley when the land itself was reborn in the spring. On ground where communities came together, the mix was greater still, as was the potential for tracing relations in the bloodlines of stock.

Cattle may have also been an important source of wealth and standing. Whether such judgements were made on the basis of the stature of individual beasts or the volume and health of herds is unclear. Each might have been stressed at different times. The right to hold stock was probably a prerogative of particular age grades, the outlines of herds also following ties of kinship. Those outlines may have been blurred. Rustling saw animals

move against the grain of social relations and many cattle were probably traded or given as gifts to others. Sometimes they made that journey on the hoof, sometimes off the bone. Often though, their passage contributed to the ties of kinship and affiliation that worked back and forth across the landscape. A calf delivered from close kin; a handful of animals married out across the ridge; a feast given in honour of visitors or of the dead.

Cattle mattered. For many communities, they brought a twist in the content, if not the shape, of the annual cycle. They were also a medium. It therefore mattered how animals fared. For people at the time, the changing fortunes of herds, the health of individual animals and success in breeding were a measure of practical experience. They were also an index against which to measure standing with the ghosts or ancestral forces that watched over the living. They had the power to help, to hinder or to turn their backs. They required respect and observance. This weaving together of practical and social values may have meant that cattle took on a more basic role as metaphors for the standing and composition of communities. Beyond the life cycle and the fortune of animals, there was the sense of bloodlines crossing and mingling when herds were brought close. Perhaps animals were marked against these events, so that a gathering signalled both the diversity and the unity of the broader group.

What of the crops in which cattle or other animals sometimes strayed? Despite the survival of pollen, and on occasion grain, we know little about the character and scale of cultivation. Some talk of gardens and forest fallow, and in many settings this may be apt. For many communities, the cycle of planting and harvesting was practised only a handful of times. After the grazing of stubble, a patch was left to regenerate; scrub, then birch and ash; leaf litter and shadow. Soils depleted of their fertility could be renewed in this way. Attention turned to other plots on other shelves, ones last used a generation or more before, their presence still traceable in the composition of cover. Pasture perhaps, or open woods where boar rooted for fodder. For others, small fields were of greater importance. Sustained over longer periods, they provided fodder, materials and grain for food and drink. Stores to keep things going over winter; the makings of a feast to give to others. In the varied conditions of the time, we should not assume that precisely the same suite of routines was matched by every community, nor that this remained constant. Diversity may have been an important dynamic in the trading and gift giving that cut back and forth between families. Whatever the case, tensions could surround fields, just as they bordered pasture. As tenure shifted from one generation to another, new paths and new clearings could cut across old patterns and old agreements. If crops needed tending, so did the relationships that lay behind the land.

Like stock, crops required attention and they raised new concerns. They need not have tied an entire community to one place for the whole year. But they needed to be maintained against the threat of grazing, while planting, fostering and harvesting required varied contributions of labour. They also added a new theme to thinking about land. Whatever the particular timing or rotation of crop cultivation, much of the work was conducted by hand, not by the plough. This may have encouraged a tendency to choose the lighter or sandier soils found on the shelves and upland basins of both the limestone and the gritstone. These would have been far easier to work than the heavier clays lower down in the valleys, many of which were, in any case, still densely wooded at this time. Conditions further up may have also been rather more open, with alternating stretches of grassland and open woodlands. With perched water tables and springs, these areas were well suited to occupation, pasturage and cultivation. Waterlogging would have also been a greater problem in the lower valleys, and we can imagine that where cattle were overwintered in these settings, things might become mired quite quickly. Where valleys were old and wide enough, raised terraces may have been particularly important.

Crops, like stock, provided a rich source of metaphor and a concern with fortune. Where seasons changed the land in such a dramatic way, the sense of the world dying back and being reborn would have been nothing new. People had been harvesting the wild for generations and made sense of these cycles in customary ways. Crops however engendered a particular form of involvement. This may have made their cycle of birth, death and rebirth a particularly vivid metaphor for the lives of people and for the renewal and persistence of the community. Stock and crops also encouraged a different attitude towards time. In a world where the continuity of the line from one generation to another was a powerful concern, they were a debt owed to the past and a legacy to be bestowed on the future. Protection of that inheritance required the passing on of practical knowledge. It also demanded a respect shown to the spirits and ancestors who held the fortunes of the living in their hands.

. . . The corn is dead. It lies there, flat and lifeless like reeds in a swamp where floods have fallen. Have they been offended? Perhaps the spirits who bring the land alive each year have not been shown the right respect. Maybe it's a ghost telling us it is time to move . . .

4 A tangle of relations
4000-2500 BC

Five Wells

Italo Calvino recounts a description of a place given to the Kublai Khan by Marco Polo. There it is customary for any meeting between people, any connection or union, to be marked in a particular way. A line must be hung between their houses, a different line for the nature of the tie. In time, relations deepen and new ties are made. The lines become more dense and movement becomes difficult. Eventually, everyone has to move and start again; the web of history making life impossible. All that is left is a dense cat's cradle that sometimes catches the wind.

So far, our path into the Peak of the fourth millennium has meandered a good deal. The focus has also been close. We have dwelt on concepts of community and close kinship and have not strayed far beyond those horizons. This creates something of a false impression. The company of an extended family and even smaller numbers was commonplace at many times. But people also recognised broader social geographies, bonds with more disparate kin and relative strangers. As Calvino acknowledged, the flow of life brings people into many combinations.

It was in the talk that turned around fires and between different families, new currents added all the time where kinship and affiliation blurred into one another. It was carried in the objects exchanged into different valleys, or in the blood of animals. Where biographies or pedigrees were known, tools and stock were testaments to the order of relations. Practical life itself brought this more extensive web of ties, alliances and obligations into view. There were planned and chance encounters, meetings on the trail and in seasonal quarries and pastures. There was work and trade in different combinations and the negotiation of tenure. Learning to work meant learning about those relations, about the ancestry of the land and the genealogies of people. Where work possessed the qualities of custom, it fostered social memory.

And things changed. Marriages between lines, tensions over access, inheritance and the settlement of disputes; each brought subtle shifts in the contours of social life. Obligations incurred and renown accrued through feasting or exchange might lead some to wield a local authority, just as elders might claim priority over the young. This was the routine playing out of ties between communities and between generations. Perhaps there were even occasions when claim and counter-claim led to feuding, raiding and other forms of graded conflict. An argument over land, stock or access to a trail; a matter of honour and blood that had run for many years; disrespect shown to the spirits of a place. Sometimes it was simply proximity to the ancestors that became a focus for competition.

There are deeper currents here. A tangle of relations ran through many aspects of life, change working on the threads of that ravel in different ways. Sometimes widespread, alluvial, imperceptible; sometimes focused, sudden and dramatic. Over generations, the fourth millennium saw new twists in people's attachment to places. This had always been important, even fundamental to the ways in which communities had thought about themselves for millennia. But as generations passed and paths crossed, different ways of thinking about land and time were worked into particular places. Tales are seldom told the same way twice.

Though it was bound up in attention to stock and crops, attachments to place went far beyond practical or calorific concerns. There were the histories that formed like sediment, whispered in the remnants of old camps and stated perhaps more clearly at sacred sites. Different parts of the landscape acquired new genealogies; read in the condition of the ground and fostered in oral tradition. And those genealogies were themselves woven into origin myths and broader senses of an ancestral past. In the cyclical use of many places, people probably understood their practical needs as a function of these historic and spiritual conditions. It was to these that they appealed as they pursued specific interests: access to pastures, plots and sources; the assertion of community or standing over others.

This takes us further along the path, towards particular places and times at which scattered communities acknowledged their links with others. But to talk solely of relations amongst the living is to catch only one aspect of the picture. There were other valued partners in the exchanges that made up life. Prominent amongst these were the dead; spirits and ancestral forces active in the world of the living.

This is difficult for us to grasp. It is common for us to see a disjuncture between the living and the dead, where memory seldom allows a continued influence. Dead and gone. An alien view in many settings, it is a conceit to assume that similar lines were necessarily drawn in the fourth millennium.

Death was important. It brought changes in ties of kinship and standing. It threatened the continuity of the social order, requiring the handing on of rights and responsibilities. It may not have had the sense of closure that we often recognise today.

. . . I use these chisels most days. I've grown attached to them, worn them into the shape of my hand. That one belonged to my grandfather. What he used it for I don't recall, his ashes were on the mantlepiece for years before it came to me. I remember the edge was resistant until reground, the angle of his hand and how he worked . . .

In the midst of life

At a time when routine experience was understood through concepts of ancestry and biography, the dead were a pervasive presence. Traced in an heirloom, in gestures and rhetoric learnt from elders, or in plots first cleared and stone once worked by long dead kin. That presence could be more tangible still. In much of Britain at the time, the physical remains of the dead were actively drawn upon by the living. Sometimes they were just bone; scattered fragments overlooked by people and gnawed at by animals. But bones were also relics that circulated, sustaining perhaps some aspect of the spirit of the dead.

Carried on the trail, the dead walked in step with the living. Displayed at important events, relics evidenced the responsibilities handed down the line and over time. Cult objects handled by a shaman, they aided communication with other worlds. Deposited in different settings, they spoke of the ties that bound a community to earlier generations and to particular places. This variety in the treatment sometimes accorded to bone was not confined to people. The remains of certain animals could also be cherished, sometimes circulating in parallel with those of dead kin; the skull of a fox or a cow, the antlers of a stag. It was not only people who had souls or spirits. In both cases, the respect shown to these relics suggests an importance that went beyond remembrance. Death brought not an end to things, but a different relation to the living. A different engagement. It is likely that communities of the time saw the dead and other spirits as forces that dwelt and acted alongside them. Sometimes in step, sometimes hostile or capricious, those forces required respect and observance. They could influence fortune, and beyond all else, they provided a crucial link between people and the landscape itself, their presence and their memory as powerful as any deed.

Many paths carried people into the afterlife. Not all left an archaeological trace. The limited volume of human bone that we generally recover suggests that there were forms of treatment accorded to corpses that we can only ever guess at. Exposure, the dispersal

Minninglow

of bones or ashes in the forest, the scattering of remains in rivers and the corruption of flesh. What we do know is that mortuary and funerary rites could often be protracted, comprising several stages and encompassing more than one place. At least some of these stages cohered around what we now recognise as the tombs that started to appear during the fourth millennium.

Our best evidence in the region comes from chambered tombs, passage graves and long barrows, the most detailed of all, a few days walk to the south-east. Near Creswell Crags, our hunger for quarried stone bit deep into a Neolithic long cairn. Known as Whitwell, the site was saved from total oblivion by careful excavation and recording. It now exists solely as archive, the land long despatched elsewhere. Less than half of the site remained to be excavated, but that portion revealed a remarkable history. At some point in the later fifth millennium, an area of ground, perhaps a clearing, was stripped of its turf. On this, a circular cairn was raised, comprising a double drystone wall with a diameter of around ten metres. At the heart of this cairn was the body of a young woman aged around sixteen or so. After an interval a second, larger, cairn was built over and beyond the first, absorbing it into its fabric. This time, the monument was trapezoidal. On both cairns, some care had gone into selecting distinctive limestone for the building of the drystone walls. On its northern side, the edge of the long cairn was broken by a passage that ran back into the mound, to a linear spread of both articulated and jumbled remains. Some fifteen men and women. There were adults and children of various ages, their bones associated with one or two sherds of pottery and a few lozenge and leaf-shaped flint arrowheads. Apparently, these bones had accumulated as the result of more than one episode of deposition, the passage being blocked between these lives.

Looked at more closely, the bones tell their own story. The spread of material suggests that several bodies and parts of others were placed in this area; corpses and partly dismembered cadavers. Subsequent episodes of activity, bringing new burials or communing with the dead, saw the movement of existing deposits, and the pushing of bones and decaying body parts to one side. Some bones may have been trampled on as particular rites unfolded. Wear patterns on the teeth of several people suggest that the occupants of the long cairn had a varied diet, one which included resources that we associate with hunting and gathering communities. Wear on the teeth of two women was particularly striking. It suggests that both had spent many hours using their teeth as tools; chewing hide or stripping fibres from plants.

What are we to make of Whitwell? What can it tell us about the ways that people perceived mortality and the dead, or how tombs themselves were implicated? Comparatively, the site has both similarities and differences with others. Like many, it has a complex sequence that saw the site remodelled or swallowed up in a larger monument over time. It also appears to have been caught up in complex rites of passage. These vary from place to place. At some, body parts arrived already stripped of their flesh having been exposed or defleshed elsewhere. A rocky outcrop, the branches of a tree, a platform or a pit. Inclusion, even for a time, may have been a privilege of kinship and descent, bones gathered up and brought to a tomb by those who shared blood ties. Within many sites, these bones are often disarticulated and jumbled, suggesting a levelling and confusion of personal identity in death. It is in this common emphasis on the collective that we have often traced a concern with ancestral forces. The customary breaking and reordering of bodies suggests a transformation on death and passage into some form of ancestral realm. The make up of body parts in many tombs also suggests that bones may have gone out as well as in, carried away to circulate amongst the living or for deposition elsewhere.

At Whitwell, the situation is a little different. Funerary activity begins with a single burial of an articulated body. Only later do rites turn towards the episodic movement of bones after flesh had been corrupted. Perhaps this was also the case at other sites, later activity obscuring these more individual foundations. In the trapezoidal cairn, some at least were laid to rest as complete corpses, only later becoming mixed as a consequence of the continued use of the tomb. However, others had already been exposed or partially broken up. For them, and perhaps for the others too, the tomb was one place in a longer chain of rites. Decay was a metaphor for the journey that a person made on death, the body transformed as the spirit moved into a different realm.

The particular significance given to older bones when people re-entered the tomb is far from clear. Though names may have been remembered, perhaps the bones themselves were now important largely as tokens of an ancestral presence. At some sites, reordering was structured and meaningful; distinctions of age, gender and experience marked by the positions bones were accorded. These distinctions were brought into focus as people handled and ordered skeletal remains; rites which involved the telling of stories about the ancestral past and the lives of earlier generations.

. . . Earth raised to make way for a coffin. The soil is rich with bone; shards and splinters of humanity passing unnoticed from dark to light then back again. He steps down from the cab and sorts over earth, removing longer bones and tossing them back in the hole that will soon be a grave. A spade or two of earth obscures their line. He will cover the spoil with green canvas before the mourners arrive . . .

Whitwell lies outside the modern boundaries of the Peak, but it is likely that the communities who respected the site were linked by kinship, alliance and exchange to those further north and west. Distances are not that great; two or three days on the trail, a handful more with the herd. We get a sense of this in the playing out of similar themes in long cairns and barrows across the Peak itself. Here though there is a problem. Relatively few of the earliest sites have seen systematic and well-recorded excavation. The majority were investigated in the eighteenth and nineteenth centuries and records, where they exist, often leave many stones unturned. This means that we cannot always take sites at face value. A long mound which appears earthen on the surface may contain stone chambers as yet undiscovered. Dates for foundations and reuse are also imprecise. Comparison with other regions suggests that some of the earliest tombs of all were relatively small chambered barrows, long mounds perhaps being built a little later but overlapping in the chronology of their use. There is also confusion over contents. Some mounds may contain no human remains at all, or deposits that were no more than tokens. This has been noted elsewhere and reminds us that the significance of these ancestral houses probably went beyond the dead themselves.

That said, the evidence is such that we can still sketch in one or two contours. Preserved by antiquarian interest or simply because they were set sufficiently apart from later agriculture and industry, there are over twenty chambered tombs and long mounds in the Peak. All known sites occur on the limestone. A visit to many today is a visit to places worked over by academic interest and by millennia of activity. Quarrying, the creation of landmarks, the bite of the plough, use as a kiln. At Five Wells for example, the early modern enclosure of land encouraged the 'borrowing' of material for drystone walls. At Long Low, prospection has also taken its toll, later pits and quarries encroaching upon the mound itself. What we experience is the legacy of five or six thousand years of respect, forgetting, rediscovery and reuse.

This reworking is not confined to the more recent past. An additional 'problem' in dealing with tombs and barrows in the Peak is that almost all, like Whitwell, show very complex histories of use, some stretching across the Neolithic and into the Early Bronze Age. Eighty or more generations as we tally them. Some even appear to have been a focus of interest a hundred or more generations later, in the centuries around the Roman occupation. Worked, forgotten, rediscovered. Though they often evoke a sense of stability and of the timeless, few monuments are constant. These long and chequered histories mean that many sites are now difficult to trace. Some are simply gone, but a few, like Minninglow or Tideslow are prominent features still. Others, like Stoney Low, are now so ravaged by time, interest and neglect that they can easily be passed unnoticed. A curious outcrop or a resilient ridge of limestone rather than the outline or spine of a tomb. A confusion of nature and history.

Green Low

What significance did Neolithic communities attach to these places? What did it mean to quarry stone or scrape up earth and turf, to contain space between timbers and large limestone slabs? Why return and extend respect across generations? Though common themes were recognised, people building different tombs probably interpreted those themes in locally specific ways. Tradition, despite appearances, is a malleable resource and we get hints of this in broader distributions. The patterns are by no means clear. Unchambered long mounds are a little more common to the north while those with passages have a distribution weighted towards the south. Tombs with chambers occur throughout the region. Time aside, it may well be that these subtle architectural differences reflect the interplay between local understandings and more widespread ideas. In one sense at least, things were not entirely set in stone. However, it is likely that these were often places where loss could be acknowledged and where a sense of kinship and community could be grounded in an ancestral order.

Tombs did not appear on blank canvases. Places were carefully chosen and were important in a number of ways. Sometimes it was the history that a place had accrued which guided the decision. An old settlement, or a clearing in which the spirits had always been strong. At Green Low, a tomb some 20m across, a single chamber was reached by a narrow passage that ran from a curving, horned forecourt. The passage had been deliberately blocked. The site was already disturbed when dug, but still contained an inhumed body and the scattered bones of animals and other people. Amongst these were sherds from plain, round-bottomed vessels. Excavation also revealed that the building of the cairn sealed older material. This included worked stone: part of a polished axe and other pieces of worked flint. Though some of this material may have been quite fresh when the cairn was founded, some was probably older, stretching back into the Mesolithic.

At places such as this, there is a sense of old associations reworked by the building of a tomb. An ancestral house built on an old hunting camp, or near a lodge once used by people watching over stock. Tombs may have been built where the hand of ancestors was already recognised, in the outline of a crag, in springs or woodland stands. This may have been the case up on Harborough Rocks. Here a badly damaged cairn lies close to a cave that was also used for burial. The chamber and passage of the tomb contained disarticulated bodies, animal bones, pot sherds, flakes and leaf-shaped flint arrowheads. Whether the arrowheads entered the cairn in or with the bodies is impossible to tell. Mesolithic flintwork in the general vicinity suggests that the distinctive crags and pinnacles of the area had been visited or passed long before the cairn was built. Perhaps the building of the cairn drew upon those older associations, incorporating them into the origin myths of those who now came to honour and commune with the dead.

The skyline of Harborough Rocks raises another possibility. Looked at today, it is often difficult to tell where the land ends and a monument begins. Though this is often a consequence of the ways that sites have been forgotten or curated over time, this blurring may itself have been important. Tombs were made from available materials: timbers, earth and stone. They were dramatic and impressive monuments, those qualities amplified where sites were remodelled or embellished over time. Even so, they may have sometimes been regarded as part of the land themselves. As people climbed particular hills, a tomb may have risen into view as if it was coming up out of the ground. Where visible, limestone kerbs could mimic the line of outcropping benches, while taller orthostats evoked crags that were a familiar sight on the trail. Mounds of stone or fresh soil may have soon gained a mantle of turf that took the tomb back into the earth.

This attention to place may also be reflected in the way that a number of tombs respect the run of the ground. At Perryfoot, a long mound around 50m in length follows the prevailing contour. Here again, excavation in the eighteenth and nineteenth centuries saw the recovery of a profusion of human and animal bones. A similar respect to the lie of the land was shown at Rockhurst, where a long mound follows the spine of a locally prominent spur. Elsewhere, references may have been made to other features. A link with watersheds as a setting for a number of sites suggests that springs were often close at hand, a connection demonstrated at the aptly named Five Wells, Taddington. Such links may have gone beyond practical need, important though this was. If the land embodied important ancestral and spiritual forces, then water issuing from below might have also been given a particular symbolic significance.

These examples hint that tombs were sometimes built in such a way that they emphasised ties with the land, perhaps even highlighting particular natural features. This might be achieved through close association or through the view that was had as one approached. Perhaps the gaze along the spine of a tomb sometimes directed attention to significant features. Rivers, hills or other forms that featured prominently in origin myths and genealogies. History and geology bleeding into one another. Stories told of ancestral houses and their occupants gained a weight from being traced back into the land and into older narratives.

These currents may have turned in the stories told while people laboured to found or embellish a long mound or passage grave. The scale of many sites suggests the work of many hands, clearings alive with talk and with knots of activity. Stripping the skin of the land, selecting limestone, felling timber, chains of baskets. Working in combination. At Tideslow and Gib Hill, work included the fashioning of low mounds or platforms of yellow clay. At Five Wells, large limestone slabs were use to create two chambers more or less back to back. Smaller blocks were used to run drystone walling in between. From each chamber, they laid a passage out to a kerb which formed the edge of the mound. Several people would have laboured to manoeuvre these slabs into position, perhaps under direction or encouragement from others. Excavation revealed that the site had already been explored, but nonetheless resulted in the recovery of bones from around fourteen people; men, women and children.

Labour directed to rather different ends can be seen at Long Low. The site is complex, with a poor record. Over 200m in length, it is perhaps the only example in the Peak of what we call a bank barrow. The site has three components: two round mounds joined by a long and impressive bank of earth and stone. There is also a shallow forecourt at the north-western end. A chamber was discovered in the nineteenth century by Samuel Carrington, who recorded around thirteen bodies, piled up on a pavement together with leaf-shaped arrowheads and the bones of oxen, pigs, deer and dogs. Carrington also noted human remains in sections across the long bank, as well as the presence of a spine of angular limestone walling and vertically set slabs. Much of the stone appeared to have been quarried from scoops that are still traceable on the surface nearby.

Long Low has a protracted history and there is much that we do not know. However, the stone arrangements speak of the prising of blocks and slabs from quarries or exposures; the hammering of wood or antler wedges and the sorting of stone for different uses. There is design and perhaps agreement; the considered placing of the spinal line and the creation of a forecourt in which later communion might be set. An anticipation of the future as well as a memorial to the past. Both form and scale suggest people working in combination to realise a project; shared labour invested in a monument that bound them to each other.

Just how the dead were regarded at many tombs in the Peak is difficult to say. There is a variety in the evidence and this suggests that there was no set or singular pattern to proceedings. Frequent references to bodies and to fragments indicate that like Whitwell, corpses often went through protracted rites; arrival, decay, disarticulation, handling and sorting. It is also likely that at least some of the material recovered over the last two centuries arrived in an already broken and defleshed state. In this variety we catch a glimpse of rites that blurred the distinction between the biographies of specific people and membership of a broader community. In some cases, these rites may have been played out against particular architectural settings. At Ringham Low for example, where five or six chambers were set in a larger mound, each setting may have allowed family distinctions to be drawn whilst still emphasising broader ties. Bodies may have also been

Long Low

placed in passages before being moved further in, to the chambers themselves. That a distinction was drawn between these spaces is indicated by the emphasis on defining a threshold, the line marked by distinctive portal and septal stones. And since access was still possible, or impeded only by blocking that could easily be removed, repeated visits to many chambered tombs and passage graves often meant an encounter with the dead. Entry was a dramatic, even dangerous, event. There would be crawling across or sorting through the scattered remains of people, the smell of decay, white bone and sometimes rotting flesh. Bones of those who had never passed the threshold into adulthood and close at hand, the remains of the elders, some so old that their names were now forgotten or invented. Transformation was not just an idea; it confronted the senses.

These encounters with bodies and bones served many purposes. Mourning, respect, and the evocation of the chain of names that lay behind a particular community. Even when direct contact was not possible, mounds threw long shadows. Forecourts defined areas where food might be shared and oratory could still turn to those who lay within. For specific lineages or small clusters of kin, these assemblages connected present and past. They bound communities together. We can only guess that these divisions respected marriage, descent and ties that stretched between the clearings of a few extended families. At times, this sense of commonality may have been more fictive than real. Rites that brought a sense of levelling in death could conceal differences of authority and fortune.

On other occasions, proceedings may have turned where the dead were held in a different relation; where people came to seek help or revelation. Conducting rites of passage, asking for help with the herd, the elders instructing young initiates. At certain seasons, entire communities may have gathered, their herds nearby, paying respect and seeking help for the year ahead. Perhaps there were times when people came alone; to make offerings, or to sleep close by the dead and catch their guidance in a dream.

Associations with bones and bodies are difficult to read. Arrowheads occur at a number of sites but are ambiguous; we simply cannot tell if they were placed with a body as later offerings, or were even the cause of death. Close identification is rare. There are also fragments of pottery and animal bones, noted at sites like Gib Hill, Harrod Low and Perryfoot. Like some of the flintwork, pottery and bone might enter a tomb as selected midden, the residues of acts of consumption undertaken close at hand. They could also be offerings. Animals, or individual animal bones may have even been accorded the same treatment as the remains of people. Roles in life might be signalled in this way, or relations between different categories of spirit. Where these potentials were recognised, in stock, game or other creatures, respect may have been important. Returning at a later season, entering a passage or gathered in a forecourt, people encountered these assemblages as the past in the present, and as a record of events in which they and their kin had participated. Here was a midden first established by the founders. There were the fragments of vessels that had once contained offerings to the dead or food shared amongst kin. Events and past relations were made secure in social memory through these encounters. They were reconciled with the present.

The past brought into focus at tombs helped bind particular communities, to land and to each other. And because of this, ancestral houses were also places where some held a local authority over others. The right to officiate in ancestral rites may have been

Minninglow

the prerogative of a family head or ritual specialist and there were probably times when access to forecourts or interiors was restricted. And as new bodies were brought, perhaps the heads of different families took precedence, providing food and oratory for those who were assembled. The order of things was by no means fixed. But proximity to the ancestors was an index of the fortune and standing of particular people. For those who were favoured, cattle thrived and children lived to carry the line.

. . . This is where our line begins and ends; where the circle is complete. We know the spirits this place holds, the times and places of their lives. We walk the same paths still. These are the threads that bind us . . .

Tombs were also set in relation to broader routine landscapes. Though small chambered sites are found in a variety of settings, there is a link with land that was often recognised as grazing country. This is a little clearer for long barrows, which were commonly set on the fringes of upland areas that saw use as seasonal pasture. Many lie on or relatively near to watersheds, on ridges or where dales rise up to meet the higher ground. Some would have been visible at a distance, yet hidden when close at hand, their presence only revealed by the final climb. Sites like Minninglow also provided vantages from which to look out in all directions, across familiar woods and clearings and perhaps towards country that was less well known. High ground far to the north, the rise of Stanton Moor to the north-east; the dark folds of valleys whose sheer sides lay hidden beneath thick woodland. Minninglow, and the ridge upon which it stands, was a prominent point of reference; seen from a distance, on the approach or passed on the high trail that runs nearby. This quality of prominence is enhanced today by a dramatic stand of beeches encroaching on the site.

In other cases, the visual catchment of ancestral houses was more focused. Those standing at Five Wells would have had dramatic views northwards, but more restricted scope in other directions. The site is set near the sharp northern edge of Taddington Moor and encourages the eye to dwell upon the land in that direction, perhaps upon pastures that lay above the Wye around Blackwell and Priestcliffe. At Long Low too, elevation meant an excellent vantage, particularly down onto the shelves around the junction between Biggin and Wolfscote Dales.

Vantage was not always important. There are low-lying sites like Gospel Hillocks, where visual prominence from any distance was not a major concern. The same is true of Stoney Low. Set in a shallow, gently sloping dale, the site is now difficult to identify, a sharp contrast to the imposing mound recorded by Hayman Rooke in the eighteenth century. But however dramatic it once may have been, the setting of Stoney Low gave no scope for extensive vantages. You come upon the site only when relatively close at hand, and it may well be that this 'hidden' quality added to the significance of the tomb as a place on the edge of things.

Vantage aside, the settings of many tombs suggest a connection with land that saw a variety to occupation; hunting grounds, pastures and trails along which both people and animals moved. Approached from dales and valleys and from several directions, the higher limestone was a part of the region where people might anticipate coming into contact with others. It was here that paths crossed. Extended families who were part of the line and others with whom relations were perhaps more disparate and less certain. Tombs were important in these settings. This was not just about claiming land; the assertion of tenure. Such rights may have been recognised, but what mattered here was that tombs emphasised the more extensive bonds of kinship in landscapes that saw a seasonal flux of people. It was here that scattered families might come close, here that herds mingled and here that tenure might come to be a source of tension. If valleys drew horizons and encounters in close, higher ground brought a broader human geography into view. Watershed locations added to this potential. Sometimes recognised as boundaries or thresholds, they might be places of transition, a quality acknowledged in ancestral rites and one that suited meetings between the scattered members of a broader kin group.

Visited after overwintering in more sheltered valleys, or in late summer with the herd, tombs brought extended families together, grounding their connections to the land and to each other through ancestral and funerary rites. And as seasons turned, and one generation gave way to another, those communities returned again and again; adding to the fabric and content of tombs, weaving new threads into older narratives. Beyond all else, tombs endured. They persisted in a way that the immediate trappings of many settlements did not. Massive timbers might outlive a generation and stone itself appeared to withstand time. Because of their persistence, as much as their contents, tombs evoked a continuity that went beyond death.

Broader horizons

Tombs brought scattered kin together. Passed along the trail by others, they were a powerful reminder of customary rights of access. But they had their greatest significance for those bound by ties of kinship and descent. In the dispersed and fragmented landscapes of the time, the communities who turned around particular tombs may have been reasonably extensive. But there was an order to things that was broader still, an acknowledgement of social identity that went beyond those ties.

These broader horizons are glimpsed in the flint from sources outside the Peak. Stone axes too speak of connections, albeit diffuse and indirect, which extended out beyond the region. There is also the playing out of familiar themes in the architecture and use of tombs across Britain; a balance between local, regional and even broader traditions. How was this order possible? How did scattered knots of people recognise their place in a broader web? Once again, there is more than one answer. Where gift exchange formed ties between people, the biographies of objects drew threads across the land. Even what we might deem trading was a social act, one which involved acknowledging and maintaining partners. In this way, trade was also a conduit along which ideas as well as goods, might pass. Though we cannot be certain, it is also likely that a measure of exogamy characterised marriage traditions at the time, a practice which made at least some social boundaries more permeable or malleable.

Recognition sometimes went beyond this. In many parts of Britain at the time, broader worlds were brought into sharp relief in specific places, not just in routine encounters or in objects from distant sources. Principal amongst these were large enclosures of earth and sometimes of stone, many now bound uncomfortably together in the category 'causewayed enclosure'. Often built in woodland clearings, with one or more circuits enclosing several hectares, enclosures have varied histories. Some witnessed episodes of occupation, but most were places at which scattered groups assembled periodically to renew a broader company. People gathered, perhaps at certain seasons, perhaps when word went out, around fires and along trails. They dwelt for a short time alongside others, redrawing the contours of a broader social landscape as they moved around the margins, collecting wood or food and visiting other hearths. On this frame were woven the stories of all that went on from one valley to another. There were opportunities for trade, for the creation of new bonds and for talk. Perspective was different in these settings.

So far as we can tell, there was a rich variety to the events that took place within many enclosures. Evidence suggests feasting, exchange, and rites of passage. Crossing the thresholds of many constituted a movement into arenas of value. Boundaries drew a distinction between the world outside and that which lay within. A world of natural and spiritual forces and a land that was ordered by the histories and aspirations of different lines. Forces to be contained or called upon, commonalities and tensions to be attended to. Outside was the everyday. Though rich in ancestry and history, this was a world shaped by obligation and by tenurial claim. Usual patterns of encounter were suspended as people came together. A sense of liminality, of being apart from the common order of experience lent a weight to events and to dealings with others.

It is not easy to determine precisely why these monuments should have appeared in many parts of Britain at this time. Similar places were already long established on parts of the continent. However, this simply demonstrates a flow of ideas back and forth. It does not tell us why the idea was taken up in various ways from Cornwall to Scotland and from Cumbria to East Anglia. What we can say is that reasons would have been locally and historically specific. But in a climate of ideas sustained by extensive networks of contact and communication, changes in the character of land use certainly played their part. They raised a series of concerns for the fertility of the land and of people, and new ways of thinking about the relationship between present and past. At the same time, patterns of living associated with having herds and tending crops brought with them changes in how people understood their ties to land and their relations with others. Dispersed though the landscape was, the passage of time saw a consolidation and sedimentation of those ties. There were other themes too, ones which cannot be reduced to simple consequences of subsistence change. The negotiation of local renown and the satisfaction of conflicts of interest were also crucial; social and political relations between groups were both volatile and malleable. Enclosures provided a frame in which it was possible for communities to address those themes.

Our understanding of these enigmatic monuments is changing all the time. Work in previously neglected regions is adding new examples to the catalogue, and excavation more depth to our picture of proceedings. That work is also demonstrating subtle local and regional differences in the histories of individual monuments, a variety which has sometimes led to sites being overlooked. This may be the case in the Peak. So far there are only a few sites that are arguably of a similar date. However, some may lie as yet undiscovered; no trace left to recognise, or swallowed up in the hilltop enclosures of the Later Bronze Age and Iron Age.

One likely example is Gardom's Edge, not far from Baslow. In the recent past, the site, like many others in central, western and northern Britain, has been assigned to a variety of periods. Though it may have been known locally for far longer, its entry into the literature came in the 1940s. An intense fire removed much of the cover on the moor and made it possible for the eye to trace the pattern of the bank. A photograph of the open moor and part of the site can be found in the Clarion Ramblers Journal for 1958. Referred to as 'Meg Walls' (a field a little to the south of the enclosure was given this name in the nineteenth century), and linked by hearsay to cattle and milking, it was interpreted at this time as a 'British defence wall'. The term is by no means unusual. In the first half of the twentieth century, it was often used to attribute many elevated enclosures to a period of assumed tension in the centuries around the Roman occupation. This is probably misleading. The enclosure is overlain by Bronze Age Field systems, and its character and setting owes more to Neolithic traditions than it does to those bound up in Iron Age hillforts.

Visited today, the enclosure takes the form of a bank between five and ten metres wide and around six hundred metres long. Obscured now by birches that are a product of low grazing after another fire in 1959, it is composed of weathered gritstone boulders collected from the land around. Larger slabs have also been used, some positioned on the outer face to form a basic, if intermittent, façade. There are at least five entrances through the bank, some with signs of deliberate blocking. Much of the interior of the enclosure is heavily boulder strewn, and there are many large gritstone earthfasts outcropping through

Gardom's Edge enclosure

the heather, peat and coarse grasses. Most of the site lies on unimproved moorland, but at its southern end, the bank runs into an area of more recently enclosed fields. Here the pasture has been 'improved' and the monument has all but gone, visible only when the sun is low and shadows trail from a simple break of slope. The bank delimits one side of a large area at the crest of the edge, the other being the precipitous scarp that hangs above the Derwent Valley. Today the edge is often decorated with a colourful lattice of climbers, stretching for holds on 'Eye of faith', 'Landsickness' or 'Solid Air'.

Climbers look close. They have a focus that differentiates a place for gear, a fingerlock and a slap; intimate routes remembered as hands flex in discussion off the crag. For the Neolithic communities who moved across Gardom's Edge, there was a similar intimacy to their recognition of the enclosure, one born out of participation and close attention in building. There is a variety to the build as we see it now, some of it a consequence of much later episodes of robbing and disturbance. The bank has been cut by post-medieval trackways, and stone has been taken towards either end in close proximity to more recent walls. One part of the central area was also altered during the construction of a later sheep fold and lea wall. Elsewhere there are small delves and quarry features suggesting the sporadic use of the monument as a source of stone for various purposes. Many are consistent with turning over the outer face of the bank to obtain larger gritstone boulders and slabs. Some are the pock marks and dents of old tree throws.

Robbing has certainly contributed to the current form of the enclosure, but it has probably always been varied. In places, it takes the form of a simple pile of rounded boulders rising no more than half a metre above the ground surface. In others, it stands at one and a half metres and there are equally marked variations in breadth, reflecting different volumes of stone used in construction. The bank also rises and falls where it encounters large gritstone earthfasts. These are numerous in the immediate area, but in several places it seems that the original builders of the monument actually designed its alignment to incorporate these prominent natural features. The terminals of the bank where it meets the precipitous scarp also show the same respect. To the south, the line of rounded boulders terminates at a massive naturally-placed gritstone block. A similar arrangement can be seen at the northern end, though here the boulder is rather smaller. However, the line of the bank at this point can be extended visually across the valley to the north-west, where it falls close to the Eagle Stone, a prominent gritstone tor on Eaglestone Flat.

There are other significant variations in the build. Stretches comprising a simple rubble pile can be contrasted with others where a rudimentary outer façade has been created by placing larger gritstone slabs on end. These changes in character are frequently associated with slight changes in direction at entrances, as if particular stretches were built as separate elements, perhaps even constructed or embellished as distinct steps or episodes in the broader process. This is supported by excavations, which suggest a measure of phasing in the build of the monument over time.

Taken together, the physical characteristics of the monument hint at a varied company responsible for construction. Though people probably worked together to establish the site, a variety in form arose perhaps because labour was socially patterned. On some enclosures, it has been suggested that different elements of the boundaries were dug by distinct groups. This is also a possibility here, albeit one that we cannot explore very far. The line of the bank also suggests a distinct concern with incorporating and even highlighting prominent natural features, not least the cliff itself. Perhaps this reflects a prior significance given to these features, a significance that added to the monument and helped make it fast. As with tombs, the physical details of the bank evoke a sense of scattered communities working in a common endeavour. Days of stone getting, discussion and design.

. . . Building. Labour that brings the world in close. Scattered herds assembled in the company of ghosts. One time upon another. An arc of posts; a string of boulders; a more persistent and imposing line. The broader world remade each time we gather on the edge and add more stone . . .

Setting too suggests that the monument may have brought people together. Looking west, the view is impressive. The ground falls away at the edge and down towards the River Derwent. It is possible to gaze across the valley towards the more distant reaches of the moors and the limestone plateau. From below, the cliff marks the location of the enclosure. For those passing through the valley, the edge would have been prominent and perhaps a point of reference — a dominant feature on the skyline. The bank itself would have been out of sight from this direction. Significantly, the enclosure lies between the two main watercourses that break the Eastern Moors scarp, forming visually distinctive cuts in this dominant landscape feature. It is well-placed to be approached from a number of directions. To the north and south, the ground falls away gently towards these valleys. From the east, the approach is gentler still. Here the shelf behind the cliff runs back into dips where the underlying rock is soft shale, and to another low gritstone ridge, before rising again to the face of the higher upper scarp of Birchen Edge. Perhaps there were times when cattle mingled on this saddle; animals from different herds grazing side by side as people laboured to carry, roll and lever boulders into position.

Just what went on at Gardom's Edge is for now best left to the imagination or analogy with other sites. Acid soils mean that there is little in the way of bone or other organic remains to flesh out our picture of events. So what can we say? Frequent boulders and low artefact densities, right though they are for the time, suggest an absence of settlement of any scale or duration. Multiple entrances and the diminutive character of the bank in many places also suggest that the boundary was never designed to be impermeable. Cattle and walkers pass across its line without difficulty today, often without noticing, and if the original line was respected, it was probably for symbolic rather than practical reasons. Perhaps people came to feast and renew old ties under the gaze of the ancestors, using large outcrops to expose their dead before taking their bones elsewhere. Maybe they simply came with their herds, the smoke from many fires signalling a time when others could come to trade and perhaps to settle old disputes. Perhaps, like many others, the enclosure lay empty and dormant for much of the time. A sanctuary for ghosts until the time came for another gathering.

Imagination is almost all we have to make sense of other possible enclosures in the Peak, though there are several sites that would repay closer attention. All have been assigned later dates, usually in the absence of excavated evidence. Seen from Monsal Head, the distinctive profile of Fin Cop now bears the scars of a later promontory enclosure, probably of later Bronze Age or Iron Age date. Rich chert seams lie close at hand in the Wye valley. Against this background, the setting would not be out of place for a Neolithic enclosure, and local talk of the site makes reference to stone axes and flint blades found during ploughing on the top. This echoes a close link between stone sources and enclosures seen in other parts of Britain. This dramatic bend in the Wye had long been a place where people came into contact with others; encounters prompted by the need for good stone. If an enclosure was first established at this time, it was grafted onto long historical roots.

Carl Wark is another candidate, though it sits in the literature as Iron Age, Roman or even Dark Age. These attributions cannot be judged as there is again an absence of excavated evidence. However, the foundations could well run deeper; an earlier project added to at later dates. An earlier presence in the area is suggested by a number of Bronze Age clearance cairns to the south and an earlier burial mound on Higger Tor. Separated from Higger Tor by the dip of more easily eroded shales, Carl Wark has a dramatic stone rampart and platform at one end; the remainder of the enclosure formed by the natural scarp and a chain of boulders that incorporate earthfasts. The interior is heavily strewn with massive gritstone boulders such as 'Caer's chair'. Seen from Toadsmouth and the valley to the south, or from Burbage Edge to the east, the tor can be both dramatic and diminutive. Overshadowed by Higger Tor, it gains a prominence only when the light and the angle is right. In many respects, the build and character of the place is not unlike Gardom's Edge and this raises the possibility that it may have been begun at a similar date. Only time, and further work, will tell.

A third candidate encloses part of Cratcliff Rocks, a few minutes' walk from Robin Hood's Stride on the edge of Harthill Moor. Another undated earthen enclosure lies between the site and Nine Stone Close. Here again, boulders were set to draw upon and enhance the rough line formed by prominent earthfasts, a characteristic that sometimes makes the build difficult to trace. In places however, it is a dramatic monument with revetments, large orthostats and a height of over two metres. Given the variable character of the line, it is debatable whether the enclosure was built as an effective barrier. The interior is also heavily boulder strewn with dramatic gritstone earthfasts. Without dates we cannot be certain, but this hints at a Neolithic foundation for the site. The enclosure hangs on the crag above the valley that separates Harthill Moor to the north and Stanton to the south, the tors of Rowtor Rocks marking the other side of the dale. Like Gardom's Edge, it too could be approached from several directions, and may thus have served as a place where people might assemble. Looking south-west from the promontory, the pinnacles of Robin Hood's Stride are striking features, cut by grooves that we now recognise as erosion. Perhaps these pinnacles featured in stories even then.

Archaeology is a creative act, the fashioning of a past in the present. It is, however, shaped by evidence, and this places certain limits on what we can say, if not on our imaginations. That peakland communities of the Earlier Neolithic recognised a broader world is not in doubt. Nor is it in doubt that the contours of that world could shift and change from one year or generation to another. Where different scales of community were acknowledged — at tombs, around stone sources, and perhaps at enclosures — boundaries blurred and resolved themselves again. Perspective shifted according to time, place and company, and over time, old views were changed.

Given a paucity of excavation, it would be all too easy to fill in the gaps in our record, to define these enigmatic enclosures, and others as yet unrecognised, by reference to better known sites elsewhere. That is certainly tempting but perhaps unwise. Chronologies will float until further work is done, and if the study of Neolithic enclosures tells us anything, it is that people worked the idea to a variety of ends in different regions. What we can say is that like stone that was carried and used, tombs and enclosures were implicated in the drawing of connections between people. Sometimes close and defined by blood, sometimes a function of alliance and obligation. Lives that in their practical details may seem uncomplicated to us were played out across a social landscape that was both complex and fluid. The practices that lay behind the sites that we now catalogue were themselves the outcome of changing conditions. Arguments over access, tensions between lines or between the young and the old. And they, in their turn, laid the foundations for different strategies; new ways of thinking and working. It is one of the qualities of monuments that while they may be built to evoke a connection to the past, they can often become a resource, recruited to very different ends.

5 Circles within circles
3000-2000 BC

Gib Hill

Early morning, before the sirens of Ballidon quarry start their chorus. Climbing out of the Roystone valley towards Lime Kiln Barrow. The shadow of Medieval ridge and furrow within walls on the lower flanks; above, the crags of uncleared ground. Old paths cut by habitual hooves run back and forth between denticulate outcrops. Stone and grass still laden with dew, the hollows of old leadrakes holding the wet. Along the ridge then down, past quarries and clamps; across rail line and drove lane. Then through the last wall, a ribbon of piecemeal repairs, tumbled stone a forgotten promise to return when time allowed.

Minninglow. Mist has yet to lose its hold on the place, the outline of the circular plantation blurred until close at hand. Then the gate, the circle cut by ridges, dips and braids where wheels have pressed down or lost their purchase. Only now do the trees come into view. Grey sentinels clinging to the mound, thick roots holding fast to the slabs of forgotten chambers. New growth pushing through soil, searching for knuckles of bone. There is no horizon. Not like before. Even sound struggles to percolate through the enclosing hedge.

Time condenses; becomes heavier. The parade collapses in upon itself. The Antiquarian and the Brother from the Grange sit side by side, fascinated and frightened in their turn. Others come with offerings of coins, silver to catch the eye of local gods. And all around, the slow and steady placement of one stone upon another, the ebb and flow of stock and kin. Spectators make way for the families who have brought their dead to rest amongst the old ones. The place will not give up their names.

The foundation of Neolithic tombs served many purposes. It held people together, fostering a sense of community through reference to a past where genealogies blurred into the broader flow of ancestral time. A time that existed in both the past and the present. Scattered across the region, often in places where routine brought different people into contact, their presence also helped in renewing tenure with land visited seasonally. For the most part, these understandings were local, bound by the kinship that was itself affirmed when people gathered at their ancestral houses. In time, some of these houses merged with the land itself.

One of the qualities of many of these places was their protracted, if episodic, use. Events set around forecourts or in chambers were held apart by intervals; seasons when people worked elsewhere; longer periods when a line was broken. There were many times when tombs stood alone, hidden beneath snow in winter or in clearings blurred by birch and scrub. More often than not, families returned to renew their local world, but there may well have been times when new companies assembled. Kin groups seeking a foundation for claims to land or other rights may have reused old tombs, weaving their genealogies into a hazy or even fictive past. That this may have happened is suggested by the sheer endurance of some of these places. Histories of use, reworking and embellishment can span much of the third millennium and the entire Neolithic. At Five Wells for example, stone settings that had seen use for some time were enclosed within a larger mound. Added later, the mound cut off access to the arrangements and bones inside. This, in turn, became the focus for later acts; a pit cut into the mound and a cist on its outer edge, both containing human remains.

This sense of return and renewal is important. But reuse was not simply reiteration. From year to year and from one generation to another, meanings changed. Roll calls varied and because of their associations, tombs could be appropriated to serve particular interests. The ancestors and their powers were potent symbolic capital. Proximity, or the right to speak on their behalf, could be a privilege of position and an expression of standing. Where relations could shift with time and through the pursuit of local agendas, tensions sometimes rose around these powerful places. Architectural change was caught up in this process, reworking the encounter that people had with tombs and their contents. We catch a glimpse of this at Tideslow, high on the northern part of the limestone plateau. The pock-marked barrow seen today stands to around 2m, but is simply the form achieved at the end of a sequence. Before that was raised, there were two free-standing cists, one probably built after the other. Both contained bodies and jumbled bones. These were surrounded by an area of limestone paving that was itself laid on a prepared surface of yellow clay containing the fragmented bones of animals, people and worked stone. The mound that swallowed these features was also built in stages, growing ever larger and encompassing the line of an older kerb. And like Five Wells, the mound itself became a focus for acts of interment. Excavation revealed a pit cut near the edge of the rise, containing articulated ribs and vertebrae.

Sequences vary from one site to another, and this should discourage us from assuming that all tombs developed in closely similar ways. However, a common theme appears to be a growing distance established between the living and the remains of those long dead. Continued access was not always possible, the focus shifting to forecourts or the margins of particular mounds. Just what this reflects is difficult to say. Perhaps the bones of the old ones were no longer important in themselves, or even a source of danger that had to be contained. Perhaps it was simply enough to lay new bones to rest near at hand. Another possibility is that a restriction on direct access reflects the emergence of new currents in ancestral rites. Where the dead could no longer be seen, moved or added to, perhaps there were some amongst the living who took on a more active role in speaking on their behalf. Simply knowing who lay within may have sometimes become a more political issue.

The passage of time also brought changes in the scale at which specific places were recognised. Looked at on a map and from a perspective that would have been quite alien at the time, there are glimpses of a pattern that became stronger as the Neolithic progressed. Ancestral houses had once been scattered and probably relatively local in their significance. But while successive generations added to existing sites, they also set new foundations close by, establishing clusters of monuments. Perhaps the most dramatic example of this process is found on the rise at Minninglow. Activities here, at least those that have left a trace for us to see, probably began on the site with the building of a relatively small, perhaps circular, structure. Like Whitwell, this was remodelled as a long cairn around 35m in length and this, in turn, was absorbed into a much larger oval chambered mound some 45m across and around 2m high. A larger monument and a larger commitment of labour over time. A number of barrows also lie nearby, including the long mound at Rockhurst and the chambered tomb of Stoney Low on lower and more hidden ground. There may have been other structures too, mounds recorded by Hayman Rooke in the eighteenth century that had gone by the time that Thomas Bateman dug parts of the site a century or so later. That this complex took time to develop is supported by sherds of Beaker, dating to the final stages of the Neolithic, which were found beneath blocking stones in the passage of the central chamber at Minninglow itself.

The ridge at Minninglow is just one example of a place that accrued monuments over the course of the Neolithic. Across the Peak as a whole there are probably four or five more, among them Long Low to the south-west, and Ringham Low to the north. At Long Low, the confusing amalgam of the chambered bank barrow is probably the result of a protracted sequence. The monument also attracted others, including Stanshope and Brown Low. Pea Low, another impressive mound, lies three kilometres to the north-east. The substantial long barrow at Ringham Low lies within a mile or two of Bole Hill, a probable chambered tomb destroyed in the nineteenth century, and there are numerous barrows in the vicinity.

These complexes stand out from the more basic pattern seen at other early tombs. Though these often saw long histories of use, they did not witness the coming together of monuments in relatively close proximity and this suggests a change in the character and scale of their significance over time. Some places remained local. Others took on a new status in different parts of the region, recruited to serve broader and more structured interests. Though we cannot be certain, it is possible that this new, broader significance was marked by the bringing together of bones that had once been scattered between several older tombs.

Pea Low

Work on the setting and character of these monument complexes has identified some interesting trends. They have a strong link to watersheds, a legacy of earlier decisions. All however are sited so that they can be approached from several directions and along valleys that were likely paths of least resistance. They also sit so that they give access to distinct areas — basins, valley systems and land that saw use for pasture and cultivation. Minninglow served as a focus in the south, near the edge of the limestone and above the Wirksworth Valley. Long Low to the west is well placed for visits from the Dove and Manifold and from the broad basin around Biggin. Similar ranges may have turned around more isolated monuments like Tideslow, a massive barrow that was a focus for communities across the Buxton basin and land on the north side of the Wye. These complexes were both on the edge of things and a focus. They lay between areas which held good potential for Neolithic communities and they drew people in through their position on important access routes. Where watersheds were recognised as boundaries, monuments set close to the threshold were well placed to bring different lines together.

There were other complexes too, anchored to earlier long mounds but resolving themselves rather differently over time. Two of these, Arbor Low and the Bull Ring, witnessed the building of impressive Henge monuments during the later Neolithic. Whether these places served similar purposes is difficult to say. They may indicate that the same concerns were addressed through different rites from one part of the region to another. Alternatively, architectural sequences may suggest that henges themselves worked at a different scale and in a different way to most of the other complexes.

Bull Ring

A changing land?

Given the extraordinary lengths of time over which these complexes developed, we should be wary of reading any sudden and dramatic transformation in the evidence. If certain places changed in their significance and in the social scale of their relevance, they may have done so gradually and almost imperceptibly. For any one generation, these were places steeped in tradition. But new generations bring new interests to bear; the land does not stand still. Lines break or tangle with other threads. As part of the flow of relations between communities, some tombs became a focus for gatherings at which broader geographies could be acknowledged. Several lines were woven together. This may go some way towards explaining why there are relatively few early enclosures in the Peak. Important in other regions, they were perhaps less so in an area where the identities and interests of broader social groups were brought into focus around tombs and massive barrows.

What do these developments signify? Why should certain tombs cluster and become more prominent in the early third millennium? There are several possibilities. A common response is to see change as a simple consequence of population growth, a greater press of numbers triggering changes in how the dead were drawn upon. Another idea is that the later part of the Neolithic saw changes in the character of routine traditions of landscape use, in particular a measure of settling down and consolidation in the ranges over which people moved. The evidence is ambiguous on this point. Pollen and other environmental data show that much of the land was still being used for a varied suite of activities, herding, hunting, keeping crops and harvesting the wild. Families established on the flanks of the Upper Derwent continued to climb up on to higher ground with their stock, just as they had always done. On the limestone too, groups of close kin may have followed a seasonal pattern that still took them between sheltered valleys, higher basins and ridges. Many seams of chert were also still in use, the sides of dales echoing much as they had always done. Places still had a season.

The land was as complex a patchwork as it had ever been. That said, there are hints that traditions were slowly being reworked, a process that continued to unfold into the Earlier Bronze Age. In the Peak, as in many parts of Britain, surface scatters of stone with Later Neolithic affinities occur in areas with long histories of use. However, they are if anything more widespread, new sites appearing on soils that had previously seen little concerted exploitation. This broad pattern is supported by available environmental evidence. Although pollen cores in a number of areas reflect localized phases of woodland regeneration, the trend towards open grassland, scrub and cultivation accords with the evidence of stone. Further changes can be added to this picture. In contrast to the Earlier Neolithic, the later phase witnessed a marked increase in the size of scatters. Where these had once taken the form of focussed clusters of material, now they begin to appear as spreads of worked stone across larger areas. Despite their size, these scatters do not signal even deeper roots for the concept of the village than we might commonly suppose. Most settlements were probably still no larger than a few households. What they suggest instead is a change in the nature of settlement. This could be a number of things: a turn away from the routine seasonal mobility patterns of the Earlier Neolithic and/or the more persistent use of places for occupation.

Just such a shift may be echoed in the stone being worked at the time. In place of an emphasis upon blades and narrow flakes, we find a wider range of core forms, reflecting a variety of approaches to flake production, and a wider array of tools. In many cases, cores reflect a decrease in the level of concern exercised in the preparation of platforms and in the controlled removal of more or less standardized flakes. Multi-platform cores — struck from all sides and occasionally reused as hammers — are often larger than Earlier Neolithic cores, and flakes tend to be broader and thicker than before. Platforms on individual flakes also have a tendency to be larger, reflecting a lack of preparation and the placement of blows further into the body of the core. Material of this nature is common on Later Neolithic sites in many parts of Britain.

A move away from portable and adaptable tools, and the more profligate use of stone, might be expected where movement was no longer the routine concern that it once had been. However, it is unclear how far the details of these trends are echoed in the Peak. At a time when things could change from one region to another, analogies have their limits. Moreover, the Peak was an area poor in raw materials. Flint came from outside and local cherts varied considerably in their quality and the range of uses to which they could be put. Under these local conditions, it may well be that there was less of the profligacy seen in flint-rich areas. In a region where landscapes were so diverse, offering a wide range of potentials, a seasonal pattern of encounters with different places may have remained important for a long time. Perhaps the situation here was a mix of the old and the new; changes in patterns of movement and in ways of working stone arising as tenure became more sedimented with time.

There were other currents caught up in this flow, tides in the affairs of people that had less to do with how far they ranged and more with how they thought about themselves and others. A common theme in many accounts of the Later Neolithic (and Earlier Bronze Age) has been to take changes in monuments as a reflection of changes in the structure of society itself. The fact that some monuments are larger, reflecting an accumulated investment of greater effort, is taken as evidence for the emergence of some form of social hierarchy. Talk turns from elders and lineage heads to chiefs and hereditary leaders. The development of more signal tomb complexes across the Peak could indicate that the standing of specific people was shaped by their position in lines of descent, and by their rhetoric at tombs. However, to explain these and other places solely in those terms would be simplistic. There is no necessity to assume that the passage of time saw a linear process of evolution, where less stratified societies became more complex and vertically differentiated.

The political eminence of certain individuals had probably been an issue for many generations, resolving itself at various social scales. But it was one theme amongst many and perhaps more fluid than our simple evolutionary schemes allow. Just as important were all the more horizontal distinctions that animated life within and between different communities. Close kinship, gender, descent and age; local alliances and moral obligations.

. . . The days are lengthening. There is a new green on the hills and on the branches. The ground is still hard; old ruts and footprints still trip new feet in the early frost. But soon the land will warm to the touch; will wake again. Then it will be time to take the cattle up; to catch the sweet grass and wake the dead with our gifts . . .

The evidence of stone also reminds us that tools and techniques at this time were still caught up in social life. One of the characteristics of Later Neolithic stone assemblages is that they are often more varied than their earlier counterparts. The range of tools that people recognised and used seems to have been broader, and there is a continuum of skill reflected in working, from the ad hoc to the extraordinary. Where once a simple blade was sufficient for many needs, now there were varied knives and scrapers, many displaying signs of careful and invasive retouching. The range of arrowheads that people used seems also to have varied, from leaf- and lozenge-shaped forms to points with rippled flakes and exaggerated barbs. By the final stages of the Neolithic, the inventory of projectiles had extended to include barbed and tanged forms. These continued in widespread use throughout much of the Earlier Bronze Age. Alongside these were objects that were more unusual still, including chisels, maceheads and elaborately flaked or polished axes, many from distant sources. Though axes from beyond the Peak had been coming in for some time, it was probably in the Later Neolithic that their circulation reached its zenith. This proliferation of varied and distinctive forms was more marked in some parts of Britain than in others; it finds perhaps its strongest expression in Yorkshire. But it is also present in the Peak, and is echoed by an apparent increase in the amount of flint coming into the region from the Wolds.

It is pointless to try and explain these trends in practical terms alone. Just as axes had been for generations, many of these varied tools were made and used in routine settings. But at the same time, they were drawn upon as tokens of identity, and sometimes of value, and it was often this, as much as utility, which determined what they looked like. Their possession gave voice to ideas about the identities of people. Men and women; the young and the old; us and them. Ideas could be read in the form of a tool, the ways it was used and even the specific materials from which it was made. And because of this, they could be media for use in exchange, display and even deposition. A few may have even served as 'prestige goods'; items circulated in cycles of competitive gift giving. Worn, used and carried by particular people, they offered routine confirmation of their position within communities as well as in broader groups. This capacity may have been reinforced through constraints on where (and perhaps when) some of these artefacts could be made or obtained, or the contexts in which they could be used or worn. Passed down from one generation to another, they helped to define the position of individuals within networks of descent. A patina of handling and service may have added to that role. And beyond their use in exchange, the use or deposition of these tokens in ceremonial activity introduced various qualities or aspects of a person to that event.

Tombs and stone tools suggest complex and confusing conditions. Beyond a possible increase in population, the early third millennium seems to have witnessed a series of subtle shifts in many aspects of life. Larger numbers may have assembled around particular tomb complexes, occasions which sometimes allowed an authority to be claimed and wielded. Concepts of tenure were also beginning to change, the horizons of some activities being drawn in a little more over time. And this went hand in hand with a proliferation of tokens of identity and with the circulation of elaborate or 'exotic' artefacts. Rather than indicating hierarchies per se, these patterns suggest a blurred and complicated world. A time in which people recognised themselves in communities that operated at widely different scales. Regional, local, personal and genealogical; each woven into the other and all political.

. . . Fire sprang from the stone when it was struck. The blood of the Bear so hot that it burnt to nothing before it reached the ground. That blood runs still. See the veins that course through the blade. It is our blood too . . .

Circles within circles

These arguments bring us to two of the most dramatic monuments to be found in the Peak; Arbor Low and the Bull Ring. Places at which different communities overlapped, perhaps at scales that exceeded periodic gatherings around Minninglow, Long Low or Tideslow. Classed as Henges, both take the form of near circular banks of earth and stone with deep ditches on the inside. Both are between eighty and ninety metres in diameter with two more or less opposed entrances. Arbor Low is set on a false crest on Middleton Moor, between the Bradford and Lathkill valleys, and looks down across the Monyash basin to the north-west. The Bull Ring lies further to north-west, on the edge

Arbor Low

of the plateau above the Dove, where softer shales separate the limestone from the higher western grits of Hob Tor and Black Edge. Beyond distance as the crow might fly, the two are held apart by the valley of the Wye.

When were these monuments established? Writing in 1785, and with a very different vision of the past in mind, Samuel Pegge concluded that the banks, ditches and stones of Arbor Low were from a time that stretched back before the Danes, Saxons or Romans. For him, 'The Britons are the only people, to whom with any colour of reason one can think of ascribing this august monument; and indeed it has the air and aspect of very remote antiquity'. Since Pegge's time, excavation and comparative study has confirmed his argument for 'remote antiquity', even if we are now more uncertain about the meaning of a term like 'Britons'. Finds from excavations in the ditch and in a barrow that stands upon the bank suggest a date around the middle of the third millennium BC. Work over the last century or so also suggests a duration of use that crosses the academic divide between the Later Neolithic and the Early Bronze Age.

Recent histories make for a marked contrast in our encounter with these places today. At Arbor Low, the Henge and other monuments nearby have fared reasonably well. Much of the land around was not enclosed until the eighteenth century, and was used before that time as upland pasture; grazing being kinder than the plough. Like many areas that saw enclosure by Parliamentary Act or through the consolidation of large estates, the walls around Arbor Low are distinctive. Straight lines defining geometric fields that began life on a surveyor's map rather than on the ground. Since that time, antiquarian interest and

Bull Ring

later scheduling has protected the site to some extent, not least the stones that encircle the interior. Though a few have been removed for use elsewhere, perhaps as posts or as stone in walls, the majority remain on site. This was not the case at the Bull Ring. Here, enclosure cut close to the monument and even ran inside. When the light is right, you can still trace the line of a wall that bisected the site, running parallel to the ridge and furrow once used for cultivation. Early accounts also talk of stones inside, though these cannot now be traced. Some may lie unrecognised as fragments in nearby walls, others in gates or the footings of buildings. Quarrying has also left its scars, hollows from the nineteenth century being particularly marked in the north-eastern part of the ditch. Since then, developments that include a cemetery and the laying out of football pitches have brought further changes of setting and character.

These different forms of curation are both cause and consequence of the ways these monuments are perceived today. Arbor Low receives many visitors; couples and coachloads who walk up from the farmyard, around or up the banks and into the interior. For those who choose to calculate in such empty and commodified terms, the area has a high 'landscape value', elements offering little in the way of what we now regard as a stark or obtrusive contrast. Visiting in the nineteenth century, Thomas Bateman was even moved to suggest that the setting and views, save 'a few stone fences which intervene in the foreground . . . almost carry the observer back through a multitude of centuries'.

The Bull Ring seems very different on the surface; form and setting at odds with this particular sense of place. A common response from visitors and in guidebooks is one of disappointment and distaste for the ways that the modern has encroached upon the ancient. Appearances can be deceptive. Both views are from a modern vantage, ways of seeing with roots in a sense of land as capital, and of the rural as a timeless contrast to the urban. Looked at differently, the Bull Ring reminds us that places are never that constant. Meanings change, a flux reflected by a variety in the ways they are used over time. In any case, the pasture around Arbor Low is misleading. It tells us more about land enclosure, lead mining and improvement over the past couple of centuries than it does about how the monument or the land around were used and understood in the Neolithic. For those who stood on the banks four thousand or so years ago, if they were allowed on the banks at all, things were different. It is only when it becomes 'heritage' that the past assumes the stable and consoling form that we seem to value today.

Arbor Low was established in a setting that already had a rich and significant history. Not far is the Earlier Neolithic long mound below the round barrow of Gib Hill. Fieldwalking in the area has also recovered a rich harvest of stone tools from around the same time, even from the later Mesolithic, as well as material contemporary with the Henge. This evidence is far from straightforward. However, it hints that this broad ridge had long been a focus; camps where hunters tarried, an ancestral house where

Bull Ring

communities gathered at certain times. It was against this background, in a place where paths had crossed for generations, that the henge was established. Given its situation on the edge of the Plateau, in a location that could be approached from several directions, the Bull Ring had a similar potential and perhaps a parallel history.

These details of history and topography suggest that far from being the places of 'quiet solitude' that we now seek to conserve, Arbor Low and the Bull Ring were sometimes alive with people. A confusion of camps and animals in the environs; people moving in and out of clearings and approaching along different paths. The mess of building gangs or companies gathered around fires; cooking, eating, talking. And then, when the time was right, an order amongst the multitude; people taking their places to participate or to watch proceedings in the henge itself. A broad social geography mapped to a tight scale.

It is almost impossible for us to grasp this setting, inured as we are to scenes of vast crowds. But to come to this place in a certain season, when most of life was spent with a small company, was to confront an unparalleled number. People well-known and related by blood. Others seen only in the shadow of a tomb or on the trail, and some so different that faces, dress and speech were unfamiliar. Fieldwalking in the area confirms this sense of paths coming together. Scatters of later Neolithic and Early Bronze Age material in the fields around Arbor Low suggest a significant presence. People working and using stone brought with them to the margins of the henge; scatters all that remain of episodes of occupation. Whether or not people lived permanently close at hand is debatable. For much of the year when communities were scattered, it may have been a place to be passed, perhaps even avoided. Some of these assemblages also contain a significant number of distinctive artefacts; axes, fancy knives and striking arrowheads. These may cluster in the area for many reasons. A reflection of activities such as archery, display and fighting, or of acts of formal deposition; tokens of identity and value laid in the earth during funerary rites, or to mark a close to certain proceedings. Pits with formal deposits have been found around a number of henges and it may be that some of the material around Arbor Low was originally laid to rest in this way, later ploughing bringing it back to the surface.

If we have difficulty in imagining the shock of such a multitude, it is equally difficult to picture Arbor Low or the Bull Ring being built. Seen today, the banks and ditches curve gracefully into one another, a consequence of silting, hooves and recent management. Yet when freshly cut, the ditches at both would have been two to three metres in depth, steep sides cutting down through the limestone bedrock. The banks were also higher, up to three metres above the old ground surface and comprising stone and earth from the ditches. The angular lines of fractured limestone; darker kernels of chert still in place or tipped up on the mound. A steep and dramatic barrier that fostered a sense of containment. Children would not have rolled down the slopes as they often do today.

Just how far, and in what ways, building was under direction is a moot point. Some have taken the plan and scale of henges as evidence for some form of political hierarchy; paramount chiefs dictating design and execution. This is debatable. Broad political geographies may well have been recognised at the time. But to see henges only as monuments to leaders misses the broader and more varied purposes they served in bringing dispersed communities together. When the demands of the year allowed, people

Arbor Low

came for many reasons and these probably shifted from one visit to another. Though it was probably laid out as a single design, it may be that it took some time for the banks of Arbor Low to climb to their full height. Where people returned to a henge over time, each episode may have begun with a cleaning out or elaboration of ditches; new stone added to older mounds.

From the outset, building required people to work side by side, suspending the normal social pattern of scattered labour. More than a preamble to events, building was an act that made relations just as it made a space in which those relations could be addressed. Around fifteen hundred cubic metres of quarried limestone make a dramatic statement. There were those that hacked at the white stone with antler picks, wooden poles and axes; those who stood in lines to carry baskets up the slope and along the crest. Chains of people linked by a common endeavour, bodies made familiar by a rime of clay and limestone. It is difficult to work close and remain impersonal.

And when building ceased, when the moon had risen to its appointed place and all the players had assembled, proceedings would take a different turn. Though henges brought people close, the boundaries with their internal ditches suggest exclusion and division. A containment of forces and threatening events. These were arenas of value; places in which different regimes overlapped. Here it was possible to deal with the dead, with spirits and with others. Inside, movement could become more formal, people processing through the entrance to stand or sit in appointed places. Perhaps some could progress only to a certain point during important ceremonies while others were free to move to the centre of things. There would be feasting and display; the giving of food to the dead and to other lines; rites of initiation and perhaps of marriage. Fragmentary human remains suggest a continued link with mortuary and/or ancestral rituals, events sometimes concluded by the deposition of individual bones and other materials in ditches and in pits.

There was also exchange. Where identity and position were expressed in the possession and use of things, initiation and the circulation of people were bound up in the circulation of goods. There was probably a mess and confusion to these proceedings, a bundle of personal and moral economies that stretched from the renewal of trading partnerships to politically driven acts of prestation. Some transactions happened on the margins. Here it was possible to meet and to talk, to renew old ties and to settle new deals. As herds and people mingled on the edges of clearings, it would be possible to barter for new stock and to reach agreement. Bound up in many transactions were structures of alliance, obligation and reciprocity that had to be made and made again. Other forms of exchange were more highly charged, some perhaps focused at the centre of things. Gift giving was a means of inflicting debt upon others. Caught up in marriage rites or in more overtly competitive displays, it provided a basis for manipulating kinship ties and for acquiring renown. Within Arbor Low and the Bull Ring, it was possible to suspend some of the usual conventions of reciprocity and to give added weight to particular transactions. The potentials offered by prestation could be contained. Watched over by the spirits of the past and by the assembled company, these were pivotal moments. Not only that, the episodic use of henges sustained a sense of duration in gift giving. Convention may have dictated that certain debts could only be met at these places and times and this meant that relations would persist between gatherings.

. . . The horse fair. Some remember it still. A pivot for the year and a time when all roads rose to meet each other. Services and blessings; the veneration of Saints. Then hard trade; haggling and handshakes; games and indiscretion. And after? An empty field and a will to return.

After assembly came dispersal. When proceedings had been brought to a close, kin went back to their familiar valleys and pastures. With them went talk of events they had witnessed and the detail of those in which they had participated. With them too were new animals and tools, cloth perhaps and even new kin. Some walked with a different step, a reflection of their passage through initiation or marriage rites. Each carried an acknowledgement of those who had scattered along different paths. Then, after a year or maybe more, they would come together again, to remake ties that had been carved into the bedrock, or to resolve disputes that had festered in the intervening years.

It may have been in the context of a return to Arbor Low that the stone circle and cove were raised. This has parallels elsewhere, and work has shown that circuits of stone were often preceded by similar arrangements of timber. Whether this was the case here is not as yet known. Though around fifty stones can now be seen, some are fragments and it is likely that somewhere around forty or so limestone orthostats were originally dragged into the interior. Various questions have been directed at these stones over the years. Where did they come from? Were they ever standing? What were they for? Though the ditch itself is rock cut, this was not the source. Weathering patterns suggest that they were split and levered from pavement bedrock somewhere else. Many of the stones present two very different faces; one relatively sharp and angular, the other much older and more weathered, with curves, holes and hollows decorated by lichen. Gazing out at the bank (or at each other), visitors often sit with arms outstretched behind them, absent-mindedly tracing the contours of this ancient pavement with their fingers.

Just how far the stones travelled is not known. But with weights rising to more than eight tons, these slabs are a testament to skilled and cooperative labour. People would have had to work together to move them, just as they acknowledged a principle of design. Splitting and quarrying also meant working in combination, and it is a skilled task; seeing the shape and realising it rather than shattering the bedrock into useless fragments. Pavement limestone lent itself to this purpose, and this too suggests a close familiarity with stone.

Work in combination, perhaps with an audience, extended to the setting of the orthostats in a rough circle with an internal cove. Whether or not these massive slabs were originally upstanding is still the subject of debate. Some suggest that they have always reclined, laid out perhaps for later erection in a project that was abandoned. Excavation has lent a little weight to this view. Work at the turn of the twentieth century failed to locate stoneholes or sockets around one stone. However, it is difficult to know how far this accurately reflects the state of the ground, or whether it is typical for the circle as a whole. Arguments to the contrary work on several fronts. In 1785, Samuel Pegge recorded that a William Normanshaw had seen the stones upright a few decades before. This may be hearsay; perhaps Normanshaw said what he thought Pegge wanted to hear. However, this does accord with some evidence on the ground. In several parts of the circle, it is possible to trace a series of 'stumps', short uprights of stone adjacent to larger prostrate slabs. These may be bases still in place, indicating that the orthostats once stood upright, balanced in shallow pits or widened fissures in the bedrock. Shallow features may be difficult to recognise, and if foundations were this ephemeral, this may explain why all the stones are now toppled.

There is one other possibility, albeit unlikely at Arbor Low and uncertain at the Bull Ring. At some sites, stones were deliberately toppled to prevent their use as a pivot for unorthodox or 'dangerous' political meetings. Often an attempt to quell rural unrest or religions factions, destruction could be a calculated political act. The disappearance of the settings at the Bull Ring is most likely to have satisfied a more basic need for stone. But it is always possible that some changes were made because of what the monument had come to mean, rather than what it offered in material terms.

If they stood, as they probably did, the stones at Arbor Low had a dramatic impact on the experience of the place. Hidden from the outside eye by the bank, they came into view only on the final stages of the approach from the north-west, or as one came over the ridge from the south-east. Suddenly, in front of you were a series of tall pillars, some standing to nearly four metres in height. Entry may have also meant crossing between dramatic portal stones. And within the circle was the cove; massive orthostats arranged to create a place yet more proscribed and hidden. A tightening of the circle. The stones looked down on proceedings. They could hide important rites from inquisitive eyes. And when lit by fires at night, they might seem almost animate, evidence perhaps of the spirits they embodied. From the centre, some of the stones appeared to spring up above the bank, linking the interior directly to the sky.

Just why the stones were raised (if they were) is difficult to say; many arguments circulate. There is the symbolism of the circle itself. A form that encloses with no beginning and no end, the circle is both inclusive and exclusive; a continuous threshold. And where that line was traced by stones set at intervals, arrangements also lent themselves to ordering people. Only some could cross at certain times, perhaps to enter the cove, or to stand or sit with their backs to individual stones, faces turned to the centre and each other. No doubt there were also times when the company was more fluid, spilling out beyond the entrances as people moved back and forth around events. However, the addition of these settings may indicate that the henge became an arena for more exclusive rituals over time.

In a world where many things were bound to a seasonal wheel, where cycles were recognised in the land and perhaps in life and death, the circle also had a deeper metaphoric potential. That these readings were sometimes made is hinted at by the details of position. Some have suggested, often with good cause, that circles were set so as to catch specific movements and events in the heavens. There are a good number with strong alignments, and this demonstrates both an awareness of cycles in the sky and a desire to mark their course. Just what this attention may have brought is lost to us. But where the fertility of land, animals and people was a constant concern, such alignments allowed a connection to be made between individual lives or seasons, and the more timeless cycles that were cut into the sky. What people saw when they raised their eyes is also lost. A signal for planting or a start to a seasonal ceremony, perhaps the campfires of ancestors or spirits still following their round.

Under these conditions, alignments and arrangements served several purposes. They tied the flux of the present to tradition, and tradition in turn to the timeless. The stones themselves were implicated in this process, reinforcing statements through the fact of their endurance as well as their position. Through them, death, display and debate were reconciled with a greater order. Sometimes this was a comfort, an acknowledgement that the death of a loved one was simply a move to another state; that they, like the land, would be born again. Sometimes it was a source of legitimacy. Officiation could be an expression and a medium of authority. Being allowed to enter and to have the knowledge of these places, the stories that explained what was seen, may have been a prerogative of varied companies. Those with a certain standing; those who had reached the appropriate age; those who had made the right connections. That this was set against a backdrop of communal events suggests that participation in rituals renewed ties between people as well as the standing of particular individuals.

. . . Chinese whispers. They say, and who are they? that the ditches were once filled with jelly. An artist in the sixties; some party, who knows. What flavour? No idea . . . I've heard it from several people so there must be something to it . . .

The addition of the stones at Arbor Low may have come some time after the foundation of the henge, perhaps as much as several centuries. It is possible that their erection transformed the meanings of the place, the significance that it held for different people at the time. Entry was into a very different space, albeit one that took its inspiration

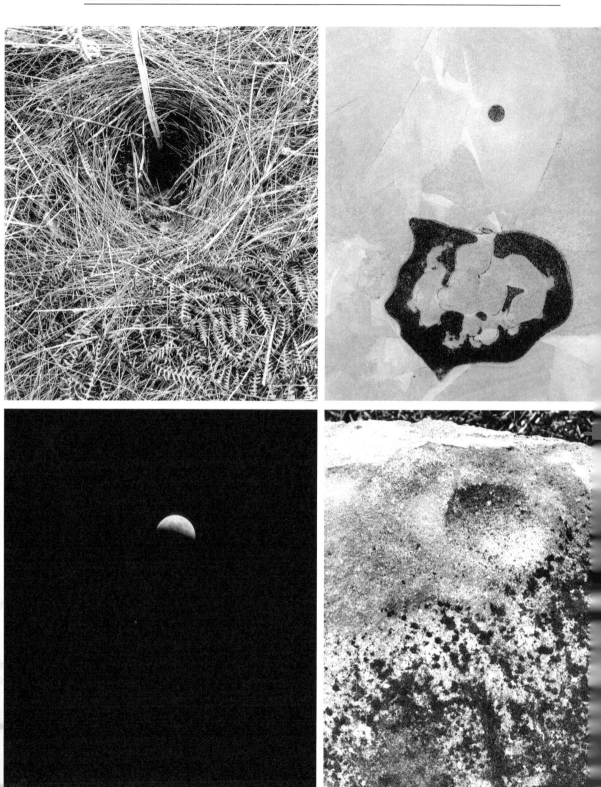

from an older line. Whether this reflects a more exclusive focus or a generally more limited company is impossible to say. In any case, we should allow that things may have been different. The raising of the stones may have simply been one event in a long line of subtle shifts of practice, a reworking of tradition that did not recognise a sharp break with the past. It was still possible to renew a sense of the collective, to mediate conflicts between lines and confirm distinctions within groups. People still assembled, affecting the renewal of their world through exchange, through dealings with their dead and with worlds beyond.

That the focus of events at Arbor Low may have shifted back and forth is suggested by one other feature. Up on the bank near the south-eastern entrance, and jutting out beyond its line, is a large round barrow. Like the mound raised on top of the Gib Hill long barrow, stratigraphy shows that a new monument was grafted onto the old. Pitted like some giant molar, the top of this mound is cratered by the scars of old excavations. These revealed a stone cist; large limestone slabs arranged to create a polygonal box with a yet larger capstone. Within lay human bones in disarray, some of them burnt; a bone pin, iron pyrites and a piece of flint. There were also two vessels with incised decorations, arguably Later Neolithic in date. What they contained, if anything, is unrecorded.

The barrow is a dramatic feature. Perched on the bank, near the threshold people crossed when moving in or out of the circle, it cast a shadow on proceedings. This is not an isolated case. Central burials were added to a number of henges and there are several where massive barrows were added nearby. So why build it here? What did it mean to raise a mound above the remains of a small number of people in a place associated with broader companies? Where the dead were honoured and perhaps active, the simple presence of these remains was not remarkable in itself. What was different was the setting. The bones of others were hidden, lost in pits and ditches or taken off elsewhere. These were highlighted by a mound that dominated the approach from the south, and stood proud of the bank for those who gathered within. Perhaps this marked a close connection for some, rather than for all. Individuals of particular renown, or members of a specific line. If this were so, burial may have sometimes been an act of appropriation. Building asserted a closer association, even an authority over the place and over proceedings. Arbor Low was a monument to ties that stretched some considerable distance. But there were times when it was worked to selective advantage. Perhaps this was a theme that emerged from time to time throughout the history of the site, as relations between people shifted back and forth.

We know little about the afterlife of these enigmatic sites. The name Arbor Low is derived from the Anglo Saxon 'Eorthburg Hlaw' which means no more than 'earthwork hill'. What else this place may have stood for by that time is a matter for conjecture, though there may be burials nearby which speak of a renewed interest. Nor can we say how far proceedings continued into the Bronze Age, though the span may not be all that long. Also hazy is our grasp of the full flow of events around and within the banks. The imposing scale of henges encourages the broader view, so that we miss smaller and more varied encounters. Perhaps there were times when people came in close companies, pausing briefly to leave offerings inside or nearby. Impossible to trace directly in the evidence, the rich crop of flintwork found outside may reflect brief moments and a close focus as well as more signal events.

. . . A boy watching stock with the old men looks towards his place in the family; how that will change when he reaches the right age. As he struggles to work a recalcitrant core, he sees the distance still to travel. Gazing up towards the circle, he sees how his line is one amongst many; part of a weave to which new threads are always being added. In time, if the spirits allow, he will make his own pattern in the weave . . .

6 Interpreting nature

Rowtor Rocks. The south-west edge of Stanton Moor. An island of grit in a sea of softer stone. Birchover Buff, the pinks and greys of the rock mottled with moss that takes your feet in a moment. Crags stacked and tumbled like cairns on a field edge.

Look. Wind and water have worked a pattern on the place; a slow and patient sculpting of the stone. Ice has wedged and splintered; fissures and hollows making faces at people on the road below. Climber's chalk flowers like lichen on grooves and ledges. All around are signatures: Melrose . . . AB . . . DW 4 TP . . . 1824 . . . 1959. Names, dates and sermons in the stone. Boredom, love, a nod towards posterity.

Look again. The crag has felt the chisel's bite; herringbone and punctiform pecks on many surfaces. There are benches, seats and sculpted shelters; guttering, steps and walls. Sharp edged hollows stride across the top. A recess once for structural timbers, they hold dark water, sodden roaches and the leaf mould of last autumn. There is even a 'hermit's cave', a black interior where thousands of chisel scars dance in the torchlight. Three seats face northwards, arms tattooed with recent names, a pentagram and an anarchist symbol. A moment held in the sharp edges of a word.

Look closer. Past the pillar on the high point and down onto stone that has slipped from the pile. Shadows collect on a ripple pecked into the grit, within the circle a dew pond around a hand's span wide. A carved line slips serpent-like across another boulder, a cup mark near the head. There is duration here. Inscriptions written one upon another, the oldest lines abraded, sharpness lost. Patterns scatter into sand grains, taking meaning with them. The stones have no rosetta.

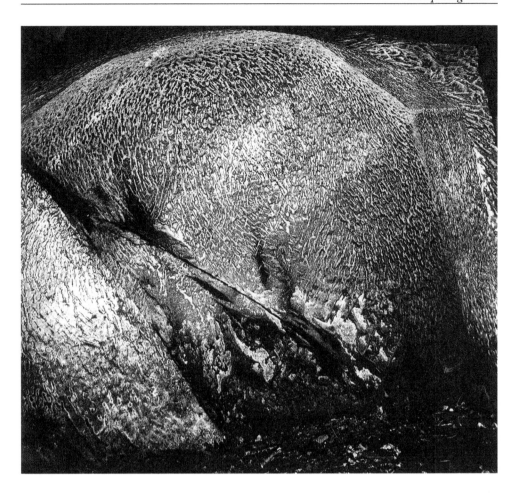

One of the stumbling blocks that we encounter in trying to understand the past is our own common sense. We forget that some of our most basic attitudes and cherished taken-for-granteds are historical; products of the recent past. It is to practical reason that we often appeal when we distinguish activities in prehistory as either ritual or routine, missing how one often bleeds into the other. And it is common sense, forged in the heat of the industrial revolution and tempered ever since, that leads us to see tools where people once read identities and histories. That same common sense also shapes the ways we perceive places as either nature or culture. Topography or hydrology on the one hand and monuments on the other. Those perceptions are far from universal. Encouraged by a century or more of disciplinary sanctions, we draw a sharp line between geology and archaeology, missing the possibility that people in the past may have drawn the line rather differently, if indeed, they drew such a line at all.

These problems are brought into sharp focus by the carvings on Rowtor Rocks. Most of the features cut into the crags are attributed to the later seventeenth or early eighteenth century and to Thomas Eyre, a member of the local gentry. Rowtor's other name, 'The Druid's Stones', probably dates to around his time; an association more romantic than historical. For Eyre, like many in 'polite society', places such as Rowtor had a particular

Foxhole

value. There was wonder at forms carved by time and the elements; new discourse on the processes that had shaped the crags. There was embellishment too; a desire to add to nature, creating gardens for diversion and seats from which to enjoy the view. To understand the balance of a scene and to appreciate good prospects was a hallmark of judgement and taste; of proper sensibilities. Those sensibilities were particular and contingent; tied to the interests of a distinct class.

These rather eccentric embellishments to Rowtor remind us that the perception of nature is never direct. It is historical and situated — a politics of vision. They also demonstrate that ways of seeing are not set in stone. The view across the valley which inspired Eyre to carve his armchair is now obscured by a tall stand of beeches. The place and the prospect have changed. Rowtor also demonstrates that what we see now as folly or indulgence can be understood quite differently when set in context. Actions are better interpreted when they are set against broader currents in the society of their time. Eccentric though they may have been, Eyre's labours were in step with fashions that shaped many parks and gardens; fashions through which people connected and competed with other members of their class. For the gentry, the idea that landscape was an object to be gazed upon or held within a frame went hand in hand with a view of land as an object to be bought, sold and accumulated.

Creating a context is difficult enough when the focus falls on the last few centuries. The leap to prehistory is often a leap in the dark. The oldest carvings on Rowtor probably date to the Later Neolithic and Earlier Bronze Age, a world utterly different to those inhabited by Eyre or by ourselves. However stable and constant they may seem to us, the crags at Rowtor were different then, seen from a perspective that erodes much of our modern divide between humanity and nature. An outcrop or a spring might mean something very different to a person who saw the land itself as an animate entity. A sacred tree or grove might be an important focus for centuries, its presence now untraceable. It is only when the respect shown to places involved material expression — alignment, avoidance or deposit — that we can take our ideas further.

Seeing in the dark

One category of place provides a good example of how our modern distinction between the found and the made may have been rather blurred in prehistory. A part of nature certainly. But at the same time, a setting that had strong ties to the dead and to the spirits that dwelt in the land. Numerous caves and fissures are scattered across the Peak. Within them, beneath the leaf litter, crushed cans and charred remains of recent camps, are sediments formed over millennia. Many contain archaeological material. Given the nature of their development, there are only a few caves on the gritstone but many in the White Peak, on pastured hillsides or in the sides of deep dales and defiles.

All this country is hollow. Could you strike it with some gigantic hammer, it would boom like a drum or possibly cave in altogether.
Arthur Conan Doyle

Caves have long been a focus of archaeological interest. The scene of many early excavations, inspired by chance discoveries or popular myths of cave dwellers, cave deposits have consistently revealed a remarkable, if poorly understood array of evidence. This complexity stems from several sources. Flooding and the accumulation of sediment are continually changing the character of deposits, biting into material that has been in place for thousands of years or masking it beneath ever greater quantities of soil. Caves have also been a popular place of residence or retreat for many animals, among them bears, wolves and foxes. Their activities led to the reworking of sediments and no doubt account for many of the bones of both predators and their prey. We have also had a hand in this process. The growth of industries such as lead mining, in particular the draining of deep shafts, has had a major impact on the water table across the limestone and thus on conditions in a number of caves. Over a century or more of excavation, much of it sketchily recorded, has also taken its toll. And there are all too many caves where records or excavated material do not survive to be examined today: Eyam Dale quarry, One Ash Shelter in Lathkill or Old Hannah's Hole in the Manifold Gorge.

The complexity of cave deposits also arises from much longer histories of human activity. Larger examples, like Peak Cavern ('The Devil's Arse") in Castleton, have been places of occupation and industry in the historic past. There are also many that were a focus for burial and other activities during the Roman period; Sycamore, Ossom's Crag and Elder Bush Caves have produced pottery and other deposits dating to this time. Some, like Fox Hole Cave, even contain material that stretches back into the Palaeolithic. Neolithic and Early Bronze Age material is also common, taking the form of human remains and various artefacts. The fact that material from these different periods is often recorded in the same levels illustrates something of the difficulty encountered in exploring how caves were used and regarded at any particular point in the past.

What did caves mean to communities of the Neolithic and Earlier Bronze Age? Around thirty chance discoveries and excavations have revealed burials, fragments of bone, pottery, beads and stone tools from this time. This may well be the tip of the iceberg. Most caves have yet to be fully explored and there are, no doubt, more yet to be found. An earlier Neolithic presence is attested by sherds of Grimston ware, and in some cases perhaps, by leaf-shaped arrowheads and axes of polished flint and stone. Later Neolithic and Early Bronze Age activity is represented by pottery and a range of other artefacts such as knives, bone implements and beads. Human bodies often appear in association with this material, sometimes as articulated skeletons but often as deposits of selected bones or weathered fragments. This variety in assemblages suggests that many caves were acknowledged as places for burial and for use in other rites.

The setting of many in the Peak suggests that caves were often places apart. This impression was created in several ways. Fox Hole Cave is set on a prominent hill, High Weeldon, which rises above the upper Dove valley. When viewed from the limestone shelves to the north-west around Earl Sterndale, or from Chrome Hill, High Weeldon dominates the local landscape. From the summit, you can look along a spine of reef limestone, a sinuous and dramatic line formed in the shallows of an ancient sea. In contrast to the prominent setting, the diminutive entrance to Fox Hole cave is situated a short distance from the top on the north-west side. It is not visible from a distance, and

High Wheeldon

when on the steep hillside one has to know it is there to find it. Visibility would have been poorer still if the hill retained scrub or woodland cover at the time. Given the steep slope here and the more general topography, people are highly unlikely to pass by accident. No paths up, down or across the hill are likely to have come close. A prominent hill but a hidden cave.

There are parallels with other sites. Neolithic and Early Bronze Age material has been recovered from fissures that are difficult to locate at the best of times, and there are many cases where access to the cave mouth was difficult or obscure. This was probably the case on Carsington Pastures, where a recently excavated cave has revealed multiple burials and other deposits. Were it not for cavers exploring new routes, these would have remained hidden. Other caves evoke this sense of being set apart in different ways. Cheshire Wood and Seven Ways, two of several caves along the Manifold, are located high on the sides of the limestone gorge. Similarly, Dowel Cave lies up on the side of a small, steep-sided dry valley, north-west of Earl Sterndale. It is found near the lower end, immediately above where the narrow defile opens into a small amphitheatre-like valley. Passing through this bowl and out between two reef limestone crags, one enters the upper Dove. The cave has a small entrance that is today hidden by nettles and the branches of trees. If the valley was heavily wooded and intractable in prehistory, as seems likely, the cave would have also been well hidden then. Even without the vegetation, it is a diminutive feature, set above the line of sight, difficult to approach from below and near impossible to reach from above. The setting is secluded and was perhaps secret; prior knowledge was probably necessary for it to be found. Calling

Ossums cave

Low is somewhat similar; a rock shelter near the top of a small, cliff-lined, dry valley which descends steeply into Lathkill Dale to the north. Today, this side valley is heavily wooded and this was again probably the case in prehistory. It provides no convenient path anywhere, and was arguably a place seldom passed through. Thick with vegetation, it may have then, as now, been difficult to enter.

To our eyes today, these settings are primarily a function of geology and geomorphology, a view very different from that held by communities at the time. Where we see faults and erosion, they may have seen the hand of ancestral forces, an ancient tomb or the features of a spirit. This is difficult to gauge. What we can say is that the settings of many caves brought a particular pattern to the encounter that people could have. They involved movement, and probably movement away from the hub of things, a climb to a hidden portal or passage into a defile or dale which was itself set off the beaten path. And through this, they suggest a sense of separation, of being set apart from many aspects of day-to-day life and perhaps the majority of people. At many caves, the topography is such that it is difficult to imagine substantial gatherings in the immediate environs or around entrances. And from these characteristics, it is a small step to the idea that for some caves, a measure of secrecy could have surrounded their whereabouts or the events they witnessed. Simply finding a cave may have involved instruction — being taken by someone or being shown the path. Once there, it was possible to undertake rites beyond the gaze of others.

After the approach comes entry into the earth. That was often difficult, and once inside it was dark, damp and frequently cramped. At Fox Hole for example, the current entrance is actually larger than it once was, explosives having been used to allow easier access while people searched for a lost dog in 1928. Passages can be tight and restrictive and there are not always large chambers that permit easy movement. Only a few sites offered a basic potential as places of occupation, and even then numbers were probably small and episodes short. What carried people into most caves was less the prospect of shelter and more a concern with the dead, with the spirits of a place and their relation to both.

What did people do once they crossed the threshold? It is here that we face the greatest uncertainties, the confused nature of many deposits allowing interpretation in only the broadest terms. Burial was certainly an important practice, perhaps from the earlier Neolithic onwards, though there are few dates or strong associations between human bone and artefacts from this time. This parallels the situation in chambered tombs. Only two — Greenlow and Five Wells — contained fragments of early vessels. At Cheshire Wood Cave, Grimston sherds were recovered in the 1950s. However, human remains in the cave appear to comprise only the jaws of two adults and two children and these were not found in direct association with the pottery. Early pottery was also found at Fissure Cave, Bradwell, but it is unclear whether vessels were put in the cave to accompany the dead or as a feature of other activities. Here, as in many other cases, there is also plentiful evidence for similar activities in the later third and early second millennia; Peterborough Wares, Beakers and other later vessels. Like the pottery, there are many other artefacts which probably date to these later phases. Rarely is it possible to link these artefacts directly to instances of burial. Indeed, it is often difficult to determine 'what goes with what' at all. This sense of confusion is actually important. Though some of the mixing we encounter is a product of other agencies, at least some of it is telling us that objects took different paths into caves. Some may well have arrived as grave goods — gifts to the dead and provisions for journeys to come. But many others were left behind for other reasons, casually discarded at the end of certain events or deposited with some formality and to different ends.

If it is wrong to assume that all artefacts entered caves as 'grave goods', it is equally difficult to accept that all recovered human bones reflect burial as we understand the term. Multiple burials have been identified in a number of caves, from two or three bodies at Wetton Mill or Mill Pot to over twenty children and adults at Carsington and Ravenscliffe. There are also single burials. At Thor's Cave, weathered climbing gear jammed into the roof hangs above sediments that contained the contracted body of a woman, deposits of pottery, an amber button, a polished axe and other pieces of worked stone. In these and in other cases, it is probably appropriate to suggest a concern with laying people to rest; mothers, children, brothers and other kin. However, it is difficult to avoid the conclusion that dealings with the dead did not stop there. Some bodies entered caves intact and remained that way, their skeletons still showing a high degree of articulation when excavated. But many others are represented by jumbled bones or careful arrangements of skulls, limbs or other elements, places like Harborough, where a cave cuts in beneath a prominent ridge of limestone pillars and crags. What we often recover may well be the results of protracted processes which saw bodies or other more fragmented remains re-excavated, handled and moved around. There were also cases where that presence was only a token, people represented by highly selective deposits; a handful of jaws; skulls placed in recesses; limbs pushed into narrow fissures.

We find this variety within individual caves. In the outer part of Dowel cave, in a section of passage about three metres long, were the bones of at least seven people and two dogs. Many of the bones were jumbled but there were concentrations of long bones from two people, and six out of the seven skulls recovered were placed near the right-hand wall. The skulls looked into the cave rather than out towards the entrance. Nearby was the headless body of a dog. In at least three cases the skulls appear to have been surrounded by rings of protective stonework. In one example, the skull had a perforation with wear on its inner edge, suggesting to the excavators it may have been 'carried on the end of a spear or stick'. Near the skulls was the lower trunk and legs of a flexed skeleton, together with an ox bone and two flints. Further in, where the cave starts to narrow, the passage was purposefully blocked to the roof by a crude wall of stones. In a low passage behind these stones were two inhumations. One was flexed and the bones were largely in their correct anatomical positions. However, one tibia was placed across the chest, as if this part of the leg had been removed to place the body in the confined space. Behind these burials was a second wall of stones to the roof. This sealed the continuation of the cave, which here was less than thirty centimetres wide. Behind the wall a child's skull had been purposefully placed. The lower jaw was missing and a small flat stone supported the palatal region, perhaps to stop it rolling down the sloping floor. Accompanying the skull was half an ox mandible and there was an ox femur and humerus in the soil above the rest. The bones of wild cat, dog, badger and fox, as well as many small mammals and birds were also found, suggesting the presence of other predators.

The evidence from Dowel demonstrates how people responded to the 'architecture' of caves, using it as a frame across which to map different deposits and activities. It also shows how they sometimes added to those arrangements, building divisions or markers out of stone. This was undertaken on several sites: at Falcon Low Cave, and at Ravenscliffe. At Calling Low Rock Shelter, limestone blocks formed two open cists against the back wall. One contained a jumble of disarticulated bones, mostly from one person, but with the skull missing. A further three or four people were also represented by a small quantity of bones. Scattered amongst these were sherds of Peterborough Wares, a transverse flint arrowhead and several flint and chert flakes. Whether these individuals' bones had been buried after their bodies had lain elsewhere in the rock shelter, or whether they had been brought from elsewhere, is not clear. The other cist contained a single tightly-contracted inhumation of a woman, the front part of the skull apparently having been purposefully pierced. Immediately outside this second cist was a flexed inhumation of an adult woman and nearby that of a young child. Elsewhere under the shelter was a group of six inhumations, all young children and all buried close to each other. In a niche in the back wall was a human pelvis and a fox skull.

Structural features were also added at Fox Hole. Today, the narrow entrance is a comfortable squeeze at the top of a short drop into a small chamber where it is possible to stand. After a short but narrow section, at just over nine metres from the entrance, a second somewhat larger chamber is reached. Beyond this, the passage narrows and it is possible to stoop/walk a further fifteen metres before reaching a third and larger chamber with a higher roof than the first. From here, three passages continue, one straight on, the others to either side, superficially resembling the chamber arrangement of a cruciform passage grave. From the entrance chamber inwards there are extensive and sometimes beautiful stalactite deposits coating the walls. Patches of charcoal and scorched clay on the floors of some of the chambers reflect the presence of hearths and a bear's vertebra with a worked hollow may have seen use as a lamp. Human remains at Fox Hole are found in the outer parts of the cave, while other artefacts and hearths stretch back further into the hill.

There are also numerous bones from other animals, some the remains of consumption or careful placement by people, still more the calling cards of other predators. Telling these apart is not easy. However, traces of working, the considered association of bones or simple oddity reminds us that many wild animals may have been drawn upon in varied rites. Nowhere is this clearer than at Thor's Fissure Cave, where Dolphin bones have been identified.

. . . What Nature meant in leaving this window open into the infernal world, if the place lies that way, we cannot tell. But it must be said, there is something of horror upon the very imagination when one does but look into it . . .
Daniel Defoe

It would be easy to become lost in the details of caves, their forms, contents and histories. Those seeking a single path will lose their way. What we can say is that events in caves had a particular pattern to them. They involved movement, separation, and passage into the ground; a place of darkness only revealed in flickering light. The passages close in, opening out into chambers that contain you once you have struggled through. The 'architecture' imposed a certain order to the way in which deposits were encountered, keeping some things hidden until the entrance had disappeared. Revelation was possible. Close by were the remains of the dead; flowstone spreading over skulls and long bones so that they too seemed part of the place. And there were the walls themselves, many taking extravagant and bizarre shapes; flowstone and erosion forming contours that scowled or smiled when the light from a hearth or torch played upon them. The orbits of skulls would have had a similar vitality. These places were highly charged and they demanded responses. Though we cannot be certain, they were well suited to the inducement of altered states of consciousness, with or without any additional help. The movement of light on stone could be mesmeric as well as revealing, and even the pitch darkness throws shapes and colours on the mind's eye after a time. For those who crouched and squeezed their way through passages, who sat silent in the dark or watched as spirits moved before them, the conditions were well suited to trances and visions.

Rowtor

In effect, a cave was a place of seclusion. Here it was possible to come to commemorate and to seek revelation in the earth. It created conditions that could often only be experienced by a solitary person, or at any rate, a very small number at any one time. Many may have been regarded as socially liminal, their association with the sacred given weight by the presence of the dead. As water dripped and shadows danced, people set themselves apart, excavated, handled and deposited certain tokens, and perhaps stayed for a time in the company of spirits. The dead were certainly an important presence at these places and times; bodies of those who were remembered as well as bones with less familiar genealogies. However, they were often the audience for other rites and the creation of other deposits. A vessel that was significant in itself, or for the offering it contained; an axe that had accumulated a rich biography; the bones of particular animals and other relics.

. . . This is how it is. The hill takes you in. It tells you what you need to hear. And when you're done it delivers you back, blinking and struggling into the world, your sight clearer than before. When you die, it will take you back again, seed corn waiting for the cycle to start over. . .

Exclusion and solitary revelation probably lent themselves to structuring various rites of passage, including those that attended the thresholds crossed in life. Given their character, the return from many caves was perhaps equivalent to being reborn. To be released, clay smeared, after the struggle from the interior was to come back changed; a successful initiate; one of the company of elders, or of a particular group. Perhaps there were also occasions when the journey was made with others, those with the authority to pass on secret knowledge as a prerogative of age and kinship. The land was integral to this process.

Periods of separation from the everyday are also a hallmark of various forms of Shamanic ritual. Here it is perhaps telling that creatures such as bears can feature prominently in Shamanic rites as can prominent landscape features, rocks, springs and so on. It is possible that certain caves in the Peak saw use by these ritual specialists — people who could move between worlds with the ability to speak to or on behalf of the spirits. Some of the 'tokens' we recover might have seen use as the paraphernalia of these rites; touchstones for entry into other worlds. Perhaps there were times when communal events were preceded by a shaman withdrawing to prepare; to seek guidance and approval in the land.

Marking time

Our understanding of caves and the significance they were accorded in the past arises from three sources: their contents, character and location. But even where the evidence is strong, understanding remains partial and fragmentary. There is much that we do not and probably cannot know. These same constraints apply to another class of evidence that is more enigmatic than most. Though by no means common in the Peak, particularly compared to Northumberland or the Yorkshire Moors, there are a number of places where outcrops or more portable slabs of rock have been decorated with carefully

Eyam Moor — Stanage barrow

pecked designs. Almost all known examples occur on the gritstone. This may be a real distribution. The limestone of the White Peak would not have lent itself to carving in this manner and if designs appeared at all, they may have been rendered in other media — pigments or paint that leave no trace. How many carvings have faded over the years and how many more remain to be discovered beneath peat or turf is something we can only guess at.

These carvings take a number of forms. The most common element is a simple 'cup mark'; a pecked hollow in the surface of a stone. These were cut into natural surfaces, occasionally onto stone that had been dressed to a limited extent. Cup marks can occur singly or in considerable numbers, multiple cups recognised at places such as Bleakley Dike and Stanage Barrow on Eyam Moor. They are also sometimes held within one or more concentric circles, a pattern seen on Calton Pasture and Rowtor Rocks. Groups of cup marks are also found enclosed within a carved border, as at Ball Cross or Gardom's Edge. Other designs tend to be rather more complex; composites of cup marks, rough spirals, linear and curvilinear carvings. Dramatic examples have been identified on Gardom's Edge, Burr Tor and again at Rowtor Rocks. Some of these bear a resemblance to designs found in Neolithic passage graves in northern and western Britain.

Dating rock art is a bizarre process. Analogy with similar designs in other media suggests that most were carved in the third and second millennia. Support for the argument comes from the fact that carved slabs were sometimes broken up and incorporated into Bronze Age monuments, demonstrating that they were certainly in existence by that time. This is a strong characteristic of material in the Peak, where slabs were used as cist covers, architectural details or simply as rubble to be added to banks or mounds. Examples have been recovered from a number of barrows, among them Stanage, Eyam Moor and Barbrook on Big Moor. Carved slabs also occur as components in other monuments; three carved stones were found in association with Barbrook II stone circle, and a complex design on a boulder was recovered from the ditch of the Late Bronze Age/ Early Iron Age enclosure at Ball Cross. These associations are a little confusing. The decorated stones at Barbrook II, Stanage or Eyam Moor may be of a similar date to the monuments, their position a calculated act of placement. The boulder at Ball Cross may be residual, reflecting the later use of stone in the building of the enclosure. No dates are entirely secure. For that reason, it is difficult to test the common argument that some of the more complex designs are Neolithic, while cup marks, also produced at around the same time, continued to be carved throughout the Bronze Age. Dates by association are also recruited on occasion, any artefacts found nearby indicating the same broad range. This also has its limits; we still toss coins in Medieval wells. Though many carvings do probably date to the Later Neolithic and Early Bronze Age, there may be some that are considerably older. Perhaps the oldest carvings of all are now the grains of sand that rush down footpaths whenever there is heavy rain.

There are many more interpretations of the meanings of these carvings than there are examples in the Peak. This may be partly because almost all are not strictly representational as we understand the term. They do not contain figures or images that can be easily equated with other objects or features. Though they may have sometimes served exactly that role, they are tied to an aesthetic that we can no longer recognise. It is this very ambiguity that has encouraged such a variety to interpretation. Maps are often mentioned, as are suggestions that carved surfaces were tallies or records of events. People talk of stellar arrangements or of carvings cut to harness latent energies in the earth. Mention is also frequently made of fertility, carvings seen as symbols of fecundity or of the forces involved in ensuring the reproduction of the world. Perhaps there were even occasions when the image was entirely subordinate to the act of carving itself, a by-product of respect shown by action rather than the 'reading' of inscriptions. The list is a long one and can only grow longer. Particular meanings are lost.

. . . A large boulder; orange brown. Across its face are carvings; circles spirals and grooves. There are other carvings too, though not so old. The bite of the teeth on the bucket that brought the boulder to light; fresh stone exposed under the patina. And all around the edge, the cut and bounce of the plough; shares raking up the slope and onto the top. The same orientation again and again; a chance reminder of the line of a wall . . .

Ashover

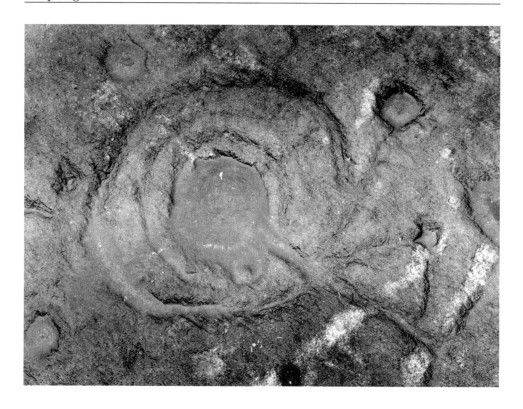

Ashover

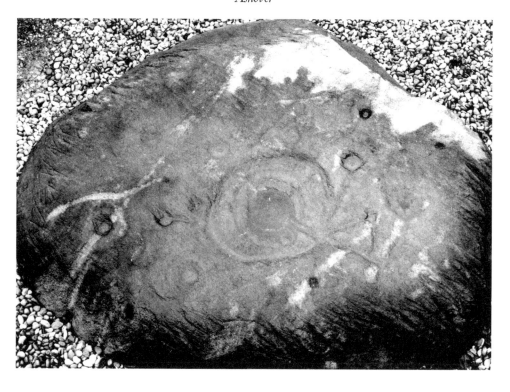

Clues as to the broad significance of rock carvings can be found in the details of their setting. One of the most common themes in interpretation is that carvings acted as some form of sign; a set of directions or a statement of claims. Some suggest that they served as markers of territory, others that they were visited as people passed though an area on their way to particular monuments. A common theme has been that carvings were often set to be on important paths of movement — along likely access routes or on the threshold between higher and lower country. A good example of this tendency can be found on Gardom's Edge. Here a particularly dramatic composite design was pecked into the surface of a large earthfast slab. Two other carved gritstones have been found elsewhere on the moor. The earthfast lies close to the Neolithic enclosure and to the banks and cairns of Bronze Age fields. Separated by a few steps and by hundreds if not thousands of years.

Visited today, the carving is convincing until touched. A hollow sound reveals that what lies at your feet is a cast, installed to protect an original that has suffered from too much attention and careless damage since its discovery last century. Opinion is split as to the merits of this installation. On the one hand, it has slowed the process of decay that has had such a rapid impact on the true stone. It also means that people can continue to appreciate the setting of the original act of carving. On the other it is a rather bizarre act, an attempt to hold back the continual process of change that is the hallmark of any landscape. It is a curious aspect of contemporary attitudes towards the past that we feel compelled to

Gardom's Edge

hold things as if in aspic, no less bizarre than many of the prehistoric rites that we now struggle to comprehend. Time passes, things fade.

What the cast does demonstrate is the setting of the carving. It is not far from the crags of Gardom's Edge itself, but is set back a little, a few minutes walk across massive earthfasts and boulders, on the dip that runs down to the east. It is not particularly prominent, lying very low to the ground. It helps if you know where it is. There are no postholes or related features to suggest that the spot was highlighted in any contrived way, and beyond clearings and paths it is likely that people may have often been brought to the place and had it revealed to them at certain times. For all we know, the slab itself might have been covered between visits.

There are hints here of a concern with revelation. Not far from likely paths or on the threshold between seasonal or otherwise periodic places, carvings were also hidden, set just off the track. A strong sense of this can be found at Rowtor Rocks, the outcrop visited at the start of this chapter. The crags are striking, dramatic forms that would not look out of place on Dartmoor. Several prehistoric carvings have been identified here; cups with concentric rings, a sinuous line, and more complex designs. The outcrop is a prominent local feature, giving views back up towards Stanton Moor and across towards Harthill, Cratcliff Rocks and Robin Hood's Stride. Yet the rock art itself is almost hidden, cut into outcrops overshadowed by others. The immediate setting does not lend itself to easy discovery. Here too, people may have had designs revealed to them, perhaps when they reached a certain age, shown and instructed by more senior members of a family. The right to attend or to add to a surface may have also been a privilege of blood or gender. Like the meanings of the designs themselves, there are many possibilities.

This idea of revelation gains support from a rather unusual source. Work in neuropsychology indicates that what we might term abstract designs can be generated in the mind's eye when conditions are right. Zigzags, spirals, chevrons and dots. Often associated with altered states of consciousness, these images can be induced by fasting, sleep depravation, trances or the ingestion of narcotics. These 'entoptic phenomena' feature in carvings and paintings in a wide variety of cultural settings and have close parallels in the decorations on a number of Neolithic tombs. It is possible that some of the designs on carved slabs and outcrops in the Peak sprang from a similar source. Contemplation of those designs may have also acted back upon the mind, helping to induce similar changes in consciousness. Where this was the case, it may be helpful to see carved outcrops, like caves, as places of revelation, where people sometimes came to seek visions or spiritual guidance.

Carving or visiting may have been understood as a spiritual act. Perhaps it was required in order to renew a connection with land visited only at certain times; on a journey, on the move with stock; returning to old hunting grounds. Traditions of carving and painting outcrops that can still be observed today suggest that this is a common theme. The meanings of images can be extraordinarily varied. They can also change according to who is present and why they are there. And they can certainly change over time. But often a core theme in visits, and in the act of decorating stone itself, is the renewal of a tie to place, the paying of respects to whatever forces are recognised as residing there. People often recognise a responsibility to look after these places, to attend to them and in the act, renew

Robin Hood's stride

their connection with the land and with each other. Who knows. The slow, rhythmic hammering and pecking of stone may have set the tempo for chants or recitation, knowledge driven into memory through repetition just as the design grew stronger in the stone. What we do know is that at least some carved outcrops were revisited and added to, sometimes cutting through older lines. At Ashover, in a parish whose geological make up mimics the broader pattern of the Peak as a whole, recent work on a school playing field brought several new carvings to light. Two, perhaps three, large boulders bear cup marks, spirals and concentric circles, some bisected by more linear grooves.

The situation may have been rather different where carved slabs were incorporated or even highlighted in built monuments. We know nothing of where these carvings originated. Some might have been fashioned for use in those settings. Others were far older slabs that had been taken out of context, bringing histories and associations with them. The fact that a number of slabs have an association with places of the dead suggests that they may have sometimes been recruited in asserting tenure with particular pieces of land. An old carving had witnessed rites which reaffirmed the spiritual link between the land and certain people. Brought to a barrow, it added its weight to the latest of those claims.

Stone of course did not need carving in order to be accorded a particular symbolic significance. A small number of standing stones have also been identified in the Peak, arguably erected at around the same time as outcrops were being carved and stone circles erected. Dramatic examples are found at Gardom's Edge and Wirksworth, monoliths of grit and limestone respectively. Just how many have gone since that time is unknown. Another, the 'Old Woman's Stone' on Bamford Moor, is now prostrate; others like it may yet lie hidden. Piecemeal 'borrowing' of stone and more concerted 'improvement' in the last two centuries has also seen many large stones uprooted for use elsewhere. Gateposts, lintels, building stone. We also know that standing stones in many areas were disturbed or toppled by excavators following tales of treasure to be found at their bases. Once prostrate, these too were sometimes broken up for use elsewhere. It is possible that a similar range of processes have contributed to the small number of monoliths still standing in the Peak today.

There is a considerable overlap in the interpretations offered for standing stones and rock carvings. Once again, and perhaps predictably, the form of monoliths has been taken to reflect a concern with fertility. Similar links are often made where stones were erected near to springs or other water sources. Folklore attached to standing stones in several regions suggests that this link has some pedigree at least, but we cannot be certain how far back it goes. Talk of women visiting or dancing around stones in the recorded past as a means of enhancing fertility may be hearsay, or a use of stones for rites that were never thought of when they were first established. The fertility of people, animals and the land itself would have been powerful concerns for Neolithic and Bronze Age communities, just as they had been in earlier times. It is simply unclear whether this led people to raise stones as direct representations of a phallus. In any case, it has been said on more than one occasion that (male) archaeologists tend to see the phallus almost everywhere, interpretation saying more about us than about the people we purport to study.

Interpretation does not have to revolve around the phallus, which is probably a good thing. In fact, there is a broad variety to the interpretation of standing stones that may be helpful. One theme that does recur is that stones were set to establish sight lines for

Gardom's Edge

astronomical observation. This has been shown to work for some monoliths set in close relation to other sites, not least stone circles. However, it is a difficult proposition to test where stones were raised or survive in isolation. We simply don't know where to look. Work has also suggested that for some stones at least, there was a seasonal pattern to the encounter that people would have had. More often than not, these arguments assume a role for stones as markers of social boundaries or meeting points. This is also difficult to reconcile with the evidence from the Peak. The Wirksworth stone stands isolated in a more recent field and we do not know its detailed relation to contemporary settlement. The stone on Gardom's Edge stands in close proximity to prehistoric cairnfields. If the stone predates much of this surrounding evidence, it may well be that it served some similar purpose. If contemporary, the relation to people may have been rather different, a monument set apart from dwellings and plots but seen on a frequent basis at times when communities lived and worked nearby.

Given present evidence, we cannot really choose one or any combination of these themes with any confidence. Besides, they do not exhaust the possibilities. Stone should have been erected to mark the place in which certain events had transpired, even where sacred trees had once stood. Like early Medieval crosses, they could have been on the edges of things, giving definition to boundaries and visited as speaking points on important occasions. And perhaps there was a significance more basic still. Certain outcrops of rock had long held a spiritual and symbolic importance; residues of ancestral tasks or the remains of the ancestors themselves. These understandings were implicated where people used that stone in the making of tools, or built monuments that were inspired by or incorporated natural forms. Perhaps for people at the time, these monoliths were not stone at all, but a manifestation of an important ancestor or spirit. This is not as surprising as it might sound. Folklore again reveals a common tendency to anthropomorphise, to recognise people in the stone. And where early Medieval crosses bore inscriptions or depictions, people often saw not a representation but a direct and immediate spiritual presence. We should not assume any direct continuity with the prehistoric past in these readings. However, they do give some sense of the different ways in which contemporary imagination could have pivoted around the rock.

Echoes

Sound does strange things in caves. It can be absorbed almost instantly, the stone soaking up your words. It can also reverberate, the faintest footfall or trickle of water gaining new cadences. Echoes are soon lost when you struggle back out across the threshold. This quality also played its part in the performance of various rituals. Sonorous voices and the sound of spirits weeping for the dead. There were different sounds in other places. The drumming of hammers in the carving of designs; the reverberant responses where people chanted near to upright stones. All of the senses contributed to the ways these places were held in social memory.

How long those memories were sustained is difficult to say. Many caves saw similar uses between one and two thousand years later, and it is tempting to trace in this a continuity of meaning right through to the Roman period. However, we do not know how far history had turned into myth by this time, a cave recognised as significant, but for reasons that would have hardly been understood by earlier communities. We get a hint of this fluidity in the names that adhere to many caves and barrows today. Some make sense, tied as they are to origin myths and local traditions that we still acknowledge. Some are less clear, their significance already eroded beyond recognition. Some have no names at all. Though these landmarks seem permanent, their meanings are not. In any case, those earlier communities had themselves inherited caves. Stories and traditions handed down from older generations, worked and reworked with each passing year. Even stone can flow and change its shape with time.

For now, we must accept that there is much about the history and significance of caves that eludes us. That will always be so. New excavations and new radiocarbon dates may bring a much-needed clarity to particular questions. But they will never be enough. The same is probably true of rock carvings. There will always be a flux to interpretation, an uncertainty at odds with the confidence of those who sometimes claim to have cracked the code of meaning in these enigmatic designs. A similar confidence may have been claimed in the past, by those in a position to say what histories or forces were condensed in and

Wirksworth

around a particular stone. But even then perhaps, there were other meanings and different views. And as time passed, meanings changed, designs were recruited to different ends or simply became anachronism; scratches passed unnoticed.

Given the extraordinary variety in contemporary attitudes towards what we regard as nature, it would be remarkable if prehistoric communities recognised the same sharp boundaries of classification that animate so much academic work today. In a region where names like the 'Devil's Arse' or 'Madwoman's Stones' are still written on maps, such an argument requires special pleading. Given the pattern of life at the time, the importance of ancestry and closeness to land, we should take it as a basic axiom that people recognised history, myth and powerful forces in the landscapes they inhabited.

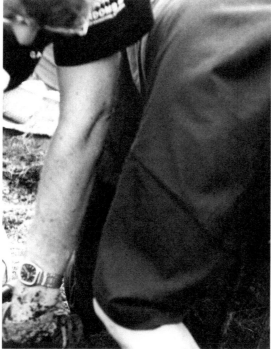

Arthur's Cairn – Eyam Moor

7 Traditions of dead generations
2500-1500 BC

Liff's Low

It has been a long day. The tractor has laboured on the heavy clay, the plough more an anchor than a blade. Eyes turn towards the next line, automatic hands bringing wheel and engine around. The lad faces home for the fifteenth time, the wall no more than two strides to his side. The last run, then through the gate, blade lifted, and back to the yard.

He does not notice the mound. Had the ground been dry, the light less tired, he might have seen the change in the soil. A pale circle against the darker earth. Stone gathered long before, reduced by frost to shards and crystal; flint the colours of a magpie's throat. It is only felt in passing. A slight swell in the stomach as the wheels rise and fall, one undulation amongst many. The blade follows, jumps and chatters across a hidden slab.

The plough moves on, its wake a ridge of fresh earth that draws the gulls down. Eager for worms and roots, their bodies pitch and toss as if still at sea. They pay no heed to the slivers of burnt bone, nor the stab and drag line on the vessel that has risen to the surface. It is only clay; the pattern cut by the sharpened fibula of a crow.

In 1843, Thomas Bateman undertook the excavation of 'one of the most interesting barrows ever examined in this vicinity' at Liff's Low, near Biggin. Published five years later in his *Vestiges of the Antiquities of Derbyshire*, Bateman's account paints a vivid picture. Recovering a few sherds of 'coarse urn' and fragmentary human and animal bones as he cut through the mound, he finally came upon an octagonal limestone cist.

. . . Within lay a fine human skeleton, whose knees were drawn up, according to a general custom, prevalent in the most remote ages. The extreme antiquity of this interment is demonstrated by the simple form and material of the weapons and tools which were, with one exception, deposited behind the shoulders of this early denizen of the Derbyshire moors. The skull which is fine and intellectual, lay on the left side so as to look towards the west and in the angle formed by the contraction of the knees, was placed a hammer head ingeniously constructed out of the lower part of the horn of a noble red deer; one end of this instrument is rounded and polished, the other is cut into a diamond pattern, somewhat similar to the wafer stamps used by attorneys. The articles before alluded to as being placed near the shoulders were of a very miscellaneous character, and highly interesting; as showing, after a lapse of several thousand years, that the savage Briton reposing in his cairn had cultivated the art of making war amongst the inhabitants of the forest in preference to molesting his fellow savages; as almost the first observed articles were a pair of enormous tusks of the wild boar, the trophies of some, perhaps his last, sylvan triumph; next came two arrowheads of flint, delicately chipped and of usual form; two flint celts or chisels, beautifully chipped and polished at the cutting edges; two spearheads of the same material; two flint knives polished on the edge, one of them serrated on the back, in order to serve as a saw; and numerous other pieces of flint of indescribable form and use . . . with these utensils were found three pieces of red ochre, the rouge of these unsophisticated huntsmen which, even now, on being wetted imparts a bright red colour to the skin, which is by no means easy to discharge. Upon the summit of the little heap, formed by this accumulation of relics, lay a small drinking or incense cup of a novel and unprecedented shape . . .

The first recorded excavation in a sequence at Liff's Low that runs through into the 1980s, Bateman's account is important for many reasons. It tells us what he recovered, and in some detail; not only what was found but also where. The record varies depending on where you are in the mound, but the description gives a valuable picture of a body laid to rest with accompanying tokens. His account also catches something of the intellectual frame of the time. There is his delight in the craft displayed in various pieces, and in the immediacy of materials; that the ochre could still redden the skin. There is also the importance of comparison, familiarity with other sites and the work of other scholars, that allowed him to dub artefacts as 'typical' or 'unprecedented'. There too is the linking of stone tools to 'the most remote ages' and to discussion of savages. Faith in a view of progress as technologically driven.

Bateman was by no means the first of his kind. At his most active during the middle of the nineteenth century, his library contained notes and publications on the work of earlier generations of antiquarians, among them his own father, William. People like Samuel Pegge or Hayman Rooke, who explored the region on horseback in the eighteenth century, and who traced in the earthworks all around him the hand of ancient Druids and Romans. What sets Bateman apart from many of his predecessors or contemporaries was the sheer scale of his efforts, and, at times, his attention to detail 'with the utmost care and preciseness'. He and his associates were responsible for digging over three hundred barrows in the region, and his accounts provide an invaluable record.

Precision was not always his watchword. Like his colleague Samuel Carrington, Bateman dug voraciously and sometimes with little time or eye for detail. He apparently got through four cairns in one day on Hind Low near Buxton and records being 'obliged to clear out the grave by candlelight' at Rusden Low. Something of the tone of his 'opening parties' can be found in the doggerel of the Reverend Stephen Issacson's *Barrow digging by a barrow knight*. Bateman features prominently, as do Carrington and the tools that were used; even Bateman's dog gets a mention. Elsewhere we get a vivid (if awkward) picture, of workmen shifting earth, and of long, rich and heavy lunches. There is also the sense of a close social group, of welcome visits by gentry and the more unwelcome attentions of other locals or 'aborigines' as Issacson calls them. In these lines, as in Bateman's books and manuscripts themselves, there is both material and milieu. A discipline forming out of the interests of a particular class. A discipline in which distance in space, succession in time and even distinctions of class held a close equivalence.

There is much about the work of Bateman and his contemporaries that we now question. Though remarkably perceptive in their comments, there is usually little information on the structure of a mound or even a precise location. Bateman often steered clear of maps. More basic still, there are the crude evolutionary schemes, the drawing of tight parallels between prehistory and the contemporary world 'outside' the West. Such schemes were not independent of their times, and in one sense at least, helped justify a view of the empire as the acme of progress. How far this mattered (or even occurred) to Bateman is not known. For him, as for many others, a passion for antiquities was a fascination with many things. There was the order of the past, classification itself a passion and a valued contribution to knowledge. There was the history of familiar country, learning more about the regions with which one had a personal connection. And running through both was a fascination with mortality itself. The keen interest shown in barrows was more than the oft-painted caricature of a lust for treasure. Older attitudes to death were being redefined, reason and fashion chipping away at old certainties. It was the same shifting interests that were to transform so many graveyards that led Bateman and his contemporaries to focus so strongly on places where human remains could be anticipated. There are hints in the writing, a grim fascination with the form of bodies; the 'promiscuous huddling' of skeletons, and the degree of charring on cremations. The language of many records blurs the line between objects of a scientific curiosity and objects of desire.

The positive legacy of Bateman's time can be found in the archives. Patchy though they are, his records are a vivid portrait of the heart of many monuments; inventories of artefacts found, described and classified. Few of the well-known sites in the region escaped his attention, and the tailing off of excavation after his death reflects not a loss

Barbrook

of interest but a difficulty in finding new places to dig. Records also show that Bateman had a subtle and detailed grasp of differences in the rites that created many of the sites he explored. Answering a plea made by Pegge almost a century before, he was one of the first to systematically document a change in the ways that the dead were treated; a change that resolved itself during the course of the Later Neolithic and Earlier Bronze Age.

Liff's Low captures much of this change in a single place. Recent work has shown that prior activity on the site stretched back into the early stages of the Neolithic. It is also clear that the mound itself took time to develop, growing in a series of stages, each accompanied by rites of commemoration and perhaps interment. But it is at the heart of the mound that we find evidence for a shift of attitudes. A body was laid to rest and left undisturbed. Accompanying the body were objects, some the belongings or trappings of the deceased, others perhaps gifts from mourners. Dating to the final stages of the Neolithic, the burial reflects a concern with the individual in death. Unlike many earlier tombs, there is little to suggest a desire to subsume that person within a community of ancestors, passage marked by the mingling of bones.

This difference in the character of respect is not in itself so remarkable. Even in some of the earliest passage graves and chambered tombs, disarticulation and the jumbling of bones may have come some time after a corpse had been left to decay. There are also objects, some perhaps tokens that were left with the dead by those who attended their interment. What makes Liff's Low important is that it signals a shift in funerary ritual that became remarkably widespread in the later third and early second millennia. It is part of a pattern that was to repeat itself many times.

. . . They've been up there again. The carriage went straight through the corn without a by or leave. Gates wide open; typical. Me and the lad offered help with the digging, paid of course. But he'd brought his men and all the while he kept his eye on us, I could tell. I don't know why they bothered. Sam says old Rooke was in there years ago, he didn't miss much . . .

Traditions of dead generations

The long history of interest in barrows has created a remarkable distribution pattern. More than five hundred have been identified in the Peak, most dating to between 2500 and 1500 BC and thus to both the final stages of the Neolithic and the Earlier Bronze Age. The majority are also more or less round. A density and character at odds with the tombs and long mounds of earlier generations. The original figure may well have been significantly higher. Records are not always reliable and land use since then has bitten deeply. On the limestone, barrows are relatively rare in areas where the pattern of Medieval strip fields can still be traced, suggesting destruction by the plough from then on. Many have also gone with the advent of more 'industrial' agriculture over the last two centuries, which probably accounts for their relative scarcity in enclosed land on the grits. The process continues to this day.

These factors aside, densities do seem to vary across the region. Barrows are certainly found on the grits, beyond the boundaries of enclosed land, across moors and along prominent edges. But the greatest densities are found on the limestone, some in isolation, others in clusters. Relatively thinly spread in the north, particularly on the higher ranges, they increase in density as one moves south, with prominent clusters on the southernmost fringes of the plateau.

Why are there so many? From a certain point of view, the question seems misplaced. After all, round barrows were being built for over a thousand years and in that frame, the number seems less dramatic. That duration also demonstrates that not everyone was buried in these settings. As before, there was probably more than one path into the afterlife. What is important is the contrast that these round barrows offer to earlier monuments. In their form and in their frequency, they signal a change in the ways that the living thought about and drew upon the dead.

The term round barrow is generally reserved for broadly circular mounds of earth or stone which have no chambers but clear associations with the dead. Where built primarily of stone, some also use the term 'cairn'. Though we define them as a type, there is a remarkable variety in round barrows. The size of mounds varies considerably, and where the plough has dragged a barrow outwards, calculations are difficult. However, diameters seem to vary from around five metres up to twenty metres. Diameters of between twenty and thirty metres have also been recorded, the largest being the massive and in some respects distinct group of later Neolithic barrows noted earlier; sites like Tideslow or Stoney Low. Excavation has also revealed an extraordinary range of architectural variations as well as diversity in the histories of individual sites. Much of this diversity is now lost beneath a mantle of grass and scrub, a cover which belies the striking appearance of many

Above Glutton

mounds when first constructed. A heap of upturned turf and earth; a stark memorial of angular stone that shone when wet. Entirely earthen mounds are rather unusual, and have their greatest densities in the southernmost parts of the region. Mounds of stone, and sometimes earth and stone, are far more widespread. Reporting on work on Ilam Moor, Bateman himself describes a mound 'composed of alternate layers of earth and loose stones . . . there being no admixture of stone with the earthy layers, or of earth with stony ones'. Variations in building techniques were often a function of available materials, though in instances such as this, we may be catching glimpses of very localised architectural traditions.

Some barrows were also provided with kerbs. That this was an embellishment and not just a way of retaining material is suggested by the careful placement of contiguous stones, as at the remarkable triple cairn on Beeley Moor. A sense of design can also be detected in the creation of concentric kerbs, as at Aleck Low, Stanton Moor or Longshaw. Some, like Crow Chin, had flat-topped platforms on top of the main mound. Others, like the reconstructed mound near Barbrook I stone circle on Ramsley Moor, had low platforms appended to them. In this case, the platform covered an urn containing the cremated remains of a child. Some of the most unusual sites in the region are more or less square, though very few are known; Hob Hursts' House and Rod Knoll on the grits and Gallows Knoll on the limestone.

Beeley

Many other barrows contain specific settings, such as oval or rectangular cists, their edges marked by slabs of limestone or grit. These can still be seen on Stanton, Calton Pasture and at Wet Withens on Eyam Moor. An equivalent perhaps for a cist was the rock-cut grave, a recess created in the bedrock identified beneath the mounds of more than sixty sites, among them End Low, Cronkstone Low and Harland Edge. At Shuttlestone, a rock cut grave descended to over two metres. On the bottom lay the contracted body of a man wrapped in a hide and ferns. Near the body was a bronze flat axe, a dagger of the same metal, a bead of jet and a flint scraper.

The popular image of the round barrow is of a mound raised over a body; a singular instance of bereavement and building. Such an image is not altogether wrong. However, it does little to catch more complex and protracted histories. In many places, a clear association with the dead had been established some time before the mound we see today was built. At Bee Low, at least seven burials had been laid to rest before the mound was built. One, the body of a young adult, lay in a rock cut grave together with a fragment from the skull of a small child. Close by was a Beaker, some of the earliest pottery associated with round barrows. Human bone was also recovered from a pair of cists constructed on the old land surface; adults and children, some bones in a disarticulated state. There is a sense of bones being handled and disturbed by people some time after they had been laid to rest; of relics moved aside to make way for new additions. And near the centre of the area, near other scattered bones and fragments of Beaker, lay the contracted body of an adult with four bronze awls. In their character and variety, these deposits suggest some duration to events before even the thought of a mound was raised.

Cremations inserted into the mound also suggest that the building of the barrow did not bring proceedings to a close.

Variations on this theme can be seen elsewhere. Longstone Edge, a limestone ridge now falling into a lead rake, saw the definition of an area by a kerb within which bodies were exposed. Here birds and other scavengers may have come to pull at flesh, corruption a requirement and a metaphor for the journey being undertaken. A similar pattern of birds wheeling above a rise may have been seen at Hind Low and Wigber Low. At Wigber, an exposure platform was established on a low mound. It was only later that the cairn was raised, sealing the small bones of over twenty people that had probably scattered and fallen unnoticed amongst the stones. A similar sequence unfolded on Longstone Edge. We have no way of knowing how common this practice was, or of what antiquity. It may well have stretched a good way back, but it is one which by its nature leaves little in the way of an archaeological signature. What we can say is that some of these exposure or excavation sites remained important enough to become the focus for mound building and what we more readily recognise as burial.

Phasing in the construction of many mounds also suggests enlargement and elaboration over time. On many sites, there is a sense of episodes and intervals; of deposits accumulating; turf and moss on older mounds being buried beneath a fresh mantle of earth or stone. Like older tombs, many barrows were places to which people returned. These patterns may have had a particular significance at the time. One possibility is that intervals separated different forms of ceremony and different ranges of participants. Inevitable though it may seem, death is seldom that predictable. Perhaps the laying of a body to rest happened soon after death, an event attended by those who were close. By contrast, barrow building and the ceremonies that attended construction might have involved more people. Where it took time to arrange proceedings and accumulate food for feasts, an interval may have been essential. In other cases, the raising of a mound may have been in step with other matters — the restatement of claims to land in the face of competition or a commemorative act. Perhaps there were also times when the interval was simply a mark of respect, allowing time for the spirit to escape the ashes or the flesh. Once established, the mound itself became the focus for further events; new burials and acts of commemoration played out across the years.

As these examples suggest, there is a considerable variety in the treatment accorded to the dead, something best seen on the limestone, where bone fares better than on the grits. On the more acid soils of the moors, bone tends to survive only where it has been altered by cremation or other forms of burning. Where survival is good, the remains of anywhere between five and thirty people can be found; bodies in rock cut graves and cists on old land surfaces, in the make up of mounds and in burials added some time later. There are cremations as well as inhumations, some in vessels and others tipped into cists or hollows. And often, a scatter of loose human bones, their articulation lost before coming to a mound or as part of the process of opening and reusing sites. The casual nature of references to these scatters in early accounts suggests that they were sometimes overlooked or went unrecorded, indicating that they were probably common if not ubiquitous.

That many barrows have multiple burials cautions us against assuming that a sense of the collective and protracted use were no longer important. We are dealing here with trends and shifts of emphasis, not a sudden and dramatic break with the past. What matters is that these later mounds reflect a marked concern with specific individuals and often the persistence of that concern beyond death. Where bones had actively mingled as a feature of ancestral rituals, barrows now held the identities of specific people in sharper focus. Not only that, there are simply so many more of them. Earlier communal tombs may have seen use over a similar length of time, yet they are rare by comparison. This suggests perhaps a diminution in the number or range of people for whom a barrow held a particular significance.

This change of scale could mean a number of things. Burials within round barrows may have been overtly concerned with specific genealogies; lines of descent and inheritance that stretched back behind particular families. A narrowing of focus and a pulling in of social horizons. Where older tombs and ancestors had brought broader communities together, barrows stressed close kinship, tracing those ties in a more recent and recounted past. The protracted histories of many barrows suggest that those genealogies could be recalled time and time again; as new burials were added, or as people stood on platforms and recited the names that were tied to particular mounds.

Here we must be careful. It would be easy to oppose these two different forms of respect shown to the dead, treating each as the signature of a distinct period of time, one following the other in neat succession. That was not the case. There is a considerable overlap in the histories of these sites; indeed, some of the oldest complexes continued to be used in the Earlier Bronze Age. This suggests a variety to the ways that the dead could be drawn on, and sometimes a desire to trace the roots of new attitudes into the past.

. . . Wolfscote. A sharp hill between two dales and on the crest a barrow, hemmed in by limestone benches. Cist and cairn hold the dead in place so that they may watch over their own. Then, after an eternity of silence, another monument. A concrete trig point; a tapered obelisk that pins the barrow like a specimen. Two monuments, one place. The first a memorial and a vantage for ghosts. The second a fixed point in a cartographic imagination. SK1370 5832: 1272 feet above sea level. Forgotten genealogies between the two . . .

Object lives

At least some of the issues addressed during funerals took their cue from the tools, weapons and ornaments that we recover from mounds, sometimes in direct association with the dead. This material is not always easy to interpret. Some artefacts in the make up of mounds or on old land surfaces may be considerably older and have little to do with later funerals or commemorative rituals. This may have been the case for some of the oldest material found at places like Liff's Low or Hognaston. If it served any purpose at all, a scatter of weathered stone and clay was a reminder that a place had a history that stretched some way back. However, it is equally possible that some material was scooped up unnoticed in the raising of a mound, its significance already lost.

Wolfscote

This was not always the case. The deposits at Liff's Low which exercised Bateman's imagination demonstrate that objects were often buried with some deliberation as a feature of funerals and other rituals. The range of finds from the site are quite exceptional. Like Green Low, where the burials of a man and a child were accompanied by a Beaker, a flint dagger, arrows, knives and other objects, it contains an unusually high number of artefacts, some of them finely crafted. The edges on the axes hold a line so straight that you know they have been held up close to the eye; worked and worked again until true. Though graves in the Peak can contain no artefacts at all, there are many with a small number of simple tools or a single clay vessel. Just what these deposits meant at the time is difficult to determine. A common tendency in recent interpretation has been to rank the relative 'wealth' of grave goods, using this as an index to measure the status of burials and thus the complexity of society at the time. Such studies have their value. But they often lead us to assume that the laying of people to rest within or under many mounds was necessarily concerned with the signalling of political authority. This is not a particularly new idea. Describing stone tools, pottery, bones and ashes recovered from an impressive mound near Fin Cop, Hayman Rooke reached a similar conclusion, that 'the barrow was the sepulcre of the chieftan and his relatives'. In the Peak, this may have been the exception to the rule. Though the living recognised differences of standing or renown, what shaped many deposits at barrows were more localised concerns. No doubt some funerals were signal events, involving the coming together of many people. Most, however, were probably witnessed by much smaller groups, those bound by more immediate ties of kinship. In these circumstances, objects deposited by mourners may have spoken of values and identities that had little to do with the broader discourse of renown or political standing.

Grave goods could be drawn on in varied ways. Some entered graves on the body; fittings and adornments which spoke of the personal history and identity of the deceased. Some, like Collared Urns, entered mounds as containers for the cremated remains of the dead. But like Beakers, many artefacts were added to the tableau. A quiver of arrows, a dagger or a battle axe; a clutch of scrapers or pins; bone objects and elaborate or exotic items of jet, bronze and faience. Some of these assemblages reflect the provision of artefacts for use by the dead. Scrapers, knives, arrows, strike-a-lights and cores or flakes may have been interred for use in the tasks that people were likely to perform in the afterlife. Some of the Beakers and Food Vessels found next to bodies may have contained food for the journey. Many tools bear traces of use, and it is possible that they were elements of the personal gear that had been worn and used by particular people. In these situations, it was perhaps appropriate that objects with strong biographical associations should make the same journey as the body. Perhaps some of the deposits of objects that have no associations with burials made the journey to a barrow for similar reasons. Though the body was absent, objects that 'stood for' a person tied their passing into the narrative of the family line and fixed them to a particular place.

Various purposes may have been served where objects were made specifically for display or burial, elaborate or finely-made variations on everyday themes. Placed by the mourners, these artefacts may have been cues for the interpretation of the dead person, and his or her association with specific concerns. Exotic items may have signalled the existence of distant alliances and the position of particular families within broader social networks. Adornments made of jet from the east coast, or from stone carved many days to the north. These had passed through different hands and had carried people with them, people who were remembered when a necklace was worn or a macehead displayed.

This process of definition had important consequences among the living. The burial of particular artefacts drew attention to the rights and influence that had been held by a person in life, as a way of passing on those rights to particular descendants. The placing of objects with a body may have also been seen as a form of exchange, in which a mourner established a lasting relationship with the dead. This confirmed close kinship ties where the right to 'give to the dead' was restricted by blood. It was also a medium through which different mourners could demonstrate their own standing as well as their links to the deceased through generous gifts. Although bodies may have sometimes lain exposed for a time or were transformed in spectacular cremations, these acts of giving to the dead were often seen by only a few, and for a short period. For those who were present, the harnessing of objects to a body provided a medium through which local understandings of descent and identity could be acknowledged.

The inventories of a number of graves raise other important issues. These are some of the first contexts in which metalwork appears, often alongside tools made of stone. In addition, a number of the objects that appear in graves, when there are objects at all, can be loosely classed as weapons. What lies behind these patterns? As with stone, it is unhelpful to assume that we can understand the appearance of metal artefacts, or their deposition in graves and other settings, in practical terms alone. Some daggers or axes may have seen some practical use, though they were by no means all that strong or necessarily stronger than their counterparts in traditional materials. Some of the first metal items were also what we would class as adornments. These characteristics suggest that the reasons behind the first appearance of metal objects were as much social as they were functional.

As with stone, what things meant mattered as much as their utility, sometimes more. Metal artefacts were well placed to serve as tokens of identity and value, and this may be why they were incorporated into traditions of exchange, display and deposition which stretched back into the Neolithic. In the first place, metal provided a potential for control over important tokens. Where the possession and circulation of items like daggers or axes served local political ends, there might have been a premium on demarcating the channels through which they could be obtained. Metal lent itself to this. Ores are not found everywhere, and the knowledge required in working them is complex. As Gordon Childe pointed out many years ago, extraction, the processing of ore and the working of metal were skilful and dangerous tasks. Transforming ores and mixing metals; the poisons, danger and drama of smelting. These qualities often encouraged the view that working was a spiritually powerful or magical act, one to be shrouded in complex prescriptions. Metalworkers in different settings can be a separate caste, polluting and threatening, or of elevated stature. Alchemists, magicians or the lowest of the low. Sometimes they are just like everyone else, changing only for a while when they turn to ore and hearth.

It is likely that many of the metal artefacts found in the Peak were introduced from outside. Like flint, their presence reflects the persistence of broader webs of contact and communication. It is however possible that some originated closer to home. The limestone heart of the region is rich in lead, though there is no direct evidence that this was exploited in the Early Bronze Age. Copper could also be had. Recent work in the Medieval and later copper mines at Ecton in the south of the region, resulted in the discovery of a digging tool made on an antler tine. Radiocarbon dating gave an Early Bronze Age date, indicating that here at least, exploitation began at an early stage. For now, this is all that we know. Later mining has destroyed many traces and as yet we cannot say how working was organised, at what scale nor for how long. What Medieval miners thought as they struggled through passages and encountered old workings has gone unrecorded.

Beyond the knowledge and perhaps the magic used in working, metal had other qualities too. It could be decorated or embellished in a variety of ways, and modifications to moulds offered the scope for reworking forms. Not only that, metal could be recycled and manipulated in ways which had no counterpart in stone. The exhaustion, breaking, destruction or burial of most stone artefacts effectively removed them from systems of circulation. A dagger could be turned back into liquid and rendered into new and varied forms. This greater scope for reworking introduced a new twist into established traditions of circulation and deposition. It allowed the manipulation of the physical characteristics of artefacts as they circulated in different settings and moved from one 'regime of value' to another. Traded goods could be turned into appropriate gifts, and artefacts could be refashioned in keeping with local custom. Perhaps beyond everything else it was the simple potential of bronze or gold items to catch the light and hold the imagination. Specific adornments or weapons may have sometimes even had names, recounted and embellished in oral tradition. Though it was finally written down much later, the names and histories of the swords and shields in Beowulf are powerful examples of how the biographies of people and things can be bound up with one another.

> *Weohstan kept that war gear for a lifetime,*
> *the sword and the mail shirt, until it was the son's turn*
> *to follow his father and perform his part.*
> *Then, in old age, at the end of his days*
> *among the Weather-Geats, he bequeathed to Wiglaf*
> *innumerable weapons.*

What of the link with weapons? The tie is not perhaps as strong in the Peak as it is in other regions, not least because many bodies were laid to rest without accompaniments. But it is there — manifest in barbed and tanged arrowheads, daggers, maceheads and axes. Not all, perhaps, served as weapons. Some may have signified a connection with other activities such as hunting, itself a practice through which skill might bring renown. Perhaps hunting was the preserve of particular people within the community, progression through life marked by the polishing of skills in tracking, stalking and taking game. Fighting though may have also been implicated. As before, outright conflict may have taken many forms, from raids and skirmishes to more formal, even ceremonial bouts of fighting. Burial was often concerned with the definition of specific families and the priority of their claims to land or other rights. Under these conditions, the presence of weapons in a grave was a potent reminder of the role that people had played, or were expected to play, in achieving standing and protecting interests. And where those objects held biographies, the two themes of genealogy and expectation mingled and made their presence felt at the graveside.

Locating the dead

It is an understandable tendency for archaeologists to emphasise the things that are visible at the expense of those that are not. We should not forget however that there were many ways of dealing with the dead at this time, only a few of which leave a clear signature. This point is brought home by places like Eaglestone Flat near Baslow. Found by chance on

Rushup

Mam Tor

this gritstone shelf, Earlier Bronze Age burials had been deposited on their own as well as in stone settings, leaving very little sign on the surface. Not far away, on Stoke Flat or Big Moor, it is possible that at least some of the stone cairns that we attribute to agricultural clearance at the time were also places in which bones or ashes were laid to rest. Many bodies have passed entirely unnoticed.

It is also perhaps a mark of our own values and preconceptions that we are often quick to look for high status or clear divisions of labour in the character and 'wealth' of grave goods. For people at the time, such concerns may have been secondary, if they were present at all. Often what was paramount was the evocation of genealogical time; the reiteration of a family line that could be traced back. The bodies of men, women or children could be the medium through which this was expressed, a new deposit placed in a mound with each generation, or in the face of a crisis that required the renewal of links with the past.

In a curious way, our difficulty in making sense of barrows may stem from looking too closely. Though individual sequences are fascinating, they can draw attention away from the broader landscapes in which barrows were set. Once again, there is a strong sense of variety, suggesting that a concern with genealogies was caught up in many different aspects of life. Claims to land and other resources, to traditional ranges and even to other monuments. At a regional scale, the varying density of barrows is probably a broad clue to the density of population and to the character of land use. The fact that densities are lower in the more elevated ranges of the north suggests if not an absence of settlement, then certainly a low intensity to the use of these areas. Barrows on rises around Kinder may have marked kin-based claims to hunting grounds or seasonal pastures, and may have been set so that they were seen or passed as people moved in and out of the area. Further south, and particularly on the south-western part of the limestone plateau, the densities are far greater. This may, in part, be tied to basic population densities. But it may also, as before, reflect the greater need to mark traditional ties to land in areas where contact with others and access to seasonal pastures was both common and at times competitive. The clustering we see may be more a reflection of the frequency with which such claims were made and made again by different families.

On the limestone, barrows tend to occur in two types of location: on crests and hilltops, or on the edges of land that held good agricultural potential. Terraces and perched basins that sat above or on the sides of deeper valleys. Barrows can often be found on the edges of these areas, or on ridge tops that rise above them. In these cases, it is as if the dead were never that far away, but still set apart, on the boundaries of many day-to-day activities. Those in elevated positions looked down to where many tasks unfolded, as if the dead watched over the living, their presence a reminder on the skyline. Many of the largest barrows are in elevated locations. Though few are visible from a great distance, they were dramatic when relatively close at hand.

Barrows could address different audiences. Seen or visited seasonally as people followed their herds up from below, some confirmed traditional rights to particular areas. On the edge of an area of settlement, others were a more frequently encountered reminder of earlier generations and the debt that was owed them. The dead could be set for other reasons too. Approaching and moving around the henge at Arbor Low, barrows are prominent on the tops of many nearby ridges, creating a cluster on our maps. A relationship with seasonal pastures or otherwise productive land can again be suggested, but here at least there were additional factors at work. At a place where people had come together for periodic ceremonies for some time, the place of kin groups within the broader social landscape may have been an important concern. Because of their settings, these mounds were visible signals of those relations. References to particular lines or renowned individuals to be cited in proceedings or acknowledged as people camped nearby. It is difficult to say. Some mounds may actually post-date the main phases of ceremonial at the henge, and thus had significance for much smaller companies.

. . . Up above the Derwent, a small cairn marks where a young shepherd died in bad weather. Found several months after his death, his body would have been passed unnoticed had he not scratched the words 'Lost Lad' on a nearby stone . . .

The settings of barrows could also work on people at a fine grained scale. On the East Moors, barrows were often on the edge of things, a pattern seen quite clearly around Bamford Moor and Stanage Edge. The majority are found on the shelves that overlook the eastern side of the Derwent valley, smaller numbers to the west. Many lie close to other evidence for settlement and agriculture; areas of clearance cairns, small fields and building platforms in places like Stoke Flat, Gardom's Edge or Big Moor. Kept at a respectful distance, the dead were nonetheless close at hand when people lived and worked on these shelves. Some are also set close to ringcairns or stone circles, and though we cannot usually establish precedence or interval, it is possible that this link was deliberately made. The dead of a particular line were an important presence during the performances conducted in these settings. This close and intimate relationship is not apparent for all barrows. Some appear quite isolated, a number set close to watersheds. These more isolated mounds may have been set on boundaries — lines reinforced by their presence and passed as people moved away with stock or on other journeys across land traditionally held by others.

On Big Moor and Gibbet Moor, we find a combination of these patterns and exceptional evidence for occupation and agriculture. Much of this evidence may post-date the barrows themselves, reflecting the protracted use of these areas throughout and beyond the Bronze Age. However, the settings of individual barrows play upon the details of local topography to influence their prominence from different directions. Some at least may have marked boundaries that were important for a time. Walking upstream along the Bar Brook on Big Moor, barrows hang above you and are some of the first monuments to be encountered as one climbs up onto the flats on either side. A barrow also sits perched above the southern end of the field system at Stoke Flat, a short walk to the north-west. A related situation can be seen on Gardom's Edge, where a large barrow lies beneath more recent walkers cairns: 'The Three Men'. Set close to the edge, it was marginal for the communities who worked out their claims in the immediate area. The barrow is certainly wide, but not very high at all. As such, it would not have been a prominent marker from below, only coming into view as one walked along the edge or took a path up eastwards through the gritstone and onto the shelf that runs back toward

Hollins Hill

Birchen Edge. In this case, standing on the barrow today suggests that what could be seen from this spot was more important than prominence from elsewhere. The site gives exceptional views to the west, into parts of the Derwent Valley and across towards Eaglestone Flat. Perhaps this setting allowed the broader landscape to be drawn into the genealogies that the barrow held.

The settings of a number of barrows also show a concern with the past. Many were located so as to draw attention to the genealogical ties that bound people to particular places and resources. Even where the living were not present all year round, they strengthened claims to land by tracing ties back along a particular line. And sometimes those claims were reiterated, new mounds added close by to form small clusters. Pairs of barrows can be seen on Stanage Edge, where they look down on traces of prehistoric occupation, and also on Beeley Warren and Bamford Moor. Even closer associations are found on Highlow Bank and Raven Tor. In the latter case, three cairns with pronounced kerbs are physically joined, an architectural expression of close kinship or at least an assertion of the idea.

Links were also made with the more distant, perhaps mythic past. An old theme as well as one which took antiquity as its object. There are places where the line went further, back to the time when long mounds and great chambered tombs had bound scattered communities together. Above the Roystone valley, a series of barrows were raised along the ridge to the south and west of Minninglow. One of these, dug by Bateman and deemed by him 'tolerably perfect', revealed the burial of a child and other scattered bones. It also showed evidence of reuse for burial in the Anglo Saxon period. The primary burial in the mound was not recovered until well after Bateman's time, a cist containing cremated human bone and a flaked flint knife. The site is now capped by a wall built in the last few centuries and can be seen in section beneath the lowest courses. Another mound, known now as Lime Kiln Barrow, lies at the southern end of this spread and has also seen excavation. As the name suggests, this saw relatively recent use, one of many where elevation and the presence of a heap of stone made it a suitable place to quarry and sometimes construct a kiln. Excavations here produced a similar picture: a primary burial in a cist, and the later insertion of other deposits; a Collared Urn containing a cremation, disarticulated bone and other vessel fragments.

This place works at several scales. Up close there is the sense of personal histories and tight geneaologies; a founding grave and a return with others over time. After the drama of a cremation, the laying to rest of ashes and charred bones with those who shared close ties. That return sometimes meant handling the bones of older kin, or simply remembering the dead whilst looking out across the land they once worked. In looking out, the eye was also drawn along the ridge, where it fell on other mounds. Though we cannot be certain, that ridge may have been recognised as a small cemetery. Like the clusters found on Osmaston Fields or on Long Low, the barrows on this ridge extended genealogical time still further, the frequency of mounds a record of the line. The dead cast strong shadows here, their names were remembered. Going further, the rhetoric of events at these mounds may have even drawn Minninglow into focus; a monument that was perhaps as much a part of myth as it was of history by this time.

The idea that this 'ancient monument' could have still been a point of reference for the later barrows at Roystone finds support elsewhere. One of the interesting aspects of funerary traditions at this time was the practice of raising round mounds close to much older sites. Several later round barrows lie very close to Minninglow itself, a pattern also seen at Stoney Low and Ringham Low. There are also places where the link was even stronger. Perhaps the most striking example is found at Gib Hill, where a round mound containing a stone cist stands proud on the end of an earlier long mound. Bateman found the cist when it dropped through the roof of a tunnel that he was driving into the side of the long mound. A similar pattern is found at Long Low, Longstone Moor and also the Bullring, where another large barrow lies to the south-west. This too may be a combination of one mound upon another, elevation and a sense of family roots in close proximity to a place of public ceremonial.

Instances such as these confront our expectations about the strength of oral traditions. We might often see these as malleable and fluid. But it is a defining characteristic of many that they draw some of their strength from references to the distant past. The veracity of those references is not always at issue, though it can be contested. Like objects handed down over time, places can be important cues or props in the telling. Just how these long mounds and chambered tombs were remembered when perhaps smaller numbers of people came to build upon or around them is difficult to say. They were clearly important, but we cannot say with any confidence what for. What did they stand for by this time? Part of history; a great chain of names stretching back into the very distant past? Part of myth; places where names had been forgotten but spirits were still acknowledged? In all probability, the answer lies somewhere between the two. Whatever interests were served by the raising of these later mounds, funerary and commemorative oratory drew upon the stories of the place and sanctioned those interests in the reference.

We are back at Liff's Low. A mound to which stone was added over time. A mound that for the last two centuries has been bitten and reduced by the plough and by archaeological interest. We are in no better position than Thomas Bateman when it comes to determining just who the occupant of the cist may have been. Oral traditions that hung around the hill have lost their hold; names have been forgotten or replaced. What remains is the setting; near a path between two knolls, a prospect over land to the north and the south; Biggin and Coldeaton. Standing by the mound today and looking north, the profile of another, End Low, can be clearly seen. Whatever the ground cover, it is likely that eyes raised four thousand years or so ago would have been drawn to the same point.

. . . Upper Derwent. Out on the bus from Sheffield. They walk over the barrow; step forward and down into the kiln. The cut on the side that faces the river has assumed a gentle curve. Wet twigs bend and slide underfoot. They look for reddened stone, a sign of firing. Thoughts stray. Towards the dead that once lay below, to the paths that wound around the place and on. Did the kiln workers notice the old bone? Now it is only the two of them. Thoughts stray again, and they follow.

Nine Ladies — Stanton

8 A sort of hefting
2500-1500 BC

Late July; the first clear day for more than a week. Flocks have been gathering for some time, the word spread that shearing will start around ten. Sheep swirl down the moorside, trailed by dogs and by men walking off to one side. Others watch from landrovers, creeping along the road from Curbar Gap and shouting to their dogs from the window. Drivers on the Baslow road slow at so much stock, a contrast to the routine scatter against the moor. The rise and fall of the wall takes the action in and out of view.

The sheep swarm. Flocks jostle and turn; the broader swell alive with smaller currents. Handfuls wheel within the rest, chaotic patterns that break off and spin towards quieter ground. Flashes of black and white dart back and forth, turning eddies back into the flow down the hill and towards the gate. The yearlings turn more than most. Calling to lost mothers, they move less predictably. They have no experience, no smell of the place in their memories. Only when the call is answered are they reconciled with the tide.

In the Peak they call it 'hefting'; how flocks attach themselves to country. Given time and continuity, sheep know where they are; where to go. Lambs learn at the teat and at the feet of their mothers; where the grass is not just good but familiar. The high ground of summer, the folds of winter or lambing in the spring. With cattle it is much the same. Where blood is maintained across the years, herds know which paths to follow; when to move. And when seasons change, they draw as much as they are driven. Memory carried on hoof and tongue.

The older animals lead the way. Driven through the gate and up the lane, the flow is channelled through pens where young with little yet to shear are separated from those with heavier burdens. There is no room for manoeuvre here. Flanks press one against another, hooves turn into the turf beneath a mantle of wool; a vast and tangled skein. Green soon turns to brown. The field will have a dark corner for days to come; nettles next year.

It is quieter now; the plaintive pitch of the young has lost its heavy drone accompaniment. Animals pressed in a mute huddle till their final thrash through the hurdles and onto the shearing stage. The two men stand ready. Down from Cumbria that morning, their hands and thighs carry the lanolin of flocks from distant fells. A new smell to infiltrate the snouts that search the air nearby. Flicking half drawn cigarettes over the wall, they turn to the task and step over the first two. Clamped in the triangle of knees and feet, the ewes are resigned and still. Hands take hold. And then, as blades are poised, the taller of the men flicks a switch on the stereo hung from the gate. The pause is shattered by the pulse of banging techno; the pace set for shears that plough furrows through the wool. Skin folds back like clay off a moldboard.

Tradition and change

Tradition is a deceptive word. It implies stability, a constancy of attitude or meaning over time; an anchor that does not drag. This is seldom the case. Traditions are always being redefined, by accident as well as by design. Values shift almost unnoticed or undergo dramatic sea changes that are nonetheless justified by reference to the past. It is one of the hallmarks of much modern political rhetoric that tradition is often stressed when older values or relations are being challenged the most.

This quality to tradition is something that we often overlook in our classification of the past. We assign monuments to specific categories, give them names, and in the process assume a constancy of purpose in their building. This is probably the case in our treatment of barrows. Looking at their distribution today, it is easy to overlook both the duration and variety of the traditions that lie behind them. A thousand years or so and more than forty or fifty generations. At the beginning of that sequence, in the third millennium, genealogies and older ways of thinking about the past still blurred into one another. Barrows were built near ancient sites to acknowledge the past, at the same time introducing new twists to the tale. But new mounds were raised in other settings too, and as the second millennium unfolded, the histories of particular families, rather than the broader community or the ancestral past, became the clearer concern.

For many families, acts of burial, rather than commemoration, may have been signal but infrequent events. Once in a generation, when new land was claimed, or when people argued over the inheritance of particular rights and authorities. The death of a person of some standing still brought the wider world and questions of political inheritance into sharp relief. Broader worlds were also still acknowledged in routine movement and encounter; in shifting networks of allegiance and exchange. Such things mattered. In death though, the focus was often close; a family line drawn around a moment when one of their own was laid to rest or simply remembered by those who returned. With time, many names were lost or replaced, a function of the changing fortunes of different families and the fluidity of social memory. Some probably came to be as dimly remembered as far older tombs.

There was no prime mover for these changes; no single cause. However, it may be that dealings with the dead changed in step with broader shifts in attitude; towards the past, and in particular, towards land. Stock were still important, as was the growing of crops and the rich harvest of the wild. What may have been changing was the nature of access, the forms of tenure that people recognised. A sort of hefting.

Where things had once been more open and perhaps more fluid, boundaries were now more sharply drawn and at a closer social scale. As the second millennium wore on, the fortunes and alliances of families shifted and changed. Customary claims to trails and country were reworked, just as the renown of big men came and went from one year or generation to another. Some lines simply came to an end. There was still room for manoeuvre. But, as generations passed, routine traditions became more sedimented. Residence became more fixed, in places extending over seasons, years and even generations. Grazing lands became more persistent, kept open and perhaps enlarged; families making a commitment to each other by marriage and alliance, by trading stock or sweating together to clear scrub or trees.

What evidence is there for this shift of attitudes? Clues are once again to be found in pollen from peat and from buried soils in several areas. The mix of grains creates a picture at odds with our common assumption that the passage of later prehistory saw the slow, steady and inexorable clearance of woodlands. Such a view is only possible from a great distance and from a perspective that measures change over several millennia. On the ground and at more human scales, the conditions of the second millennium were far more varied and dynamic.

Making sense of this evidence is difficult. Woodland can act as a filter, blocking out the rain of pollen from cereals and grassland and creating a very localised picture. And when cover and conditions are right, the reverse can hold. Pollen grains can be carried great distances; up slopes and on the crest of wind flows to be deposited in settings far removed from their parent vegetation. Some parts of the region are also better served than others. The gritstone moorlands are rich in peat with reasonable potential for pollen survival; elsewhere the chances of recovery are lower, and in all areas, pollen recovered from buried soils may be altered or destroyed, leaving little for us to go on. As if this were not enough, there are also more fundamental problems of recognition. Dating of pollen cores is often far from precise and this makes it near impossible to spot the tell-tale signs of specific forms of land use that operated on cycles from a year to several decades. In many parts of the Peak, it is likely that alongside the management of stock, communities cleared and turned cultivation plots by hand, rotating these in complex fallow cycles. Ground could be left for a time to be enriched by stock or abandoned for years or even decades to allow the regeneration of scrub and tree cover. Though they worked on different timescales, these regimes allowed people to cope with problems of loss in soil fertility, and in some areas, the loss of soils through wind and water erosion.

Such regimes brought a complexity to the ways that specific places were occupied; some seasonally, others for a handful of years or in a still more persistent manner. Just how these cycles were understood is beyond us. Where we see the need to maintain soil fertility or to keep land open, communities of the time may have recognised a more spiritual responsibility to maintain country in particular ways. Rooted in traditional concepts of tenure, cycles of working were not only basic to the attachments to land that people recognised. They were also crucial for the ways that communities thought about their past and about themselves. To be a member of a particular line was to know the names of the ghosts who dwelt in specific places; the forces that were harnessed in a cave, at a barrow or an old rock carving. That knowledge was fundamental to identity. Traditional cycles of activity were a form of respect that fostered a sense of belonging to the community, knowing one's place in the broader social scheme of things. Not only that, the pattern of dwelling followed by particular kin groups was woven into the broader fabric of others. Decisions on where to go and when to move involved an awareness of, and an involvement in, still broader social and practical geographies.

The diversity of evidence from different parts of the Peak reflects the complexity of those geographies. However, it is also a product of the varied impact of much later histories of occupation and land use and these need to be considered where we find gaps in our distributions. We cannot always take absence of evidence as evidence of absence. That said, there are patterns here that give hints of the manner in which certain landscapes were occupied and understood. In the earlier second millennium, a walk west from Black Edge, around Combs Moss and over towards Hanging Rock, would have been a walk across changing ground. There was heather moorland on some of the higher grits, scrub and extensive areas of rough grazing. There were dips and small bogs, some the beginnings of later and more extensive spreads of peat. Here was land where people brought their stock or came to hunt; ground more or less common to a number of communities. Access may have still been a concern, but things up here were perhaps quite open.

Moving partway downslope, things may have been a little different. Here again, there is little to indicate a real intensity to settlement, grazing or cultivation. Like the Trent Valley to the south or the Plateau to the east, there were areas that saw little persistent occupation, and a pattern to land use that was extensive and perhaps cyclical. Badly drained ground, land with a poor aspect or narrow, steep sided valleys. In other places, a presence was more deeply ingrained. Barrows and clearance features can be seen on some of the lower terraces on the grit, and on raised land near the heads and sides of the Dove, Goyt and Manifold Valleys. Much of this material is poorly dated but many of the barrows probably date to the second millennium. Some mounds rose near grazing land or along passes used at certain seasons. Others were set on the fringes between sheltered shelves and higher ground; on the edges of places that saw residence. Here at least there was the breaking of the earth with mattocks, digging sticks and hands, or the hooves of quartered stock.

These shelves and terraces were occupied in ways that mixed seasonal tasks with longer cycles of settlement and cultivation. And there were woodlands too, fringed by the scrub that pulled the trees back onto ground when it was left unattended for a handful of years. From these still came fodder for the winter, forage for pigs, fuel brought down by the wind and a wealth of other resources. More extensive forests still held the spirits that walked as wild animals, or the hidden places into which people would withdraw at certain moments in their lives. Paths still mattered here — it would not do to lose one's way. Above though, open woodland gave way to heath and grassland from which people with their stock and others moving through looked across darker valleys and onto the limestone or up towards the higher reaches of the Dark Peak.

The Dark Peak took the trends of the Western Grits to their logical conclusion. Once again, the overall density of material is quite low, whether it be barrows or scatters of stone that speak of camps and more persistent settlements. This is probably a more reliable reflection of the nature of occupation the higher up you go. Elsewhere, the working and reworking of land, on the sides and bottoms of some of the valleys, has cut more deeply into traces of prehistoric activity. Ploughing on the low ground; improving pasture on the flanks. Even on the tops, the picture is far from clear. Prospection for lead has tattooed the land with rakes that run back in chains and isolated scoops from where the limestone meets shale and grit. On Bradwell Moor and around Dirtlow Rake, as elsewhere on the limestone, old spoil tips masquerade as more ancient burial mounds.

Communities working across the Dark Peak took some of the terraces and the better drained sides of valleys as places of settlement. A low density of barrows and chance finds in the upper reaches of the Derwent and the Edale Valley are all that remain to suggest

Gardom's Edge

a presence. They may have also made use of some of the larger caves in the area, though later use by lead miners, industry and tourism has left little for us to trace. From these settings, they followed paths of least resistance up onto higher ground, perhaps through cuts like Winnats Pass to Windy Knoll or along streams and past waterfalls like Kinder Downfall. Sometimes led by cattle or sheep, sometimes in step with other purposes. Crossing over lower rises, they dropped down into valleys where other kin might be met.

Above dwellings and more heavily grazed intakes, much of this higher ground was occupied in a fluid and probably seasonal manner, customary ranges acknowledged as much by the hefting of flocks and herds as anything else. Beyond habit and custom, there were scant reminders. A stand of trees cut back some time before, scatters of chert and flint from the previous year, and patinated stonework eroding from beneath much older peats. Beyond these signs were more solitary barrows on Kinder Low and around Mam Tor — 'the shivering mountain'. On high ranges where things were more extensive or close by natural routes between valleys.

Closeness of identification became less marked with altitude, the distances between significant places greater as one climbed. Used periodically, the higher ground may have sometimes been recognised as a boundary or threshold between the ranges of different groups of communities. Here too, people left more familiar areas on longer journeys, or to climb in search of game or other resources. Scrub, heath and rough pasture; extensive peat and places so wet they were largely avoided. Places where you were set apart or across which you travelled to meet with others. The return to more familiar ground brought many things. Game and raw materials; news and new ideas; gifts and new relations. Maybe a change of standing after 'pilgrimage' to a sacred site that lay beyond or perhaps within the hill.

Occupation of the Limestone Plateau was also varied. Valleys like the Wye were still the dramatic breaks they had always been, though paths across the divide were perhaps more deeply carved by this time. Many smaller dales and defiles were still probably thick with dark woodland, a contrast to the more open heathlands of the higher limestone, where scrub pasture and grassland now dominated. There were also high terraces and basins where occupation or grazing over generations had held the trees at bay. Below were the rich seams of darker chert that still drew people in.

Just how people lived across these ranges is difficult to say. Here, more than anywhere else, history has involved the erasure of almost all traces of occupation save scatters of worked stone. Protected by elevation, by respect, neglect or fear, barrows often stand as lone testaments to a close identification between people and place. It is here that the plough has cut the deepest, here that veins and pipes of lead ore have encouraged a reworking of land on a colossal scale. Nowhere is this more clearly seen than on Bonsall Moor, where a convergence of footpaths draws you onto land where rakes a few centuries old lie close to pit heads, cranes and spoil tips from more recent working.

. . . The cattle don't do well in that field. I played there sometimes as a child but avoid it now. It's cold. Funny though. It always catches my eye when I come out of the churchyard with the old flowers. Just tucked away behind the side of Haven Hill . . .

This process of erasure stretches a long way back. Many parts of the limestone still display the terraces and platforms of settlements from the first few centuries AD. These often survive in small areas of land that have been set aside as marginal to modern cultivation. Raised and level areas in otherwise steep-sided valleys; stoney ground on the rise between dales. Often called 'Romano-British', a name that reflects the colonial experience of India rather than the composition of communities at the time, these settlements are often found in places that offered good potential in prehistory. Unfortunately, few have been excavated on a scale or in a manner that would allow us to see how far the roots of occupation stretched back beneath these later farmsteads and their associated fields. Many may have seen occupation in the first millennium BC and it is possible that some were embedded within far older cycles of movement and residence.

A glimpse of this can be seen near Deepdale and below Taddington Field, where a settlement from this time rests in the elbow formed by the turn of the Wye around Fin Cop. Moles are now the principal residents, their tunnels cutting through the rammed earth floors of buildings and the deeper soils of terraced fields and yards. The 'barrows' thrown up by their tunnelling frequently contain shards of worked chert and even retouched tools, which suggests a significant presence. However, we don't really know what forms this presence took. Camps from generations of journeys to a good source of workable stone. A more sustained connection; a commitment to place made in the raising of buildings, the planting of seedcorn and the quartering of stock. Probably both of these and all things in between.

The sheer density and distribution of barrows on the limestone leaves us in no doubt that many communities had close ties to the area. Those ties arose from a seasonal pattern of encounter, a pattern that had kept its broader contours from much earlier times. Some of the highest ground on the plateau continued to be used in this way throughout prehistory. It is in elevated settings such as these that a handful of enclosures of earth and stone have been identified; places like Pindale, Dirtlow and The Holmes. The oft-quoted suggestion that these sites were palisaded remains unproven by excavation. Though dating evidence is thin on the ground, some of these enclosures may have their origins this far back, arising perhaps from the need to manage stock on high pasture before bringing them down to more familiar ground. Similar enclosures have been identified on the Grits, on the edge of Beeley Moor and on Gardom's Edge, inviting comparisons with the Bronze Age stock pounds of Dartmoor and the Yorkshire Dales.

With time, places of more persistent occupation were consolidated where conditions were right and acceptable. Some old, some on new ground. Here the seasonal encounter gave way to a more continuous relation between the living and the dead, renewed each time people left on the trail or returned home after days or months away. On Roystone Rocks, the other side of the valley from Lime Kiln Barrow, a walk amongst the spines and pinnacles of outcropping limestone appears at first glance to be a walk across land with little potential. Yet in one or two places, people have worked to open patches of ground, breaking and moving stone to the edges of small and irregular plots. Near the crest of the ridge, these plots lie close to a simple line of massive boulders that work with the rock face to create a small enclosure on a natural terrace. A vantage down across step-like crags and more gently sloping ground, the area had seen use by people since the Mesolithic. By the second millennium, the terrace that had once held small camps now gained a pound for stock or a yard in which simple buildings stood. We do not know exactly how the place was used. However, small windows cut through the rough grazing on the hill have revealed a rich array of flintwork suggesting a variety of tasks at this time, similar material recovered to the south-west, near Twodale Barn. The vantage is extensive; across to the barrows on the other ridge and up towards Minninglow itself.

At Roystone as elsewhere, there was probably a variety to tasks and to cycles of residence that took a child to adulthood or one generation into another. Much the same kind of pattern may have unfolded in areas like the Upper Derwent, where scatters of worked stone suggest a mix of episodes and more protracted occupation. Barrows here are by no means as common or as densely spread as they are on parts of the limestone. But they can be found, along the rivers and perched on the edge of good ground. You can still see a handful of low barrows in Chatsworth Park, where they lie alongside the ridges of later field systems, all subsumed within the sculpted 'natural' landscape attributed to Capability Brown.

One part of the Peak, perhaps above all others, provides our best insight on the character of life in the second millennium. The East Moors are covered by an extraordinary array of upstanding prehistoric archaeology. Barrows, clearance cairns and banks of earth and stone; house platforms, stone circles and ringcairns. Much of this material survives because the acid soils of the moors have for centuries been regarded as marginal — used for extensive grazing or as playgrounds for exclusive shooting parties. The bite of industry and agriculture can certainly be traced; in coal mines, quarries and in the bright green of improved intakes on the flanks of higher ground. Here though, incisions are separated by broad stretches of country that have fared reasonably well.

If the East Moors offers a relative embarrassment of riches so far as evidence is concerned, it is evidence just as intractable as that found elsewhere. Good survival means that we can map a wide variety of features; those that we see and those we stumble across in the heather. However, it is often unclear exactly when or why many of these features were established. Part of the problem here arises from the history of archaeological research itself. From the earliest antiquarian investigations onwards, attention has tended to focus on more distinctive barrows and ceremonial monuments, amongst them stone circles and ringcairns. Where records survive, this work has been valuable and has given us most of our radiocarbon dates for prehistoric activity in the area. By contrast, relatively little attention has been paid to the more complex spreads of cairns, enclosures, platforms and banks which arose from varied traditions of occupation. Much of this material has been mapped, and this takes interpretation some way along the path. Systematic excavation is, however, rather rare. This imbalance has been addressed in the past few decades, most notably in the work of John Barnatt. However, question marks still hang over both the chronology and the character of activities in these areas.

Here we hit a major hurdle. We cannot say with any confidence just when this shift occurred, nor the particular ways in which it was expressed from one part of the East Moors to another. The imbalance of archaeological interest has left too many stones unturned. One argument, derived largely from survey, would be that this process of sedimentation began relatively early. Support is derived from the fact that many

Barbrook 2

cairnfields and other traces of occupation are relatively close to ceremonial monuments dated to the second millennium. Good examples include Barbrook 1 and Barbrook 2 on Big Moor, Wet Withens and the ringcairns on Stanton Moor or Gardom's Edge. This idea has many attractions. Clustering can be quite pronounced and it is tempting to read in this a contemporaneity between the dwellings of the living and the arenas in which local communities dealt with more powerful verities. At the other end of the spectrum is the argument that this clustering is a consequence of quite different traditions of land use. From this vantage, the barrows and ceremonial circles date to a time when the land had not been settled, where there was still a strong sense of flux and seasonal variety in the ways that people worked across the area. It was only later that a more sustained form of dwelling gave rise to the copious stone and earthen features that we see today. Here then, the clustering of remains suggests not contemporaneity, but a desire on the part of later communities to anchor their attachments to a place by grafting themselves onto much older monuments.

We do not have to choose between these two alternatives. To do so would be to suggest that things unfolded in a singular manner when it is far more likely they did not. Changes in the use and perception of different parts of the East Moors were neither identical nor synchronous. There were places where a seasonal pattern of encounter gave way to more persistent settlement at a relatively early stage, others where this happened only towards the end of the second millennium. There were still more where it never happened at all. There may also be some contemporaneity between monuments and other classes of field remains.

However, the density and full distribution of the latter suggests that much of this may indeed be later in date, perhaps showing respect for monuments that had long since fallen out of active use. Put simply, there was little unity to the conditions under which the East Moors were inhabited in the second millennium. There was still a measure of flux to things, a moving back and forth between places from season to season and over longer cycles.

How did people live across along these edges? What were they doing and how was it organised? Pollen from places like Leash and Lucas Fen, from Stoke Flat and Big Moor suggests the same varied picture seen elsewhere. Heathland broken up by scrub, woodlands on the edge of things. There are also the signals of grassland and of crops, and a mix of species which may reflect hedgerows. Compared to the limestone, clearance may have remained rather more patchy on many parts of the eastern grits, the extensive opening up of land taking considerably longer. Here again, clearings would be lost beneath scrub if left to their own devices for long enough. The soils on many of these moors were not the leached, acidic podzols that we see today, and much of the peat post-dates the second millennium. At the time, what people found was light yet fertile earth, a sandy matrix interleaved with clays where the grits gave way to shales. Enriched by woodlands over thousands of years, these soils were not altogether robust. However, they were more than sufficient for the growing of crops and for the working of pasture; they could be tilled by hand and were far better drained than heavier clays. What we now see as marginal ground was then an attractive proposition.

Against this background it is probably best to envisage a mix of routines and cycles of occupation. Seasonal dwellings or sheilings bound up with the movement of stock. Fields and buildings used for a handful of years before attention turned elsewhere on the moor; new houses and new plots opened up within a generation. There may have even been places that remained constant over longer periods; land rotated from more fixed points of settlement. Even here though, it is likely that members of households and of broader communities followed routines that carried them down the dipslope or across the Derwent Valley and onto the limestone. Pulled by the demands of their herds or by the obligations that bound them to people on other ranges.

Just how much of this had been set in place by the beginning of what we call the Early Bronze Age is difficult to say. Later Neolithic and Early Bronze Age material has certainly been found; sherds of Beaker, Collared Urns, thumbnail scrapers, plano-convex knives and arrowheads with barbs and tangs. Unfortunately, much of this has no secure context or it is associated with funerary cairns and other monuments. At Swine Sty, on the edge of Big Moor, the situation is little better. Work has revealed evidence for buildings and associated yards, garden plots and field enclosures. Material recovered during excavations last century has yet to be published in full. However, there is a spread of pottery and stone tools here that stretches back into the third millennium and runs forward into the first. Cultivation has certainly taken place nearby, the working of land attested by rough lines of clearance cairns. However, it is difficult to establish just when certain features were built or how long they lasted.

Whatever their origins, the features scattered across many parts of the East Moors often seem to reflect a protracted and non-intensive quality to activities. If persistent occupation began at a relatively early stage, it was probably based as much on stock management as anything else; crops grown in plots and rotated over varying timescales. There may even be hints of this in individual clearance cairns. Few have been satisfactorily dated, if at all. But excavation sometimes reveals a pattern or structure in their makeup. There are many where the first stones to be set in place are massive gritstone slabs; products perhaps of initial phases of clearing ground. Many are so large that they required a sharing of labour and a pooling of effort. These are frequently overlain by smaller and generally rounded pieces, pushed into gaps between slabs and accumulating as low mounds. These are perhaps indicative of clearance as an ongoing task during cultivation; a back bent and a hand outstretched to toss another rock out of the way and onto the older pile. In some cases, these cairns received much larger slabs again; pitched against the sides of the older mound or heaved onto the top. Here perhaps we are seeing the sign of another plot being opened or older plots consolidated with a renewed vigour. Whichever it may be, this pattern suggests that some clearance features were accumulations rather than 'builds', the results of working that remained episodic over long periods.

Can we talk in terms of numbers? What sorts of populations would have lived across different moors? Though it is probably the most common question that archaeologists are asked, it is one to which there can be no satisfactory answer. We have little to go on and given the evidence, any specific calculation would assume a constancy to occupation which may have been the exception rather than the rule. The overall density of building platforms on many parts of the East Moors is sufficiently low to talk of a dispersed pattern of dwelling and of relatively small communities. Standing on Big Moor in the second millennium, it may have been possible, if the fog allowed, to look across to smoke rising from a handful of buildings on Gardom's Edge and beyond, on Gibbet Moor. Beyond seasonal and other periodic gatherings, numbers were probably low and settlement dispersed. Fifty? One hundred? Perhaps no more than that and often rather less.

It is all too easy to slide from these crude 'guesstimates' to an image of scattered extended families; small groups bound by kinship and by a shared tenure with particular tracts of land. That is certainly tempting, but the picture may be far more complex. Where people recognised themselves as members of several different scales of 'community', there may have been a considerable variety to the ways that they lived and worked. Time spent solely in the company of women or men; time in small parties or alone; time in the company of many. This may have applied not just on special or more ceremonial occasions, but also in the cycles of activity that made up routine experience. Working plots, hunting or herding; each may have had quite different roll calls.

At Eaglestone Flat, down steep crags and across the Barbrook from Gardom's Edge, excavations on a cemetery from the second millennium reveal hints of very different ways of living. Here, not far from a prominent tor, a diffuse cairnfield and a ring cairn, a series of deposits comprising the ashes of around fifteen people were identified, only some marked by stone settings. In some cases, the ashes were still hot when they were laid to rest. Cremation itself took place here, smoke rising above the edge, the heat of dramatic pyres transferred to the surrounding soil. Other ashes, particularly those in urns, had been brought from elsewhere. As noted before, these largely unmarked cemeteries are usually found by chance; another was identified on the south-western edge of Stanton Moor during quarrying, other clusters found around Beeley and elsewhere in the Derwent valley.

So far, study of the ashes deposited at Eaglestone Flat has shown them to be exclusively the remains of women and children. Several factors may have influenced this pattern. However, it alerts us to the possibility that occupation, perhaps for part of the sequence at least, could have been undertaken along lines rather different to those that we might tend to assume. Parallels are not that hard to find. In many societies, including our own, it is not uncommon to find that gendered divisions of labour go beyond specific tasks and manifest themselves in patterns of living and common association. Perhaps there were times when women occupied buildings on the moor for a season, growing crops or tending stock while many of the men were off with herds or for other reasons. Even if this link was not exclusive, it may have been that some of these areas were more closely linked to women and it was thus appropriate that their remains should rest nearby. This was so important that it required not just cremation on site, but a final journey back to the cemetery for those who had died elsewhere. Perhaps it mattered that death required a return to the place of one's birth — a closing of the circle. There are so many possibilities, most of equal plausibility. What we cannot assume is that modern concepts of the nuclear family were necessarily recognised.

It is one thing to talk of flux, and of occupation switching on and off from one season, year or generation to the next. It would be quite another to suggest that dwelling respected no broader pattern. In fact, there are hints of subtle differences in the ways that specific parts of the East Moors were used over time, glimpses of quite localised traditions of occupation. Though clearance cairns can seem scattered at random, they sometimes form rough grids or clusters. There are more linear arrangements too, some worthy of the name 'field'. Though these patterns probably developed over long sequences, they suggest that people returning to an area would have often been returning to land that was fixed in social memory. Familiar banks and hedges; old plots still visible through the scrub; a building that had not felt the warmth of a hearth since the previous year.

Even within these relatively fluid conditions then, it is likely that people often identified quite closely with particular ranges. Things were not fixed in perpetuity; communities were probably never that constant. New lines wound across the moors, taking on responsibilities for land and to local sacred sites. Continuity and change in a single moment. There would also be tension and conflict; disputes over access and traditional claims. Often though, there were customary links. These were fostered in oral tradition and could be traced in the state of the ground; in the presence of a barrow or a particular sacred site. In all probability, there were many of these; not just monuments as we define them, but also springs, trees and even rock outcrops which we will never recognise.

We should also allow that the land itself lent a pattern to things. Bisected by rivers in several places, and by other changes in relief, the eastern grits were broken up into a series of distinct areas. Some of the thresholds between these had been marked by barrows from an early stage. Perhaps an identification with country, whenever it began, relied as much upon 'natural' as other more 'constructed' features. The line of a prominent crag; a stream which turned to boiling orange in times of heavy rain; a fault in the rock which created broad steps.

Doll Tor

Locales

What you see when you walk out today depends to a large extent on what has happened to the land since prehistory. On Stanton Moor for example, only the highest ground on this island of grit has escaped enclosure and various scales of improvement. Only Doll Tor, a stone circle, sits below the line, protected in the recent past by a plantation of trees. The heather and birches on the top sit above the high water mark of agricultural incursion, though even here, historic and more recent quarries make their presence felt. Any approach to the high ground today is an approach through spoil tips and discarded stone, reminders of the labour that laid the foundations for both Stanton and Birchover.

The pattern of survival here is biased heavily towards monuments that served relatively specialised roles. The same may be the case on the higher exposed reaches of Raven Tor to the north-east. On Gibbet Moor too, more specialised monuments look down upon extensive cairnfields and banks. Scattered across the top on Stanton are burial mounds, ringcairns and the embanked stone circle known as Nine Ladies. Much of this material has been dated to the earlier second millennium; some may be a little older. Vestigial

cairnfields suggest that the lower flanks of the moor may well have seen various forms of occupation at the time, the highest ground reserved for grazing, for the dead and perhaps for certain moments when people gathered at their ceremonial circles.

How far did people have to travel in order to be a part of those moments; an hour, half a day or several? What place did stone circles and ringcairns occupy in their lives and imaginations? Around forty of these monuments have been identified in the Peak, the vast majority on the East Moors. Once again, we have to allow that some at least were constructed and encountered against the backdrop of seasonal cycles of movement and activity. However, it is likely that many of these small enclosures of earth and stone came to have a particular significance for those who lived relatively close at hand. It is unlikely that we are dealing here with places that drew people in on scales similar to those once

161

seen at Arbor Low, the Bullring or other complexes in the later third millennium. Here the focus may have been rather smaller; catchments reduced. Local.

There is a measure of variety in these places. They range in diameter from around five to thirty metres, many near the middle of this span. Some, like the Seven Stones of Hordron or Nine Stone Close, take the form of free-standing stone circles. In most cases though, circles of upright stones are associated with a form of low embankment that either frames or contains them; sites like Barbrook 2 or Brown Edge. In addition, there are a variety of ringcairns, sites like those on Birchen Edge, Bamford Moor and Cicely Low which have embankments but no prominent orthstats. These are generally penannular arrangements of earth and stone creating small circles of enclosed space. Many have one or two entrances though there are some, like Ash Cabin Flat, where the bank appears continuous.

The history of excavation at many sites is, as elsewhere in the Peak, rather patchy. Pegge and Rooke paid attention to some of the monuments on Stanton Moor, but records of these and other investigations in the eighteenth century are fairly thin. Often all we have are sketches and uncertainty over levels of artistic licence. The situation is not that much clearer for the nineteenth century, when at least some ringcairns were identified as hut circles or 'British houses'. Not surprisingly, Thomas Bateman's name has been attached to one or two sites, notably Doll Tor and Nine Stone Close, but it is likely that this is only the recorded tip of the iceberg. We simply have no record of many investigations, and for some sites at least, no clues left as to what they would have looked like. Lost circles include Handsome Cross on Bradfield Common, Woodbrook and the Seven Brideron on Matlock Moor, their erasure most likely a function of enclosure and improvement in the last two centuries or so.

Many other circles lost orthostats and kerbstones at around the same time. At least seven stones were recorded in the area of Nine Stone Close on Harthill Moor. Now only four are left standing in an arc; a fifth was reused as a gatepost and can be seen in a nearby wall. Read in sequence, antiquarian and later accounts of the embanked stone circle at Wet Withens on Eyam Moor suggests a dwindling of orthostats over time (if also a tendency to miscount just how many were present). Dismemberment here seems to have been casual and piecemeal in character and this may have been a pattern seen elsewhere. Information is still patchy though generally better for twentieth-century work, most recently that associated with the restoration or conservation of sites like Nine Ladies or Barbrook 2. Even then, there are many sites for which we have no information other than that to be gleaned from their outward form and setting.

The strongest trend in the setting of circles and ringcairns is their common association with cairnfields and other field systems. Often on the edge of things, and sometimes just out of sight, they are rarely found too far from these traces. Many are also perched on ledges or cut into slopes so that they look down across particular areas of ground and a number lie close to streams. As noted before, this close association may mask significant variety — a good deal of the cairns and related features in the vicinity of sites like Stoke Flat or Ewden Beck may be significantly later in date. However, the link is so strong that it suggests a measure of overlap. Though many circles eventually became archaic features, respected out of half-remembered custom by later generations on each moor, they initially had more vibrant links.

Nine stone close

. . . The girl stood near the circle. In her arms the windfalls for the fire that would feed them all that night. Over her shoulder, the two pinnacles with their deep grooves. She'd known them all her life, a silhouette that told her it was summer. Her grandmother said that the cuts were from the old time. The spirits who had walked then used to pause on their round, grinding and polishing axes before moving on . . .

What did these circles enclose? What went on in the middle and on the edge? Though they served relatively local groups, many may have seen the gathering of people from time to time. These may have been drawn from dwellings nearby and perhaps from neighbouring moors. Set on the edge of plots and pasture, often on the edge of the land itself, they created a threshold between different ranges, their form a further tightening of the line. Though people crossed each other's paths at many times, these were locales where that encounter might become more highly charged.

As with larger gatherings at Arbor Low or the Bullring, it may not be appropriate to seek a solitary purpose for these monuments any more than it would in the case of more recent churches. Here too, it was possible to link different kinds of cycle; those in people's lives, in the land and in the sky. Thresholds were crossed at certain moments, to seek help and to pay respects. And, if communion fostered community, it also allowed distinctions to be drawn in terms of who could enter and who could speak. Local distinctions; momentary flashes of local authority.

Whether the knowledge involved in creating and using these places stretched into the recognition of complex mathematical principles is a moot point. Various ratios and relationships have been claimed for sites across Britain though these are difficult to uphold in the Peak. Most, and probably all, sites in the region could easily have been laid out without recourse to careful calculation. Though they were no doubt inscribed

Hordron Edge

with complex values, these 'circles' did not revolve around a fascination with numbers per se. Similar uncertainties surround the possibility of strong alignments, most often claimed when circles have entrances or one or more prominent orthostats. Many of the entrances on Peakland sites are orientated north/south and few cut across this line. This is a strong pattern and may be in step with values given to the cardinal points. However, it is also possible that where they were orientated at all, circles fastened upon other features, landmarks and perhaps settlement itself.

Links become even hazier when we look towards the sky. Beyond occasional alignments on the midwinter sunset, there are few strong and unequivocal links between stones and sun or stars. If people did catch celestial cycles in the arrangement of events, they did so in ways that left little trace. One possible exception to this is Nine Stone Close, where the surviving arc contains some of the most dramatic stones still standing in the Peak. Some flared and angular, others pitted with deep erosion scars; bespattered with dung when the spreader works across the field or when cattle rub their heavy flanks. Those stood here at midsummer in the second millennium would have seen the full moon framed in the twin pillars of Robin Hood's Stride. Though the names and stories were different, perhaps these dramatic pillars were even then the stuff of legend; oral tradition tethered to myths that went back beyond the first cattle. Those who gathered at that moment may have listened while others took a role in recitation, linking the stories of the place to the lives of those who stood within or around the perimeter. It has even been suggested that chanting or drumming in certain ways can make the stones ring out in sympathy. If this was the case, it would have added yet another texture to the experience of the moment; another voice to attend.

Strong alignments on celestial events may be relatively uncommon, but this should not really matter. We may be missing certain links and should not assume that the drawing of a line between earth and sky required the levels of accuracy that we tend to search for today. In any case, events may have turned on other matters. Changes in the seasons, problems with the land or with stock; a threshold to be crossed at a particular point in life. It is probably unwise to assume that all of these places were used and understood in similar ways simply because we have chosen to group them together in an academic category. Though they may reflect the recognition of a common theme, that theme may have been worked to different ends. What they stood for and how they were used or respected probably varied depending on who it was who stood within the circle or passed close by.

Circles, like the events they witnessed, could be exclusive as well as inclusive. If arguments about access to these sites today tells us anything, it is that societies are made up of communities of interpretation — groups who attach varying degrees and different forms of significance to a place as a function of their identity. Perhaps this was also the case in the past, albeit along very different lines.

Amongst seasonal celebrations and other rites, it may be that many circles developed an association with the dead. This is implied by cairns and pits within many, most of which contained the ashes of men, women or children. Once again, there is a question of time depth. At least some of the cairns may have been additions to circles that had existed for some time. This may have been the case at the embanked stone circle on Brown Edge. Possessed of one of the widest banks in the region, around 3m from inner to outer kerb, the circle contains an oval cairn and two pits. Associations with these features include collared urns, a so called 'pygmy cup', the rim of a limpet shell with a worn or polished edge and several flint scrapers. Each contained cremated remains; two men and one woman. Given the character and setting of these deposits, it is possible that the circle had already been set in place and used for generations before the arena welcomed these remains. The same may be the case at the more southerly of two ringcairns on Beeley Moor and also at Doll Tor. In both cases, stratigraphic relations and patterns of architectural survival suggest the addition of cairns over time.

Unfortunately, the relative paucity of well-recorded excavations makes it difficult to determine just what this appropriation of certain circles grew out of. Perhaps many had always had an association with mortuary rites; caught up in cremation ceremonies, even providing the setting for the transformation of the body by fire. Mentions of charcoal and ashy deposits at a number echo notes of scorching on similar monuments elsewhere. At Barbrook 2, recent excavation revealed that fires had been lit around pots containing ashes, not cremation itself but a form of treatment that was perhaps not unrelated. Perhaps all we can say is that though death and the changes that it wrought may have been a common concern within the circle, it was probably only one theme amongst many. Perhaps the circle was also important because it mimicked the form of contemporary buildings, or because it held certain forces in a particular arrangement. Whatever the case, there was often an order to events, and from this came expressions of the standing of particular

Stoke Flat

people; orators, elders and ritual specialists who moved between different moors. Perhaps those roles and events were remembered as people dug on plots nearby or sat outside their buildings working stone. The state of the ground and the health of people and stock was a measure of how well proceedings had gone the last time the community had walked to the edge of things and gathered at the circle.

Only after some time, a duration perhaps of many generations, did associations at certain circles shift towards the formal burial of the dead. A similar link may have been made where impressive funerary cairns were raised nearby. Examples here include Offerton Moor, Wet Withens and Barbrook 1, where a substantial cairn and associated platform were built just upslope. Whether this added to or broke with established tradition is unclear. We should probably anticipate both. Events at many circles were crucial to the negotiation of a variety of issues and relations. With the dead, with the land and with others. That made them powerful, at least at a relatively local scale. They were thus a likely focus for strategy and appropriation where claims of access to land or authority were sometimes made.

That links could be made with the past, perhaps traced back along genealogies, is suggested by the alignment of several of the monuments on Stanton Moor. Arrival at each one brings the next into view. This lent an order to encounter as one moved across the Moor, an order that may have helped to sustain particular narratives about the ties between the living and the dead. Alternatively, these were the circles of different communities, each with a customary claim to access. If this were the case, the alignments may have spoken of the links that bound these different communities together.

In time, many of these circles probably lost their prominence in social memory. They were still there and perhaps important as local landmarks. However, for people living around the end of the second millennium, many were no longer the pivots they once had been. Excavation has yet to reveal significant quantities of Later Bronze Age or Iron Age material within any circuits. This could mean many things. Perhaps some circles were more or less forgotten, others avoided or kept at a respectful distance by fear. Maybe some were also still significant, reminders of the ever-deepening roots that joined people and place. We shouldn't assume that all were held in the same regard.

That monuments can change in their significance is demonstrated all too clearly at Nine Ladies. There were ten stones here, possibly more. The name has a different derivation, a link to folk traditions that saw an importance in the number and circles as women frozen in the act of dancing. How far back these values go is anyone's guess; older names have long since faded. Close at hand is an outlier — 'The King Stone'. Enclosed by a Victorian wall until 1985, the circle has watched the ebb and flow of birch woodland, the building of a nearby folly and the arrival of Himalayan Rhododendrons blown in from a formal garden. It has also become the focus for a variety of events in the past few decades. Visited by locals out with their dogs, by hikers pushing through and those clutching archaeological gazetteers, the circle also sees regular gatherings around seasonal thresholds. In certain years, the signature of these can be traced in a broader circle of charred and shallow fire pits, each associated with the debris of celebration. Some come alone to hold their own communion, others to party; attitudes running from political or religious conviction through to romantic whimsy.

For many, the circle is a broad church, with the capacity to be interpreted in a variety of ways, not least because we know so little. In their shared fascination for these places, others express their dissatisfaction with the crass materialism of the present. For some though, meanings are more fixed and more dogmatically asserted. Claims are made that there is a 'truth' to the place, a truth held exclusively that establishes priority over others. When such claims are made, we may be catching a faint echo of statements heard in the second millennium. However, that echo is a similarity of tone and assertion, not of content. There is little in these archaeological or sacred 'truths' that can be traced back much further than the Victorian era.

It is easy to get lost in the details of individual circles, so much so, that a broader question is often left unasked. Why are there no small circles and ringcairns on the Limestone? One answer would be to suggest that we are simply too late; circles were present on the Plateau but they have been lost to enclosure and improvement. This has some attractions but is unlikely to be sufficient. Given the lateness of enclosure and the sharp interests of eighteenth-century antiquarians, we would know if densities had once been comparable. In other words, the absence of evidence does seem to be evidence of absence.

What lies behind this pattern? One possibility is that the limestone and the grits had very different histories. On the white ground, there were long-standing traditions of gathering at monuments or monument complexes; henges, barrows or older tombs. These were largely absent on the grits, or revolved around features that we now no longer recognise. From this vantage, at least two possibilities present themselves. There may have been quite different traditions of social interaction across the region — large scale on the limestone and more focused on the grits. Alternatively, it may be that the second millennium saw more local concerns addressed right across the Peak, a possibility supported by the proliferation of barrows. In other words, the pattern we see today reflects the playing out of those concerns at 'ancient' sites in one part of the region and at newly established monuments in others. This may well have been the case. Perhaps Arbor Low itself saw a diminution in its catchment over time. Numbers had once run into hundreds; people drawn from many lines and across broad areas. Now, the scale of events was smaller, their relevance more closely appreciated. In this contrast between limestone and grit we catch a glimpse of what may have been important differences of identity and tradition recognised within the region.

. . . It has been good to get the trench finished. Cash in the pocket before Christmas. The ground has been hard and the attention wearing. Few features and few finds save fag packets, glass and a piece of flint. The three of them link arms as they stamp the turf back down; a simple jig to mark the close . . .

The King Stone

9 Belonging to country
1500 BC-AD 100

A winter evening; late afternoon. The reservoir is almost full. Water drawn down from Howden Moor, down Linch Clough and Slippery Stones into the Derwent. After months of heavy rain, the water laps against an ancient river terrace cut when the valley was young. Flakes of flint and chert are scattered amongst cobbles and sand, a beach exposed where the grass has washed away. Stone from cliffs beside the Wye; stone from the coast. The water is still. No breath of wind to scatter the reflection of the quarry track that cuts a sharp diagonal above Ronksley Wood. No movement and no sound. No echo of the calls once raised as the old men and the children took the cattle past the barrow and up to higher ranges in the north.

The silence absorbs more recent histories. It is less than a century since the thirst of nearby towns brought over two thousand navvies to work on the dams; the air alive with voices, hammers and industry. Drawn from Wales and Devon, and from a community that lay on the edge of society, many of the Navigators were housed at Tin Town, below Birchinlee Pasture. A walk eastwards through the village now is a walk through young trees and between faint platforms. Past the mission house and police station; the tobacco shop and huts for unmarried workers on the right. Dormitories, each with their own keeper. To the left, the houses for the married, the street leading on to the recreation centre, public baths and the school. The schoolmaster's house lies upslope to the north, behind it a grid of old allotments.

There is a pattern here at odds with older Navvy camps. Workers settled according to a plan, a design for living that was also a moral order. Philanthropy, social engineering, and a concern for productivity; each one a foundation stone. Navvies were different. They had their own customs and language; networks that cut across the sedentary boundaries of 'decent society'. Here, after a century or more of lives spent building the infrastructure of the industrial world, were all the institutions that enabled 'improvement'. Drawn from Burrator and Rhayader, migrants looking for work on the project met with a mix of welcome and mistrust. After arrival and delousing, accommodation in the village meant living in a microcosm of society, a model of social relations that tempered older solidarities. The geography of class and social position in nearby towns drawn to scale in the setting of houses and services.

It lasted over a dozen years. A moment in the history of the valley. A vision of society imprinted on the ground. When work was finished on the dams, the village was cleared, George Sutton, the missioner, the last to leave in 1915. By then, Tin Town had a history of its own, a place amongst other villages. A frame for the biographies of many families, this model of an ideal order had been reinscribed by more personal senses of identity and belonging. Houses that had been decorated with possessions and with memories were pulled down and taken off for use elsewhere. Some still stand on allotments across the region.

Trying to understand prehistory involves working with several different forms of time. There are individual moments or episodes; a body laid to rest, a house erected or a boundary set across the ground. There are also more persistent traditions and institutions; attitudes towards the dead or forms of tenure that shift almost imperceptibly across many generations. Those institutions may include attitudes towards time itself, concepts of cycles or a collapsing of past and present at odds with our common, linear, sensibilities. There is also a timescale broader still; the time of the land itself, and the yet more gradual shifts of character that worked behind short-term clearance or cultivation. Narrative arises from exploring the interplay between these different scales.

There is also another form of time that plays its part — the time of the here and now. Though it is sometimes no more than lip service, archaeologists generally acknowledge that the pasts we write are responsive to the present. The questions we ask and the answers we accept are shaped in some respects by the attitudes, values, fears and desires of our time. Ideas about the self, about gender, trade or society may have once been understood very differently. This matters even when we talk about activities that seem self-evident or easily understood; things like farming or specific features; fields, boundaries and dwellings. We might often take these for granted. But when we do, we miss how even in our own lives, the mundane is intimately bound up in the fabric of social life. Concepts of property, social identity and personal memory are woven into architecture, into the tasks we undertake and the tools that we routinely use. It is often our inability to see the values bound up in the practical fabric of life that makes those values so resistant to challenge or change. That is what makes a place like Tin Town so remarkable. Here the mess and complexity of life was shaped by the imposition of a moral order that for once is explicit and visible.

These observations matter here because they have implications for the ways that archaeologists have dealt with a series of shifts in our evidence in the later second and early first millennia BC. For many years now, it has been acknowledged that a contrast can be drawn between two broad phases in prehistory. On the one hand, we have the Neolithic and Early Bronze Age, an archaeological phase dominated by ostentatious monuments to the dead and other places of public ceremonial. Settlements across this span are ephemeral and difficult to trace. This can be set against the evidence that survives from the middle of the Bronze Age onwards. For the most part, our evidence here consists of field systems, land boundaries and settlements; the dead are by no means as visible, and places of public ceremonial less easy to identify.

At first glance, the more familiar aspects of this later evidence means that we often take it as read. After all, we assume we know about agriculture and more sedentary forms of living. However, that familiarity soon starts to evaporate when we ask what may have prompted the change. One view is that the increasing prominence of field systems, settlements and broader land divisions in the second half of the Bronze Age was a product of the wealth economy. In other words, agricultural production was geared not just to subsistence, but to the creation of a surplus that could be used in feasting and other forms of exchange. This had probably always been the case to some extent, the movement of stock in particular an important thread that ran between groups. But by the later second millennium, networks of exchange also carried a range of metalwork; weapons, jewellery and other items of bronze bound up in displays, in cycles of gift giving and in acts of hoarding and conspicuous consumption. In other words, exchange was crucial to local and regional politics; a medium for cementing alliances and affiliations; a means of inflicting debt and subordination; even on occasion a form of tribute to be paid to a powerful leader. Against this background, involvement in the wealth economy, as either a dominant or subordinate player of the game, increasingly required lineage heads or other powerful individuals to generate and mobilise an agricultural surplus. This, in turn, led almost inevitably to an intensification of production: the enclosure and dedication of land to specific tasks and shorter fallow cycles, the use of the plough and the more careful maintenance of soils.

These arguments are important. They remind us that practical life at the time was caught up in webs of social and political relations, bonds that were continually worked upon. That said, they are not without their problems. In many areas, including the Peak, it is difficult to find evidence for an intensification of agriculture. Not only that, the timing and character of developments seem to vary from one part of the country to another; traditions shifting from region to region.

An extension to the argument has been that the changes we see relate to more fundamental shifts of perception. Beyond exchange and display, it had once been customary to acknowledge the past and present order of things through elaborate funerary rites and public ceremonies conducted at dramatic monuments. Through these places and times, people forged a sense of who they were, traced the roots of their communities in relation to the dead and acknowledged their place in the broader social order. Control over ritual itself may have been a powerful basis for authority at local and regional scales. These practices did not disappear altogether. Older barrows could still be a focus for memory and myth, as could other monuments. But with the passage of time, these concerns came to be addressed in other ways as well — in the division of land, the consolidated working of fields and the more persistent inhabitation of settlements. Each requiring labour at varied scales of social resolution; dwellings, fields and land boundaries became the monuments of their time. In attending to land, communities attended to themselves, their ties to others and to the past. And against this background, the agricultural cycle itself took on a greater significance. Always an important concern, it increasingly came to be the principal source of metaphors for cycles in the lives of people and the order of relations in society.

Belonging to country

It would be easy to overstate the case, creating an opposition between 'world views' that missed how one set of conditions gradually gave rise to another. In practice, no one generation witnessed a transformation of the world. It took centuries. Not only that, the stimulus for change stemmed from regionally varied sources. The growing depth of genealogical ties to land; the playing out of relations between different tribes or clans, even shifts in climate or population density.

Just how these developments unfolded in the Peak is difficult to determine. Evidence varies from one part of the region to another, the best preservation, as always, to be found on the Eastern Moors. There is a good deal of complexity here. The land has been inscribed and reinscribed many times and this makes it difficult to 'read off' neat arrangements of activity or clear sequences of change. That said, there is little in this evidence to suggest the marked intensification of Later Bronze Age agriculture claimed for other regions. What there is suggests something more subtle; a closer identification with land; an intensification of focus if not of productivity. By the end of the second millennium, attitudes had shifted in many areas towards a more sustained sense of territory. This arose not as a sea change in people's lives, but as the result of a more gradual reworking and adjustment of traditional attitudes over centuries.

This process was more marked in some areas than in others. There was still country which lacked a closeness of identification; far flung reaches, higher ground and land that lay between customary ranges. But there were also tracts of land where settlement had become more sedimented and secure. Places where people lived all year round and measured their attachment in generations rather than seasons. The mess and confusion of upstanding features across the Eastern Moors today is a consequence of this variety. Seasonal visits, consistent occupation, land abandoned and ground taken up again. The ebb and flow of animals and the reworking of relations from one generation to another.

The duration of activities across the moors can be measured in millennia. What we walk across today are palimpsests and these are by no means easy to take apart. Features lying next to one another on a moorland shelf may be contemporary or separated by a thousand years or more. We get a sense of this where survey reveals overlapping patterns of land use and land division. Contrasts between different stretches of moorland also suggest that the character and duration of prehistoric activities varied from one part of the area to another. The scattered cairns seen in areas like Winyard's Nick or Toadsmouth below Carl Wark create a very different pattern to the more diverse banks, fields and cairns on Stoke Flat or Gibbet Moor. In places this variety is tied to slope, aspect or water. Some stretches of ground were simply more favourable than others and this played its part in shaping how land was occupied and valued. These different potentials also meant that some areas were used over thousands of years, others for shorter sequences, or in episodes with protracted intervals.

. . . A stone dwelling. Built for the estate, it held four rooms and eleven people. Stone and flesh tied to the family whose titles went beyond the horizon. The old Duke died. Land was sold and the house became private. Names changed; persisted for a generation or two then changed again. A link maintained and made anew across the years. Then the land around shifted, came to be valued as retreat and as unchanged. The house became a cottage. Prices rose again. Out of the reach of the children born beneath the roof . . .

That there were differences in the duration of different cairnfields and field systems is suggested by an interesting trend. Though there are extensive remains on many of the lower terraces and shelves, evidence tends to be more limited the higher up you go. This can be demonstrated in a simple contrast revealed by climbing from the shelf of Gardom's Edge onto the higher ground behind Birchen Edge. Here, by the three tors that bear the

names of Nelson's ships, you can look down to the west and onto more than a thousand different features: a rich array of cairns and banks. Looking east, what survives is rather meagre by comparison. A ringcairn or two, and a lower density of stone and earthen features, some forming small fields and plots. This is a trend seen elsewhere on the East Moors, on Bamford Edge, Stanage, Raven Tor and on Sir William's Hill above Eyam.

This pattern was a product of several things. Some higher ground probably has a limited range of evidence because it was largely set aside for the dead and for ceremonial activity or because it was seen as a boundary area. However, this was not always the case and a more likely explanation for the general trend is that altitude set some limits on what people did and for how long they made use of different patches of ground. In other words, settlement and related activities persisted for far longer on many of the lower terraces. The relative timescales involved are unclear. Plots may have been worked on the lower shelves long after those above had been abandoned. Alternatively, communities did not take these areas into their rounds of dwelling and cultivation until quite late in the sequence. Both arguments have their attractions, though the presence of Early Bronze Age ringcairns on the higher reaches lends a measure of support for the former.

If this is right, our evidence could suggest a change of land use over time. Some have argued that such changes were driven by a deterioration in the climate around the turn of the millennium. Ground became wetter and the first dwellings to be lost beneath scrub and encroaching bog were those in the most elevated and exposed settings. This makes some sense. But these simple cause and effect arguments relate to processes that unfolded on a timescale that went beyond generations; there may have been other factors at play. In

180

any case, there is a good deal of evidence to suggest that many upland areas continued to be used long after the climate had worsened.

Another possibility is that the later second and early first millennia saw the consolidation of dwelling on lower and more favoured terraces and a change of use for higher reaches. Increasingly, many settlements identified with their own patch of more elevated ground for use by stock or where firewood and other resources might be collected. By the early first millennium, many of these more lofty edges had probably come to be regarded like the higher ground of the Dark Peak; grazing land broken up by scrub and patches of regenerated woodland. Some were open ground where stock ranged away from crops and dwellings. Others were no more than 'places in between' — uncleared and largely untended land to be crossed on the way. By the early first millennium, a view down from some of these higher ledges would have been a view down onto land that bore a stronger stamp of order. It is generally in these more low-lying and sheltered locations that we find the greatest density and variety of features, and the most clearly defined fields. Built up over many generations, these features run from scattered cairns, house platforms and plots to true fields and extensive banks of stone and earth. We can see this at Beeley Warren, where more linear field boundaries and cairns lie on lower ground south-east of more scattered barrows and cairns.

We find both in most places. On Big Moor, the land to the east of the Bar Brook has scatters of cairns on the higher ground and ringcairns and barrows on the edge of things downslope. Across the water to the south-west there are similar cairns, but these cluster amongst more linear and clearly defined fields comprising low banks of earth and stone. Work on some of these boundaries suggests that they were sometimes deliberately built to enclose land and to trap sediments washing downslope whenever the rains were heavy. It is also possible that many banks supported hedgerows and there is evidence that some were maintained and augmented over time. There was order here, a history of landholding that could be traced on the ground. Plots may have been rotated within the areas defined by these banks while some fields saw consistent use for the close quartering of stock. The two patterns also overlapped, close quartering bringing the manure that could enrich depleted soils.

This was not always the case. Some of the more linear banks that cut across several moors have an appearance of unity on the surface that belies their true development. Some were not 'built' at all. Instead, they reflect the gradual accumulation of stone along a line defined in the first instance by a fence or a hedge. As the seasons turned, these lines acquired stone in a piecemeal fashion. A basket of pebbles picked from plots by hand and tipped along the base of the hedge; larger slabs and boulders manoeuvred and dropped into position by two or three people who were opening new plots close by. To talk of these boundaries as walls is to miss how their creation was a collaboration that extended over several generations. One stone placed upon another; in the space between the two, a grandchild became a grandmother. This sense of a piecemeal and protracted development to cairns and banks probably applies to features that are both early and late in the sequence. Cairns added to on seasonal visits or augmented where plots were opened again after long periods of fallow. As noted in the last chapter, individual cairns can reveal a structure that reflects this duration and a shift in the nature of stone clearance over time.

Sometimes the sequence in specific features tells a slightly different story. On Big Moor, the stratigraphy of one oval bank shows familiar phases of slab moving and the more casual and unconsidered tossing of stones to one side. In places though, gritstones no larger than two hands lie across the cairn in a regular order. Here there is a sense of rock being stacked; a person standing at the end of a line of people passing stone along from the plot to be piled out of the way. A morning's work. Though we may tend to think about these features in prosaic terms, piles of cleared stone had some of the qualities of monuments for people at the time. They arose from work in different combinations — individuals, close kin and different families — and could be read as a record of those bonds. Some boundaries also needed to be maintained, and this meant negotiation and the balancing of interests. And because they often grew over time, they were a reminder of the debt that was owed to earlier generations of kin. With time, this too became an important expression of belonging.

One other line of evidence may indicate an increasing closeness of identification. We have already seen how some stone circles and ringcairns on the Eastern Moors acquired cremated human remains. The link with the dead may have been much older, but in cases where we have some dates, these deposits sometimes relate to events late in the second millennium. By this time, these circles may have shifted in their significance. Whatever they had once stood for and how long they had been respected, now they were an appropriate setting when it came to burying certain people 'close to home'. Like the alignment of a field system on an old barrow, this too was a way of tying the present to a more distant and perhaps more mythical past.

Sometimes the link was even closer. In keeping with evidence from other areas, there are glimpses of an attitude towards the dead that removed even local senses of separation. On Gardom's Edge, excavation of a building thought to date to the Late Bronze Age or Early Iron Age revealed a cremation beneath the floor. The site of the building had been ridden over by carts and carriages moving along a track established by the order of the Duke of Rutland in the eighteenth century. Fortunately, the ruts had not cut down to the level where a shallow pit contained the ashes of a young woman. These may have been interred in a bag; the feature topped by a timber setting. Work revealed an arc of stakeholes, probably from a single phase timber building. Whatever the structure was used for, it probably stood for no more than a couple of decades, if that long. The apparent absence of a hearth within the arc may indicate that it did not serve as a dwelling, or if it did, only on a seasonal basis.

The presence of these ashes suggests that for people at the time, it was customary to keep the dead close. After the more inclusive event of cremation, ashes returned to rest in and around the dwellings of those who were tied by the closest bonds of blood and descent. They were part of the foundations upon which close identification with land was built, their presence marked by household shrines or simply acknowledged when people lay close to the ground to sleep. With the morning, and the walk out to tend the plots or check on animals, that presence was still strong, in a nearby cairn or in the old circle. Perhaps it was to these local ghosts that the living appealed to ensure the fertility of the land.

. . . Our kin are here; they watch over us. Their blood is in the land and they will not let us go. We belong . . .

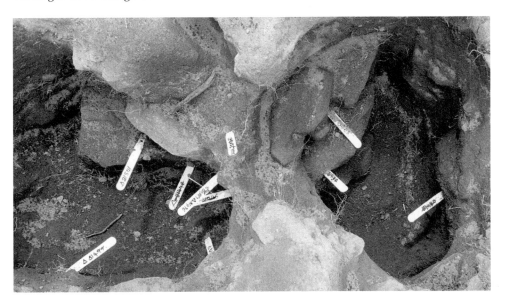

Post-holes

That links with many places were now more sustained and perhaps continuous is suggested by a second building found on Gardom's Edge. Here the pattern of post and stake holes suggests the renewal of the building over time. Timbers that had become rotten at floor level were removed and new post holes sunk to take their replacements. Large quantities of pottery, chert and burnt stone outside the building attest to a dwelling and a range of tasks, perhaps even midden slowly accumulating to one side. Though few houses have been excavated, this example may reflect the persistence of a dwelling across the divide that we place between the Bronze Age and the Iron Age. Just how far this site is typical of dwellings across the Peak is impossible to say. Built of timber and seldom of stone, the houses of the time are difficult to find, particularly on level ground where a long fallen circle of timbers leaves little or no sign on the surface.

On occasion, we do have clues as to the presence of dwellings; markers that can be traced because of the ways that the site of a building was marked after it had fallen out of use. At both of the buildings investigated on Gardom's Edge, it appears that stone banks were piled up around each structure at the end of their active lives. This could have been clearance, a convenient place to dump stone out of the way as people tended later plots nearby. Another possibility is that these banks effectively closed off buildings that were no longer used, their presence a barrier to continued access. Why this may have been done is difficult to say. Where buildings had a strong association with particular people, death may have meant an end to not just the person but also to the dwellings they had used in life. Another possibility is that in building these arcs of stone around buildings taken out of commission, people were making an architectural reference to old but still recognised ringcairns; places that were themselves associated with the dead.

How long these patterns of occupation persisted is not known. Much of our evidence is referred to as Bronze Age, and attention usually focuses on how much is early and how much late within the period. This may be warranted, but should not set artificial limits. At least some of our evidence reflects a persistence of occupation well into the first millennium and the Iron Age. If it tells us nothing else, this extraordinary time depth is a testament to skill with which communities worked the land. Given soil conditions, it would have been all too easy to push the ground beyond its limits, stripping nutrients and encouraging erosion. That this did not happen over several millennia suggests that however it was understood at the time, people recognised the problem and knew how to deal with it. This may have become even more acute as the climate worsened in the early first millennium. Yet people still managed to keep the balance, rotating land through fallow cycles and using grazing as a way of enhancing fertility and keeping country open.

Here again we have to be careful. One of the dangers of any single narrative written from this evidence is that it can create a sense of unity at odds with the lives that once unfolded across the Peak. For example, it is all too easy to infer a constancy to patterns of occupation and landholding, an image of a land and a society that was stable and unchanging. This says more about us than it does about the communities of the time. Our tendency to accept such a caricature is probably encouraged by the rather romantic way in which we have come to regard rural life as essentially small scale and constant. In fact, communities who live in what we would now regard as far flung, isolated and 'marginal' settings have no difficulty in recognising that they are one place amongst many; part of a broader order. Though that order took different forms, this was also the case in the first millennium.

The complexity and confusion of many survey plans is a reminder that things were not necessarily stable. Things changed, customary ties reworked and land claimed or abandoned as a consequence of many factors. Within a handful of years there were changes of fortune, shifts in networks of alliance and even competition between groups. All probably played their part. Over generations, there were changes in the state of the ground. More water than the elders remembered; old clearance cairns stood on land that was no longer amenable to planting; bad ground where once the pasture had been strong.

In one or two places, we get hints that the passage of time saw a shift in the character of land use and perhaps in patterns of landholding. There are a few more extensive boundaries that appear to have been constructed quite late in the sequence. Banks of stone and earth built deliberately to break up or divide the land. The most dramatic examples are found on Gardom's Edge. One of these is a long stone bank which runs more or less east-west across the shelf from an area of marsh to the edge of a scatter of cairns and fields. The bank takes a 'dog leg' in the middle where it overlies a sub-rectangular enclosure that may have seen earlier use as a stock pound. Stone appears to have been taken from this enclosure for use in the bank, and the change of direction in the middle may indicate that the line was built in stages. The building of this bank did not mark an end to cultivation. A few clearance cairns are piled against it, indicating that such activities continued. However, it may be that it was designed to break land up into broad stretches for different forms of use. Another possibility is that it was built to draw attention to changes of tenure and responsibility as one crossed the line.

A hundred or so metres to the south, another boundary feature runs almost parallel to the bank for over 350m. Here though, the line was drawn by digging into the ground rather than building upon it. Part of the boundary takes the form of a ditch cut into the underlying mix of leached sands and clays. You can trace it now by the coarser sedges that thrive on the wetter conditions in the ditch. For much of its line however, the boundary is rather more striking, taking the form of a long chain of pits, each between one and two metres wide and not much less in depth. Now filled with the wet peat that developed sometime after the area was all but abandoned, the pits also provide the conditions favoured by sedge. The upcast mounds and banks of soil cut out of the ground in making and maintaining the line can still be seen running parallel to the dips. This is the only example of a pit alignment so far found in the Peak. Several examples have been identified in the Trent Valley to the south, where they often have a close association with watercourses. Where evidence is found, many appear to date to the latest stages of the Bronze Age and to the Iron Age.

What were pit alignments for? No two archaeologists will give you the same answer. Most would acknowledge that they could serve as boundaries, not least because many were augmented or subsumed by later banks and ditches. However, details of form are more difficult to pin down and nowhere is this more of an issue than on Gardom's Edge. Work so far suggests that most, if not all, of the pits in this alignment were originally lined with a fine grey-white clay. This enhanced a tendency already seen on clay-rich patches of ground for cut features to hold water. Why do this? One answer would be that the line served as a ready and convenient source of water. However, there are much simpler and more effective means of achieving this end and it is difficult to envisage quite how this would have worked in practical terms. Though it is tempting to conjure an image of stock stood side by side at watering holes, it would not have been long before sliding hooves destroyed the integrity of the line. Another possibility may lie in the suggestion that stock are often reluctant to cross their own reflections without some form of encouragement. In other words, the alignment was less an attraction for animals and more a boundary that kept them to one part of the shelf. This last idea also has its attractions, but we should perhaps acknowledge that stock don't always seem to be aware of this rule. If the line was recognised as a boundary, it may have been a social one. A line across which rights rather than resources could be seen to have changed.

Just why this line needed to be defined by water is far from clear. Beyond practical concerns with access to water (not a problem on the shelf) or links to other processing activities, it may be wise to acknowledge that Later Prehistory was a time when people recognised water in powerful terms. It was, after all, crucial to so much of life and to the renewal of the land. It was also the medium into which people threw dramatic hoards of metalwork — gifts to gods or acts of conspicuous consumption that enhanced the standing of those who could afford to be so generous. There is also evidence from several regions that rivers could receive the bodies of the dead; a different route into the afterlife. Given this, a chain of ponds that sometimes caught the light may have had a spiritual or symbolic significance that added considerable weight to the divide.

Once more, we must accept that there is more than one way of interpreting these patterns. Larger scale land divisions may have been a feature in different parts of the Peak from a relatively early stage, and agricultural plots and other activities rotated within their lines. However, the sequence at Gardoms Edge suggests that different forms of land use and perhaps new forms of landholding may have emerged during the first millennium.

A broader vantage

So far we have dwelt upon the localised ways in which communities recognised that they belonged to country and to each other. Bonds reiterated in the sharing of food as well as the sharing of tasks. There was, however, a bigger picture. Brought into focus by stock, by marriage and other forms of alliance, a broader world was also acknowledged where different communities came together to work on land or to celebrate important events.

One class of evidence, often literally above all others, brings the focus back up to this broader scale. Scattered across the Peak are nine or so enclosures thought to date to the centuries around the first millennium BC. Among them are Mam Tor in the North, Castle Naze (Combs Moss) in the West, Ball Cross to the East and Castle Ring to the South. Many are set in elevated topographies, on hilltops or prominent ridges with boundaries defined by imposing ditches and banks of earth and stone. Only Crane's Fort, near Youlgrave and the river Lathkill has a more low-lying setting, though little is known about the site. Almost all sites are univallate, having a single bank and ditch, one principal exception being Castle Naze which has a double rampart. Some, like Fin Cop, are set on dramatic promontories that tower above lower valleys and basins. Here, natural escarpments or steep edges form part of the perimeter, augmented by earthworks only on the more open upland side. To this list may be added a number of other enclosures on false crests and plateaux; places like Eldon Hill, Dirtlow or Harthill Moor.

Referred to in the literature as hillforts, these are difficult places to understand. Few have seen systematic attention or the scales of excavation that would allow us to talk in detail about the chronology and character of their use. Even in the better cases, such as Mam Tor or Ball Cross, we can say little more than that they may have their origins in the final stages of the Bronze Age, persisting in use into the first millennium and the Iron Age. There are some, however, where foundations could be considerably older. At Carl Wark, which appears in the literature as a hillfort, activities in the first millennium perhaps involved the rediscovery and reuse of an already ancient monument.

What do we mean by 'hillfort'? Two themes tend to dominate interpretation: settlement and defence. Early in the twentieth century, few were in any doubt that these enclosures were built largely for defensive purposes — to protect those within from those outside. Sometimes it was a resident population, sometimes a gathering of tribespeople who sought common shelter in times of stress. An attack by other tribes or by the armies of occupation who arrived with Caesar. Classical sources played their part in shaping these views, among them the writings of Tacitus and Caesar's own propaganda. Such accounts made sense at the time. Many with an interest in hillforts had military backgrounds, and

Fin Cop

the contemporary political situation across Europe fed a vision of invasions, warfare, sieges and succession. It was because of this that accounts often focused on specific themes: the engineering of defences and evidence, where it was found, for assault, violent death and destruction. As the century passed, this idea became firmly embedded in the archaeological imagination. Though many hillforts were shown to be far older than Caesar, the image of fortified islands elevated above all else still chimed with the time. Hillforts or 'British camps' even featured in propaganda during the Second World War, creating a sense of deep, if fictive, roots for 'Fortress Britain'.

Who was being defended? Once again, interpretation has been quite singular, particularly in the second half of the twentieth century. More often than not, hillforts have been cast as the residences of elites who exercised control over, and drew tribute from, subordinates on scattered farms. The literature is stuffed with references to paramount chiefs and subordinate lineage heads, or to kings, lesser nobles and more lowly client farmers. Though the titles change between accounts, it is common to find hillforts at the pinnacle of an assumed settlement hierarchy, those within holding sway over production and exchange across broad 'estates' like some hybrid feudal system. Put simply, the scale of many hillforts and their physically elevated position has often been taken as a reflection of elevated political status. Places above the common herd who were forced by fealty, debt or threat to build the very defences from which they could be kept under a watchful eye.

Work in many regions suggests that most hillforts did witness occupation. But this was extremely varied, from large scale, ordered and persistent through to small and periodic. Fluctuations between these extremes can be found in the histories of single sites and there are some with little or no evidence for occupation at all. This sort of variety is likely to be found in the Peak itself. Whatever their origins, sites like Carl Wark or Castle Ring offered very different potentials to Mam Tor or Burr Tor. Mam Tor covers an area of around sixteen acres and contains over one hundred rough platforms, many of which may have once held buildings. These stand out so well, particularly in low light or after a dusting of snow, because they are cut back into the slope. Hillforts with more level interiors may contain similar structures which cannot now be traced by the eye, often because more recent ploughing has removed all trace of older arrangements. That said, it may be that low visibility actually reflects an absence of settlement, or occupation on a very different scale. The much smaller Carl Wark is liberally strewn with massive weathered earthfasts, and Castle Ring, if it was occupied at all, would have served as little more than an enclosed farmstead. Given this, it would be unhelpful to assume that all were used in the same ways or over the same time.

The pervasive image of chiefly residences is limiting in other ways as well. It fosters a sense of a stable hierarchy that misses both the contingency of the times and the specific histories of individual enclosures. Things were far more complex and far from constant. There were no doubt important differences of status within and between different lines, just as there were important divisions of kinship or affiliation. But these were still rather more fluid than we usually allow — varied from one place and time to another and continually being reworked through practices like exchange.

Where research has been extensive, a rather different image often emerges. In some areas, hillforts were constructed in landscapes that were already ordered, providing a periodic focus for a broader community rather than a hierarchical centre. Sometimes they were established in places that had a history of gatherings stretching back across the last few centuries of the second millennium. At the meeting point between different land boundaries and community 'territories'; on common grazing land; near older communal feasting sites. Where this happened, the first appearance of earthworks may not have marked a dramatic break with the past. Things continued much as they had before; people collecting for reasons of trade, to renew relations through feasting, exchange and display, and to reach agreements on upcoming tasks or disputed land. Practical and social concerns could be addressed, as could the fertility of the community and the renewal of the land. As with far older enclosures, there were times when a multitude gathered and times when interiors were all but deserted, wandered into by stock on the higher ranges of the summer. For communities of the time, a raised eye from settlements or from more distant pasture brought these dramatic monuments into view, a constant reminder of the broader pattern of the social world. In this, many of the enclosures of the first millennium display a far more consistent concern with visual prominence than their Neolithic counterparts. Perhaps this itself is an indicator that conditions were now more open.

It was only after several generations that things changed, enclosures becoming the focus for settlement. Even then, it is not easy to talk of hierarchies. Some with a penumbra of smaller satellite farmsteads may have been of elevated status, or came to assume that role over time. Others actually appear to be the home of almost all of the people responsible for working the land around. A sense of the collective, of a shared identity that encompassed boundaries, fields and stock. There may still have been differences of standing and authority even here, but they were not mapped in such a simple and direct way across the landscape as a whole.

Why was it necessary to make such a statement at this time? Why invest such massive quantities of labour in the cutting of ditches and the raising of banks; in the laying-out of dramatic earthworks that swept and folded around distinctive hills? A minimal answer would be that scattered lines had always recognised a broader world; it is simply that there were cycles in the extent to which that world was brought into focus through communal monuments or settlement on a substantial scale. Others have suggested tensions between different groups, perhaps even rival clans or tribes. Those tied by particular bonds of kinship chose to stamp their identity on an area in the creation of a refuge against the threat of physical attack. These tensions may have been exacerbated where wetter conditions encouraged changes in land use over time. This has some attractions, and gains support from the fact that inventories of contemporary metalwork show a high frequency of weapons. It has been pointed out, however, that many hillforts were so large that despite impressive physical barriers, they would have needed a vast population to make them work against all out attack. Many also seem too elaborate or over-designed for the purpose, or are set in the landscape so that they can be overlooked and easily breached. Evidence of attack or destruction can also be absent or thin on the ground.

This tempering of more bombastic statements has been necessary, though we should perhaps distinguish between baby and bathwater. In their settings and in the scale and character of their boundaries, many hillforts suggest that defence was an issue, even if it was often in symbolic terms. The fact that many seem 'over-designed' misses the point. Whatever the constellation of meanings that it carries, an elaborate or highly decorated 'display' sword is still a sword. The common arrangement of banks, ditches and ramparts suggests powerful concerns. The drawing of a line; a pattern to the approach and to entry; a barrier to access without consent; surveillance. The striking character and high visibility of many earthworks also suggests a concern with making that statement to a reasonably broad catchment. Us and them.

The extent to which these concerns were realised in outright conflict probably varied a good deal. A prime mover at some sites, a common theme at others; rare or absent at still more. Even when it was a strong concern, fighting at the time may have still been graded and rule-bound; endemic tensions and sporadic bouts or contests. What was more important was that the building of enclosures bound people together. There was the labour itself and the resulting dramatic visual statement for those who belonged as well as for others. Another related possibility is that many hillforts were a 'required barrier' because of changes in the use and perception of land. Arguments over access to different ranges may have become more strident as older, customary forms of tenure gave way to more exclusive concepts of territory. There may have been practical changes too. In many areas, the first millennium sees new patterns in environmental evidence. Though this does tend to vary, it is not uncommon to see the loss of woodlands on a hitherto unparalleled scale, extensive grasslands and crop cultivation and an increase in the scale of soil erosion. There are hints of this in the Peak. This could imply an intensification of agricultural production, but might also mean that the working of land was now organised at a somewhat broader social scale. These shifts of practice and perception may have sometimes run into other concerns: feuds, the creation of new alliances, attempts to carry authority across two generations, anxiety over the failure of crops or the death of stock. In certain places and times, there may have even been references to a mythic or heroic past, and to enclosures that had been standing on hillsides for more than a hundred generations.

These arguments are useful for thinking about enclosures in the Peak. Though we know relatively little, we can allow that there was some variety in the 'when' and the 'why' — in the conditions in which specific enclosures were constructed and used. One relatively common theme is the consistent relationship with land that offered shelter and/or good agricultural potential. Almost all sites in the Peak are set on shales and grits but have good access into a variety of landscape zones, including various parts of the Limestone Plateau. Burr Tor was raised not far from Abney Moor and from land where cairnfields, barrows and circles still show a presence of some antiquity. Fin Cop above the Wye stood close to stone sources that even at this stage were being exploited for working and trading. Chert was still finding its way to the Eastern Moors. There were also good and well-drained soils with rich potential and an outwork bank below the site may be the vestiges of a corral in which stock were brought for overwintering or on other occasions. How far these were places of persistent occupation is unclear. At least some of the material recovered from ploughed fields on Fin Cop is considerably older than the first millennium.

Variations in size also indicate that if occupation was an important theme, even if only for a time, it was not always set at the same scale. Ball Cross is characterised by a two-phased enclosure of stone and earth and encompasses an area of under two acres; far smaller than Mam Tor or Fin Cop. Castle Ring is even smaller, at less than one acre. Both could have served as heavily enclosed farmsteads or perhaps played more specialised

Castle Ring

roles. Similar purposes may have been served by other small enclosures; lines of earth and perhaps timber enclosing land in which relatively small numbers of people and animals dwelt at close quarters. One, also set on Harthill Moor and not far from Cratcliff Rocks, still bears the traces of one or two building platforms within its bounds. By this time, there were dense histories attached to these areas; the names of particular lines woven into field systems, cairns and older monuments. It may have been against this background that some of the larger enclosures were established as a way of marking the order of relations amongst a loose federation of communities.

This brings us to Mam Tor, 'mother' to the conical hills that have formed where shales have slid and weathered downslope. Set high above Castleton and looking across the Edale Valley towards Bleaklow and Kinder, the hill with its dramatic erosion scars bore the traces of earlier times. Two barrows stood within the circuit, one perhaps incorporated into the earthworks that define the perimeter. Given the lie of the land, the hill is well set on important lines of access from several directions. This may be why the barrows are here. It is also a distinctive feature for miles around, and can seem close by even from Stanage when the light is good. Two days walk with stock but so close you could throw a stone at it.

Mam Tor has some of the most dramatic features still to be seen in the Peak; details surviving because of elevation and slope. Beyond the single bank and ditch there is a counterscarp bank probably created by the routine maintenance of the ditch. There are also two inturned entrances; one to the north, the other to the south. The earthworks of the latter create a sort of funnel that leads one into the site and past one of the barrows that is set close by. Perhaps this was necessary; a way of keeping entrants under the eye and of bringing them close to a link with the mythic past. We do not know whether the barrow was still associated with the old names or had been given new ones by this time.

Looking at Mam Tor today, it is all too easy to see a unity in all the visible features; the ramparts and numerous platforms that pock mark the interior. We could however be looking at a sequence, some of the platforms older than the ramparts. What we do know is that the ramparts themselves were developed over time. Beyond routine maintenance and attendant embellishment, the enclosure appears to have been worked in phases. The perimeter started life as some form of palisade, a dramatic moment when large tracts of woodland were transformed into timber, an activity that itself involved many hands. Over time, the line gained a revetted stone rampart which was itself enlarged and augmented by the labour of large numbers of people. Seen at the time, this boundary would have been far more dramatic than the earthworks which now look as if they are being absorbed back into the hill. The making of a visual statement was a major concern here.

Only further work will reveal just how the platforms relate to the perimeter. Most are probably contemporary in a broad sense, but we do not yet know whether they represent permanent residences nor how long those dwellings persisted across the full history of the site. A visit to the hill in the depths of winter might raise questions about the sense of living all year round on the rise. Perhaps the changes in the perimeter itself suggest a change in use over time. Radiocarbon dates and artefact associations give a range that spans several centuries from the late second to earlier first millennium. These include numerous sherds of Late Bronze Age/Early Iron Age pottery and fragments of a lead rich, bronze socketed axe. The axe reminds us that lead itself was a resource that by this time had perhaps encouraged local forms of specialisation for trade and exchange.

Given the present state of knowledge, we can imagine several scenarios. Mam Tor had always been a place to be passed and a rise across which stock had grazed. The high point on a ridge that separates two important valleys, it was a place where paths crossed. Because of its setting, it may have emerged as a focal point for communities drawn from several directions. Land inbetween. Towards the end of the second millennium it took on a new significance as a more clearly defined place where various groups could meet to make agreements, trade and pass on information for the coming season. Where were the herds to be taken? Was it time to scratch for the soft grey stone that caught the light, to trade for copper from the south? What could be done to cool hot blood and appease troubled spirits? It may have been out of this sort of background that Mam Tor became a place of more persistent settlement. Unfavourable though it may seem to us, there may have been more powerful concerns that drew various lines into the place. Threat; a need to consolidate new alliances and patterns of land use in a new way of living. Maybe something of both. Even then, life may not have turned entirely around the enclosure. It probably still spread out to encompass other settlements and seasonal ranges.

Numerous platforms and a mass of pottery suggest a strong and persistent human presence at Mam Tor. That may not be something shared by all sites. Some may have started and ended their lives as places closely tied to the movement of stock, in which residence was never more than seasonal. This has been suggested for a number of smaller enclosures and for some of the larger sites such as Burr Tor and even Fin Cop. Both are situated so as to provide good access to extensive grazing and have a close link to water in the form of springs or perched water tables. Such a role may have been important where communities brought their animals together, or if the scale of herds had increased with time. Given that we know so little about the interiors and histories of these places, we cannot rule out the possibility that this sort of use persisted across several centuries. Not all took the steps seen at Mam Tor.

A new order?

Just how long places like Mam Tor remained as a focus for broad groups is far from clear. In some regions, there is good evidence to suggest that a number of hillforts continued to be important until the end of the millennium and the centuries around the Roman occupation. So far, this has yet to be demonstrated for the Peak and it may be that many local enclosures were abandoned by this time. Recognised and respected but from a certain distance.

It is against this uncertain background that some have suggested a dramatic phase of abandonment of much of the Peak during the Iron Age. Pointing to the lack of distinctive ceramics, to well-dated settlements or the sorts of material culture found in other regions, they argue that many parts of the region may have been left to their own devices, people retreating back down to the Trent Valley or into what is now South Yorkshire in the face of wetter conditions. Another 'fact' cited in this argument is the apparent late foundation for many of the settlements associated with the Roman period. Where investigated, many of these farmsteads, terraces and small enclosures reveal evidence for occupation from the first century AD onwards, and this is taken to suggest a period of recolonisation.

This argument now seems rather simplistic. Pollen cores from various parts of the East Moors, near places like Stoke Flat, point to a strong and persistent presence in the area. Though heather moorland was established on some ground, there was still plenty of maintained grassland and even crop cultivation in the area. There are even hints of a greater measure of soil loss towards the end of the period, as agricultural regimes finally put paid to extensive tracts of woodland and perhaps gained an intensity not seen before. Given the observations made above, it is quite conceivable that some of the field systems that we see continued in use a good deal of the way through the Iron Age.

Beyond the evidence of pollen, it is also likely that work on settlements of the first few centuries AD has tended to concentrate on what may be later features, or has been set at a scale inappropriate to identifying just how far the roots of occupation extended back into the past. In fact, there are places where just such evidence has been found, sites like Staden, Harborough Rocks and Chee Tor. It is also clear that many of the settlements which survive to be studied today do so because they are now on land that is considered marginal. Their counterparts on ground given different values since the Middle Ages have been all but obliterated by the plough. Coarse handmade pottery seldom survives all that long in such conditions. Beyond all this, it may be unhelpful to see abandonment simply

Ridge and furrow

because the Peak lacks the sorts of material culture found in other more extensively studied regions. Problems of visibility aside, it may well be that things were simply different here, taking another path to that seen in areas like Wessex, East Yorkshire or the Midlands.

Given these patterns, it makes little sense to imagine the wholesale abandonment of the region. The mass of farmsteads, 'Brickwork' and other field systems that threaded their way across areas like South Yorkshire at this time might indicate that some did move. Pushed perhaps by worsening conditions on higher ground or by shifts in the nature of landholding and allegiance. But these areas were not empty themselves and we should allow that our problem here is also one of recognition. Some land probably did fall out of occupation. Soils on parts of the gritstone became more acid, lost their fertility through overuse, or were washed from the hillsides in greater quantities. Grazing may have persisted even here, just as it does today. It was more that these areas were no longer 'settled' in quite the same way. This was probably not the case across the Peak as a whole. But here, the trail currently runs dry. The communities who continued to live and work across the limestone and many of the larger valleys have left little in the way of tracks for us to follow. Time and the plough have worn a hole in the pattern, and pollen gives us only a shadow.

There is a certain irony in the fact that the period of prehistory about which we know the least precedes a period where we actually have names for the first time. Often regarded as the threshold across which prehistory loses its prefix, the Roman period in the Peak brings the first references to specific tribes and to specific places. Time also becomes compressed; developments discussed at the scale of decades rather than centuries or millennia. This sense of specificity is deceptive. Because we know so little of the later stages of the Iron Age, we can only speculate about the impact of occupation on the region. We simply do not know what it meant to see new roads appear, or new forces assemble; to see old lines reworked and certainties broken.

Current evidence suggests that the Roman army and all that went with it were a presence in the Peak in the mid- to late first century AD. It is often assumed that occupation grew with Agricola's campaign against the *Brigantes* in the north. Forts were established at Brough in the Hope Valley and near Glossop; *Navio* and *Melandra* respectively. These acquired extensive settlements or *vici* in their environs, while modern Buxton also emerged as an important urban focus, *Aquae Arnemetiae*, in this case centred on the mineral springs.

Well-situated on communication routes and with good access to resources, these centres may have been grafted onto areas that had seen prior settlement. But the occupation changed things. Vici were effectively dependant settlements, ordered and on a scale not seen before. Comprising camp followers and the descendants of those who had lived in the Peak for generations, their population served the military in various ways; goods and services to the fort and probably to communities drawn in from the surrounding area. Though we know little in detail, Buxton may well have been what we would recognise as urban, a way of living quite at odds with that seen before. Beyond these centres, many smaller settlements were established in the first two centuries AD. Farmsteads with associated fields and terraces such as those still traceable on the hillsides of Roystone Grange, at North Lees or Bank Top near Hartington. Many of these appear to have flourished over several centuries; the working of land leaving the tell tale lynchets, field banks and ridges that catch the light at places like Chee Tor.

Beyond protecting lines of communication and the resources needed to support campaigns, the Peak had a rich potential. In addition to agricultural wealth, there was also an abundance of lead, as well as copper, silver and other minerals. Lead in particular appears to have been in great demand, extraction and processing perhaps operating as a dual economy for many communities across the region. Ingots or 'pigs' of lead from the Peak were exported out across the western empire, providing the raw materials for tableware, drains and other decorative items. Silver sometimes associated with lead ore was also used in Roman coinage.

If occupation changed the social geography of the region, it did so in ways that still elude us. Where landscapes were already rich in tribal and other associations, there may have been a measure of continuity; communities working new economic and political relations into an older fabric. This could serve a variety of interests. One of the hallmarks of the colonial process at this time was a strategy of grafting new attitudes, values and authorities onto older structures. Long-respected sacred sites were often appropriated and recast, a practice that implied continuity while at the same time leaving people in no doubt that there was a new order to things. This may be why we find material dating to this time left as offerings in a variety of settings; in caves and even at ancient tombs like Minninglow. How far this reflected the continuation of much older traditions of respect shown to local spirits is unclear. There may have also been times when acts of observance were undertaken to establish new claims to land and new senses of belonging. Perhaps these older spirits were now given new names drawn from a different pantheon.

Did the world change? It is possible that new forms of community may have been created in urban settings and where dependant settlement developed around places like *Navio* or *Melandra*. Patterns of residence here were no longer governed exclusively by traditional concepts such as kinship or descent. This may have remained important and was probably still a basic theme on many smaller farmsteads. But in some places at least, the new pattern of dwelling established different senses of social identity that cut across old boundaries. Just as Tin Town imposed a moral and social order on the Navvies working on the Derwent dams, so a *vicus* meant a different order to relations. A new way of living and perhaps a new way of thinking about society.

A mix of continuity and change could also be traced in various forms of exchange. The circulation and display of things had always been a way of addressing social relationships; of asserting identities and authorities. This did not stop, but it began to take on new forms as the material culture of the Roman world passed along established lines. Trade also established new forms of relationship between people, taxation and the market cutting across the essentially social bonds that had long been recognised between trading partners. Where the economy itself was reconfigured, new forms of trade established new forms of dependency and control.

For now, we must accept that there is much that we do not know. More recent colonial histories should remind us that we are dealing with complex processes. The exercise of new forms of control; the creation of new forms of community; assimilation, tension and resistance. A 'new order' that worked to the advantage of some and to the detriment of others. A political change that passed others by. It is hard to assess the shock of the new. For those who dwelt in urban settings, who dined with new forms of tableware and ate imported food, old authorities had found a new form of expression. For those who lived where they were told, encountered strange gods on every corner, and watched as roads and buildings emerged around them, subordination was different in character, but it was still subordination. Out in the hills perhaps, there were families who still maintained a distance.

. . . Time to sleep. The old man goes upstairs and into his room. Undressing, he crosses to the bed and at its side, reaches up to the window. He pulls the cord that runs out to the generator in the barn. Cuts it dead. Silence. The farmyard robbed of its steady thrum, he looks up to where the blackness of the slope gives way to stars . . .

10 Walking out

With dense fog ahead, it is sometimes best to turn back. Over a short span of words, we have crossed nearly ten thousand years. Profound changes in the character of society, and in the relationship between people and land. What emerges from the journey is an acknowledgement that the Peak is far from constant. It has been occupied and perceived in fundamentally different ways over time; landmarks worked and worked again as the social world slowly changed. It makes little sense to collapse this into a singular process, still less to call it progress. Things were simply different.

This difference is difficult to grasp, and in some respects will always lie beyond our reach. If it lies anywhere, it is in our imaginations. What we can say is that the worlds people inhabited in Prehistory were far from simple or small scale. Those we often caricature as hunters or as farmers recognised themselves in ways that were just as complex and confusing as our own.

What evidence we have suggests not just long-term change, but also cycles in the ways that people made sense of the world around them. A shift from social landscapes understood through reference to an ancestral past, to ones in which land itself emerged as a crucial hallmark of identity. A shift perhaps from a sense of tenure to be renewed, towards territory to be held. Horizons shifted too. With the benefit of long-term hindsight, the third and first millennia stand out as periods when the broader social world was emphasised in forms of communal activity that are more difficult to trace at other times. Whether or not this represents a genuine emphasis upon the local at those other times remains to be seen. Life was probably always extensive, albeit in different ways over our sequence. The crossing of trails, the working of stone and exchange amongst foragers; the circulation or display of Bronzes and the management of stock amongst small farming communities.

All of this played out across landscapes that were also historical. If life was geographically extensive, it had time depth as well. Here again, there are hints of cycles in the ways that people drew upon time itself. A sense of ancestry and the timeless past; the times of myth and genealogy. Complements rather than alternatives, these different themes seem to have been emphasised at different times (and of course, in different places). And always, running as a thread through these changes, were more local sequences of remembrance, forgetting and rediscovery. Monuments maintained, abandoned and recruited again.

One place catches this theme particularly strongly, and it is worth returning to end our journey there. We are back at Wigber Low, a limestone knoll in the south of the Peak. Just as the impression created by a visit can change according to the season, light and what we bring, so there are qualities to the relation between people and the crest over time that remain elusive. That said, there are outlines to be traced.

Our sequence at Wigber began in the fourth millennium, with the use of the knoll as a place where spirits could be liberated from the flesh by excarnation. How and for how long the place had been recognised prior to that we do not know. For the foragers and herders of the time, the crest, free of trees by then, was a place where bodies were temporarily laid within a low perimeter; stone the colour of bone itself. It was here that dead kin began their journey to the ancestral community, a journey in which animals and the elements helped in the passage. The threads of several families may have run through this place.

Wigber Low

By the third millennium, these old customs faded, though not perhaps all memory of them. The knoll became a focus for the dead themselves; bodies laid to rest more conclusively within a low cairn. It was no longer appropriate to take fresh bone back down, to circulate amongst the living or to be laid to rest elsewhere. What mattered now was that the dead should take up residence. From here, the ghosts of particular families could watch over the living as they turned on the seasonal wheel. See them take the cattle out each spring; watch over flocks on Haven Hill; remind others that the land had a specific history.

How long custom and familial memory persisted is impossible to tell. A few generations, maybe ten; who knows. There are no material signs that the place was remembered through active use during the second or first millennia BC. What people saw when they looked up is lost. Perhaps the place was lost as well.

It is this gap that makes the later sequence at Wigber so fascinating. The cairn/knoll was returned to much later, perhaps during the period of the Roman occupation. Like a number of older monuments, it may by then have been a site where offerings were left to local spirits. Different names perhaps to those that had been known a thousand or more years before. A few coins left each year or whenever the need arose; a token or what we would recognise as a hoard. But it was not until the Anglo-Saxon period, and around the seventh century AD, that burial rites trailed up the hill again. By this time, the region was known as the land of the Pecsaete, a client kingdom or satellite of Mercia. References to the region in the Tribal Hideage, written around this time, suggest a sizeable population, certainly one worth collecting tribute from.

At least five burials are known from this time; men, women and children laid to rest with a remarkable array of accompaniments. Spears, knives, gold and silver pins, pendants and brooches. In one grave, the body of a man and a woman lay side by side, the head of one turned to face the other. Across one body, a side of beef had been placed and between the two lay a fine, pattern-welded sword. In another lay a woman and a young child, a buckle from their clothing, a spear and an amber bead from the Baltic. The nature of these burials, like those in a number of reused prehistoric mounds, has led some to suggest that these were rites reserved for people of some standing. Many of the artefacts interred had their origins on the continent and their presence spoke of connections and genealogies that went far beyond the region. Swords in particular were powerful symbols with a potential for holding long biographies. Pattern welding is a long and skilful process designed to enhance the appearance of the blade. Some said that the lines on the metal resembled the scales of a dragon.

Why there and why then? What conditions prompted the rediscovery of the place and what, by then, did it mean? Perhaps local tradition drew people back at a time when burials were emerging again as important points of social reference. It has often been suggested that Anglian burials were set in mounds to act as landmarks. It may also be that appropriation by people who were new to the area was a way of laying claim to the land, of asserting a sense of belonging. An invention of tradition. In inserting new burials into a much older mound, what may have mattered was the creation of a link with mythic time. The barrow had always been there; it was part of the land. And now our dead are part of it too. Like the knoll, we are part of here.

We should also acknowledge that we are probably dealing with communities who recognised links with the cultural traditions of the Anglian homelands on the other side of the North Sea. In those traditions, barrow building was a remembered practice and burial mounds feature prominently in the literature of the time. That may be why communities in the south Peak came to fasten upon the place. In other parts of the area, they built new barrows or mistook knolls themselves as older mounds. But here, as elsewhere, the lie of the land acknowledged the presence of the dead. Where people drawn from particular lines, and/or individuals of some standing, were laid to rest in these ancient sites, connections were also being made with origin myths that stretched back across the water.

Burial mounds were a mark of respect and they required respect themselves. There are hints in sources from the time that barrows may have increasingly come to be regarded as places to be feared; associated with the threat of death and even monsters. Some even became places of execution, or the burial places of criminals and others who had offended the social code. Though it was probably not clear cut, this shift of emphasis may have accompanied the shifts in belief that unfolded between the earlier, Pagan, Anglo-Saxon

Wigber Low

period, and the later, Christian, phase. With time, the church as a political power may have seen these ancient sites as a threat to the new orthodoxy. It contained that threat by either incorporating or demonising them. Both may have happened here. Another amalgam of the old and the new.

The line at Wigber does not end there, though there is a break. The name itself persists, but we have little evidence for what the crest meant to people living and working across the area over the following thousand years or so. Medieval and later sources for the Peak contain many references to ancient monuments. Some were given names that located them within the origin myths of Christian society. A few were even highlighted; incorporated in Rogationtide processions, where priest and community beat the bounds and chased demons from the parish. And some were cast out, associated with evil and dangerous forces. This shift in the local and religious significance of stones, circles and old mounds would continue through until the reformation.

The thread gets picked up again with the interest of antiquarians, who followed Hayman Rooke's observation that there was 'hardly a crag, hill or an assemblage of rocks' that did not hold promise. It was work in the nineteenth century that brought many of the more spectacular grave goods to light. Just what this act of excavation may have meant to people like Rooke, Carrington or Bateman is itself difficult to pin down. A local interest; a duty to the discipline; a fascination with mortality. However these were combined, the act and the reporting that followed was itself a statement of identity. Disciplinary interest in the past was an expression of belonging to a particular part of society.

And then there is now. Wigber Low was excavated for the last time in the 1980s. Catalogues set great store on distinguishing antiquarian from modern excavation, largely on the basis of method and the quality of archives. But modern excavation is also a social act, one set in context. What were the motivations behind these more recent shifts in the profile of the knoll? Better understanding certainly; a clearer grasp of the material and the sequence to compare with other less well-recorded mounds. A better handle on the place; a sense of where it lay along an academic index of social evolution. The site was also chosen because of connections already made; links with people who lived and worked in the immediate area. Some of them chance — a convenient coincidence of academic interest and local availability.

The Low was also a venue for students to learn technique. Long drives out from Sheffield; wind that came uphill; several seasons in one day and never the one you expected. Laying out; cutting turf, trowelling and planning; always planning. The photographs; a particular vantage and a selection of elements deemed important. A certain point of view. People from different backgrounds working for a time as a small community. Learning how to work, learning how to get on, creating a sense of the past for themselves. Hearing how those who lived close by felt the place was cold; not understanding what they really meant.

Anatomised upon a grid, the cairn exists now as archive; the stones on the hill today a mound of our making. An old turf stack can still be seen on the rise. Each phase in its history exposed to scientific scrutiny, the site has nonetheless retained many of its secrets. What we have outlined here is no more than a shadow of events. Meaning slips through the mesh.

Like many monuments today, Wigber Low is prominent in other ways as well. It is recognised when people climb the hill on a day of escape, or by those looking for a landmark for their sense the spiritual. It is named when others draw a ruler line across the crest and on to other sites deemed appropriate for a Ley. And it is part of the day-to-day horizon of those who live locally. Often no more than a glance, but a named place; somewhere known through personal biography and the hearsay of academic myth.

Suggested reading

This book has drawn on a variety of sources, some of them dealing specifically with the Peak District, others more broad and thematic in their scope. For ease of reference, the list is subdivided on the basis of conventional archaeological periods. This goes a little against the grain of the way that the rest of the book is ordered, but it does avoid unnecessary repetition. Those looking for good introductions to some of the material and themes covered here would do well to start with *The Archaeology of Britain*, edited by John Hunter and Ian Ralston, and *The Peak District*, by John Barnatt and Ken Smith. Site specific information and more thematic discussions of the region can be found in the pages of the *Derbyshire Archaeological Journal*.

General perspectives and approaches

Ashmore, W. & Knapp, A.B. (eds.) 1999: *Archaeologies of landscape*. Oxford. Blackwells.

Aston, M. 1985: *Interpreting the landscape: Landscape archaeology in local studies*. London. Batsford.

Barnatt, J. & Smith, K. 1997: *The Peak district: Landscapes through time*. London. Batsford.

Barrett, J.C. 1994: *Fragments from Antiquity*. Oxford. Blackwells.

Bender, B. 1993: *Landscape: Politics and perspectives*. Oxford. Berg.

Bradley, R. 1998 *The significance of monuments*. London. Routledge.

Bradley, R. 2000. *The archaeology of natural places*. London. Routledge.

Cohen, A.P. 1985: *The symbolic construction of community*. London. Routledge.

Evans, J. 1999: *Land and archaeology: Histories of human environment*. Stroud. Tempus.

Fleming, A. 1990: 'Landscape archaeology, prehistory and rural studies', *Rural history* 1.1: 5-15.

Hodges, R. 1991: *Wall to Wall History*. Bristol. Duckworth.

Hunter, J. & Ralston, I. (eds.) *The archaeology of Britain*. London. Routledge.

Lowenthal, D. 1991: 'British national identity and the English landscape', *Rural history* 2: 205-30.

Muir, R. 1999: *Approaches to landscape*. Macmillan. London.

Schama, S. 1995: *Landscape and memory*. London. Harper and Collins.

Tilley, C. 1994: *A phenomenology of landscape*. Oxford. Berg.

Ucko, P. & Layton, R. (eds) 1999: *The archaeology and anthropology of Landscape*. London. Routledge.

World archaeology 1998: *The past in the past*. Vol. 30 (1).

Palaeolithic and Mesolithic

There are only a few overviews on the Palaeolithic and Mesolithic in Britain (Barton 1998, 1999; Mithen 1999; Smith 1992), and relatively little on the Peak in particular (Hart 1981). The titles listed below provide a way in to the more general literature. References have also been included to give a sense of the continental context of developments.

Barton, N. 1998: *Stone Age Britain*. London. Batsford.

Barton, N. 1999: 'The late glacial or Late and Final Upper Palaeolithic colonisation of Britain' in Hunter, J. & Ralston, I. (eds.) *The archaeology of Britain*: 13-34. London. Routledge.

Housley, R., Gamble, C., Street, M. & Pettit, P. 1997: 'Radiocarbon evidence for the Late glacial human recolonisation of Northern Europe', *Proceedings of the Prehistoric Society* 63: 25-54.

Bonsall, C. 1985: *The Mesolithic in Europe*. Edinburgh. John Donald.

Brooks, I. & Phillips, P. (eds.) 1989: *Breaking the stony silence*. British Archaeological Reports 213. Oxford. BAR.

Brown, A. 1997: 'Clearances and clearings. Deforestation in the Mesolithic and Neolithic', *Oxford Journal of Archaeology*.

Brown, A.G. & Edmonds M.R. (eds.) 1987: *Lithic Analysis and Later British Prehistory*. British Archaeological Reports 162. Oxford.

Clarke, D.L. 1976: 'Mesolithic Europe: the economic basis', in G. de G. Sieveking, I.H. Longworth & K.E. Wilson (eds.) *Problems in economic and social archaeology*: 449-81. Bristol. Duckworth.

Gamble, C. 1998: *Palaeolithic societies*. Cambridge. Cambridge University Press.

Hart, C. 1981: *The North Derbyshire Archaeological Survey*. North Derbyshire Archaeological Trust. Chesterfield.

Jacobi, R.M. 1976: 'Britain inside and outside Mesolithic Europe', *Proceedings of the Prehistoric Society* 42: 67-84.

Jacobi, R.M., Tallis, J.H. & Mellars, P. 1976: 'The southern Pennine Mesolithic and the ecological record', *Journal of Archaeological Science*. 3: 307-20.

Mellars, P. 1976a: 'Settlement patterns and industrial variability in the British Mesolithic' in G. de G. Sieveking, I.H. Longworth & K.E. Wilson (eds.) *Problems in economic and social archaeology*, 375-99. Bristol. Duckworth.

Mellars, P. 1976b: 'Fire ecology, animal populations and Man: a study of some ecological relationships', *Proceedings of the Prehistoric Society* 42: 15-45.

Mithen, S. J. 1999: 'The Mesolithic' in Hunter, J. & Ralston, I (eds) *The archaeology of the British Isles*. London. Routledge.

Myers, A. 1989: 'Reliable and maintainable technological strategies in the Mesolithic of Mainland Britain' in Torrence, R. (ed.) *Time, energy and stone tools*. Cambridge. Cambridge University Press.

Rowley-Conwy, P., Zvelebil, M. & Blankholm, H. (eds.) 1987: *Mesolithic north-west Europe: Recent trends*. Sheffield. J. Collis publications.

Smith, C. 1992: *Late Stone age hunters of the British Isles*. London. Routledge.

Tilley, C. 1994: *A phenomenology of landscape*. Oxford. Berg.

Neolithic

There are several good syntheses on the character of life in the fourth and third millennia. A good start is Alasdair Whittle's discussion in *The archaeology of Britain* an excellent introduction (Whittle 1999). Also valuable is *Understanding the Neolithic*, a significant rewriting of an earlier book by Julian Thomas (Thomas 1999). For a continental perspective, see Whittle 1996.

Ainsworth, S. & Barnatt, J. 1998. 'A scarp edge enclosure at Gardom's Edge, Baslow, Derbyshire', *Derbyshire Archaeological Journal*.

Barnatt, J. 1995: 'Neolithic and Bronze Age radiocarbon dates from the Peak District: A review', *Derbyshire Archaeological Journal* 115, 5-19.

Barnatt, J. 1996: 'Moving between the monuments: Paths and people in the Neolithic landscapes of the Peak District', *Northern Archaeology* 13/14: 45-62.

Barrett, J.C. 1988: 'The living, the dead, and the ancestors: Neolithic and Early Bronze Age mortuary practices' in J.C. Barrett and I.A. Kinnes (eds.) *The Archaeology of Context in the Neolithic and Bronze Age* 30-41. Department of Archaeology and Prehistory. Sheffield.

Barrett, J.C. 1994: *Fragments from antiquity*. Oxford. Blackwells.

Bender, B. 1978: 'Gatherer-hunter to farmer: a social perspective', *World Archaeology* 10: 204-22.

Bender, B. (ed.) 1992: *Landscape, politics and perspectives*. Oxford. Berg.

Bradley, R. 1998: *The significance of monuments*. London. Routledge.

Bradley, R. & Edmonds, M. 1993: *Interpreting the axe trade*. Cambridge. Cambridge University Press.

Darvill, T. & Thomas, J. (eds.) 1996: *Neolithic houses in north-west Europe and beyond*. Oxbow Monograph 57. Oxford.

Edmonds, M. 1999: *Ancestral geographies*. London. Routledge.

Entwistle, R. & Grant, A. 1989: 'The evidence for cereal cultivation and animal husbandry in the southern British Neolithic and Bronze Age' in A. Miles, D. Williams and N. Gardner (eds.) *The Beginnings of Agriculture*, 203-215. Oxford: British Archaeological Reports s496.

Evans, C., Pollard, J. & Knight, M. 1999: 'Life in woods', *Oxford Journal of Archaeology* Vol 18 No 3. 241-254.

Fleming, A. 1973: 'Tombs for the living', *Man* 8, 177-193.

Garton, D. 1991: 'The Neolithic' in Hodges, R. & Smith, K. (eds) *Recent developments in the archaeology of the Peak district*. Sheffield. Sheffield Archaeological Monographs 2.

Henson, D. 1989: 'Away from the core? A northerner's view of flint exploitation' in Brooks, I. & Phillips, P. (eds.) *Breaking the stony silence*. 5-31. British Archaeological Reports 213. Oxford.

Hicks, S.P. 1971: 'Pollen analytical evidence for the effect of prehistoric agriculture on the vegetation of North Derbyshire', *New Phytologist* 70: 647-67.

Hicks, S. 1972: 'The impact of man on the east moor of Derbyshire from Mesolithic times', *Archaeological Journal* 129: 1-21.

Kinnes, I. 1988: 'The Cattleship Potemkin: The first Neolithic in Britain' in J. Barrett & I. Kinnes (eds.) *The Archaeology of Context in the Neolithic and Bronze Age: Recent Trends*, 2-8. Sheffield: Department of Archaeology and Prehistory.

Makepeace, G.A. 1999: 'Cratcliffe Rocks — a forgotten hillfort on Harthill Moor near Bakewell, Derbyshire', *Derbyshire Archaeological Journal* 119, 12-18.

Moffett, L., Robinson, M.A. and Straker, V. 1989: 'Cereals, fruit and nuts: charred plant remains from Neolithic sites in England and Wales and the Neolithic economy' in A. Milles, D. Williams and N. Gardner (eds.) *The Beginnings of Agriculture*, 243-261. Oxford: British Archaeological Reports 496.

Pluccienik, M. 1998: 'Deconstructing "The Neolithic" in the Mesolithic-Neolithic transition' in Edmonds, M.R. & Richards, C. (eds.) *Social Life and social change in the Neolithic of north-western Europe*. Glasgow. Cruithne Press.

Pollard, J. 1999: 'These places have their moments. Occupation practices in the British Neolithic' in Bruck, J. & Goodman, M. *Making places in the prehistoric world: themes in settlement archaeology*. London. Longmans.

Thomas, J. 1999: *Understanding the Neolithic*. London. Routledge.

Topping, P. (ed.) 1998: *Neolithic landscapes*. Oxford. Oxbow monograph.

Tilley, C. 1994: *A phenomenology of landscape*. Oxford. Berg.

Wainwright, G.J. 1989: *The Henge monuments*. London. Thames and Hudson.

Whittle, A.W.R. 1996: *The creation of new worlds*. Cambridge. Cambridge University Press.

Whittle, A., Pollard, J. & Grigson, C. 1999: *The harmony of symbols: The Windmill Hill causewayed enclosure*. Oxford. Oxbow.

Zvelebil, M. 1998: 'What's in a name: The Mesolithic, the Neolithic and social change at the Mesolithic-Neolithic transition' in Edmonds, M.R. & Richards, C. (eds.) *Social Life and social change in the Neolithic of north-western Europe*. Glasgow. Cruithne Press.

Bronze Age

Good reviews of evidence and interpretation for the Earlier and Later Bronze Age can be found in Parker Pearson (1992, 1999) and Champion (1999). For an account that takes the entire sequence, see Barrett (1994). For stone circles and ringcairns, Aubrey Burl's work (1976) is a model of clarity and a mine of information on these monuments across the country as a whole. John Barnatt (1990) has also provided a valuable gazetteer and discussion of monuments found in the Peak. Details on the character, content and distribution of barrows can be found in Barnatt & Collis (1996). Richard Bradley's (1993, 1998) work on monuments and their character and significance is an excellent place to begin.

Barnatt, J. 1986: 'Bronze Age remains on the East Moors of the Peak District', *Derbyshire Archaeological Journal* 106: 18-100.

Barnatt, J. 1990: *The henges, stone circles and ringcairns of the Peak District*. Sheffield. Department of Archaeology & Prehistory.

Barnatt, J. 1994: 'Excavations of a Bronze Age unenclosed cemetery, cairns and field boundaries at Eaglestone Flat, Curbar, Derbyshire', *Proceedings of the Prehistoric Society* 60:287-370.

Barnatt, J. 1998: 'Monuments in the landscape: thoughts from the Peak' in A. Gibson and D. Simpson (eds.) *Prehistoric Ritual and Religion*. Stroud. Sutton.

Barnatt, J. 1999: 'Taming the land: Peak District farming and ritual in the Bronze Age', *Derbyshire Archaeological Journal* 119: 19-78.

Barnatt, J. 2000: 'To each their own: later prehistoric farming communities and their monuments in the Peak', *Derbyshire Archaeological Journal* 120: 1-86.

Barnatt, J. & Collis, J. (eds.) 1996: *Barrows in the Peak District: Recent Research*. Sheffield. Sheffield University Press.

Barrett, J.C. 1994: *Fragments from Antiquity*. Oxford. Blackwells.

Barrett, J.C. & Bradley, R. (eds.) 1980: *Settlement and society in the British Later Bronze Age*. British Archaeological Reports 83. Oxford. BAR.

Barrett, J.C. & Kinnes, I.A. (eds.) 1988: *The Archaeology of Context in the Neolithic and Bronze Age*. Sheffield: Department of Archaeology and Prehistory.

Bateman, T. 1848: *Vestiges of the antiquities of Derbyshire*. London.

Bateman, T. 1861: *Ten years' diggings in Celtic and Saxon Grave Hills in the Counties of Derby, Stafford and York from 1848-1858*. London.

Beswick, P. & Merrills, D. 1983: 'L.H. Butcher's survey of early settlements and fields in the southern Pennines', *Transactions of the Hunter Archaeological Society* 12: 16-50.

Bradley, R.J. 1990: *The passage of arms*. Cambridge. Cambridge University Press.

Bradley, R.J. 1993: *Altering the earth*. Edinburgh. Soc. Antiquaries of Scotland.

Bradley, R. 1997: *Signing the land: Rock art and the prehistory of Atlantic Europe*. London. Routledge.

Bradley, R. 1998: *The significance of monuments*. London. Routledge.

Burl, H.A.W. 1976: *Stone Circles of the British Isles*. Yale. Yale University Press.

Champion, T.C. 1999: 'The Later Bronze Age' in Hunter, J. & Ralston, I. (eds.) *The archaeology of Britain*. London. Routledge.

Clarke, D.V., Cowie, T. and Foxon, A. 1985: *Symbols of Power at the Time of Stonehenge*. Edinburgh: National Museum of Antiquity.

Fleming, A. 1987: *The Dartmoor Reaves*. London. Batsford.

Garwood, P. 1991: 'Ritual tradition and the reconstruction of society' in Garwood, P., Skeates, R. & Toms, J. (eds.) *Sacred and Profane*. 10-32. Oxford. Oxford University Committee for Archaeology, Monograph 32.

Gibson, A. & Simpson, D. 1998: *Prehistoric Ritual and religion*. Stroud. Sutton.

Gosden, C. 1993: *Social being and time*. Oxford. Blackwells.

Hart, C. 1981: *The North Derbyshire Archaeological Survey*. Chesterfield. North Derbyshire Archaeological Trust.

Long, D.J., Chambers, F.M. & Barnatt, J. 1998: 'The palaeoenvironment and vegetational history of a later prehistoric field system at Stoke Flat on the gritstone uplands of the Peak District', *Journal of Archaeological Science*. 25: 505-519.

Parker-Pearson, M. 1992: *The Bronze Age*. London. Batsford.

Parker-Pearson, M. 1999: 'The Earlier Bronze Age' in Hunter, J. & Ralston, I. (eds.) *The archaeology of Britain*. London. Routledge.

Pryor, F. 1999: *Farmers in prehistoric Britain*. Stroud. Tempus.

Radley, J. 1969: 'A triple cairn and a rectangular cairn of the Bronze Age on Beeley Moor', *Derbyshire Archaeological Journal* 89: 1-17.

Rowlands, M.J. 1976: *The Production and Distribution of Metalwork in the Middle Bronze Age in Southern Britain*. British Archaeological Reports 32. Oxford. BAR.

Young, R. & Simmonds, T. 1995: 'Marginality and the nature of later prehistoric upland settlement in the north of England', *Landscape History* Vol 17: 5-16.

Iron Age

There are several good syntheses and general volumes on the Iron Age, but little on the Peak at this time. The reasons for this, and the exceptions to the rule, can be found in papers by Bill Bevan.

Barrett, J. 1999: 'The Mythical Landscapes of the British Iron Age' in W. Ashmore and A.B. Knapp (eds.) *Archaeologies of Landscape*. London. Blackwell: 253-268.

Bevan, B. (ed.) 1999: *Northern exposure: Interpretative devolution and the Iron Ages in Britain*. Leicester. Leicester Archaeological Monographs 4. School of Archaeological Studies.

Bevan, B. 2000: 'Peak Practice: Whatever happened to the Iron Age in the southern Pennines?' in Harding, J., Johnson, R. & Pollard, J. (eds.) *Northern Pasts*. 141-156. Stroud. Tempus.

Bowden, M. & McOmish, D. 1987: 'The Required Barrier', *Scottish Archaeological Review* 4, 76-84.

Bowden, M. & McOmish, D. 1989: 'Little Boxes: More About Hillforts', *Scottish Archaeological Review* 6, 12-16.

Bradley, R., Entwistle, R. & Raymond, F. 1994: *The prehistoric land divisions of Salisbury Plain*. English Heritage monograph.

Coombs, D. & Thompson, H. 1979: 'Excavations of the hillfort of Mam Tor, Derbyshire 1965-1969', *Derbyshire Archaeological Journal* 99: 44-47.

Cunliffe, B. 1995: *Iron Age Britain*. London. Batsford.

Chadwick, A. 1996: 'Towards a social archaeology of later prehistoric and Romano-British field systems in South Yorkshire, West Yorkshire and Nottinghamshire', http://www.shef.ac.uk/~assem/2/2chad.html

Challis, A.J. & Harding, D.W. 1975: 'Later Prehistory from the Trent to the Tyne', Parts I and II. BAR 20 (i/ii). Oxford, British Archaeological Reports.

Champion, T.C. & Collis J.R. (eds.) 1996: *The Iron Age in Britain and Ireland: recent trends*. Sheffield, J.R. Collis Publications.

Collis, J.R. (ed.) 1977: *The Iron Age in Britain: a review*. Sheffield. Dept of Prehistory and Archaeology.

Collis, J.R. 1994. 'The Iron Age' in B. Vyner (ed.) 1994. *Building on the Past: a celebration of 150 years of the Royal Archaeological Institute*: 123-148.

Gosden, C. and Locke, G. 1998: *Prehistoric histories*. World Archaeology vol. 30 (1): 2-12.

Guilbert G.C. (ed.) 1981: *Hill-Fort Studies: essays for A.H.A. Hogg*. Leicester, University Press.

Gwilt, A. & Haselgrove, C. (eds.) 1997. 'Reconstructing Iron Age Societies'. Oxbow Monograph 71. Oxford. Oxbow.

Hingley, R. 1989: *Rural settlement in Roman Britain*. Seaby.

Hodges, R. & Smith, K. 1991: *Recent developments in the archaeology of the Peak District*. Sheffield. J.R. Collis Publications.

Makepeace, G.A. 1998: 'Romano British Settlement in the Peak District and North-East Staffordshire', *Derbyshire Archaeological Journal* 118: 95-138.

Grid references

A wide variety of sites and landscapes have been mentioned in this book. What follows are the grid references for many of these, so that those wishing to chase places on the map or on the ground may do so. The list is not exhaustive, particularly for later Neolithic and Early Bronze Age barrows. Those after a more complete inventory and more detail are advised to refer to the corpus by John Barnatt and John Collis (1996). Grid references and further information on other sites and landscapes in the region can be found in sources on the list of suggested reading.

Long barrows

Harrod Low	SK 09848058
Longstone Moor	SK 19797476
Gib Hill	SK 15826332
Minninglow	SK 20955728
Rockhurst	SK 21415736
Bull Ring	SK 07807817
The Tong	SK 11697698
Gospel Hillocks	SK 08637148
Perryfoot	SK 10928119

Chambered tombs

Five Wells	SK 12377105
Minninglow	SK 20955728
Green Low	SK 23165805
Harborough Rocks	SK 23895490
Stoney Low	SK 21855783
Pea Low	SK 13075646
Tideslow	SK 15007795
Ringham Low	SK 16956642
Long Low	SK 12165399
Wind Low	SK 11457517
Smerrill Moor	SK 18666080

Henges, stone circles and ringcairns

Arbor Low	SK 16036355
Bull Ring	SK 07847823
Seven Stones of Hordron	SK 21518684
Gibbett Moor North	SK 28217085
Eyam Moor III	SK 23227879
Doll Tor	SK 23856287
Nine Stone Close	SK 22546264
Ewden Beck	SK 23819664
Ash Cabin Flat	SK 26938625
Bamford Moor South	SK 22118454
Stoke Flat	SK 24957678
Brown Edge	SK 28837899
Barbrook I	SK 27857558
Barbrook II	SK 27757581
Barbrook III	SK 28337729
Gibbett Moor South	SK 28107027
Park Gate	SK 28056851
Offerton Moor	SK 21288054
Smelting Hill	SK 20278039
Wet Withens	SK 22557899
Eyam Moor II	SK 23157895
Stanton Moor I	SK 24946367
Nine Ladies	SK 24916349
Stanton Moor III	SK 24806327
Stanton Moor IV	SK 24716290

Bar Dyke	SK 244994559
Bamford Moor North	SK 20898526
Hathersage Moor	SK 25688094
Cicely Low North	SK 27528080
Cicely Low South	SK 27518078
Big Moor	SK 26957515
Ramsley Moor	SK 28957562
Birchen Edge North	SK 28517346
Birchen Edge South	SK 28177239
Gardom's Edge	SK 27447239
Beeley Warren NW	SK 27776872
Beeley Warren NE	SK 27946888
Beeley Moor North	SK 28536769
Beeley Moor South	SK 28536767

Hillforts and other enclosures

Fin Cop	SK 175710
Mam Tor	SK 128836
Ball Cross	SK 227691
Burr Tor	SK 108783
Castle Ring	SK 221628
Combs Moss	SK 055783
Carl Wark	SK 259815
Cratcliffe Rocks	SK 228623
Gardom's Edge	SK 278733
Markland Grips	SK 519752

Round barrows and cairns

Eldon Hill	SK 11548114
Bull Ring	SK 07807817
Snels Low	SK 11897942
Cow Low	SK 10277297
Wind Low	SK 11457517
Withery Low	SK 10177650
Dirt Low	SK 15558229
Tup Low	SK 18717699
Cop Low	SK 18697725
Hay Top	SK 17707310
Hay Dale	SK 18267276
Longstone Moor	SK 18887328

Longstone Moor	SK 19007365
Longstone Moor	SK 19797476
High Rake	SK 20887342
Fin Cop	SK 17447093
High Low	SK 08297148
Chelmorton Lows	SK 11407062
Slipper Low	SK 14107065
Sheldon	SK 16836925
Grindlow	SK 20066734
Haddon fields	SK 21726617
Grin Low	SK 05397174
Brown Edge	SK 06896787
Glutton Hill	SK 08076723
Nether Low	SK 10886917
Chelmorton Thorn	SK 11866955
Cronkstone Low	SK 11706631
Pilsbury	SK 12086395
Lean Low	SK 14966223
Moneystones	SK 15086163
Moneystones	SK 15176152
End Low	SK 15606056
Aleck Low	SK 17495947
Bank Top	SK 12846145
One Ash	SK 16626437
Middleton Moor	SK 15296384
Gib Hill	SK 15826332
Calling Low	SK 17486487
Bee Low	SK 19166473
Lark's Low	SK 20086260
Kenslow Knoll	SK 18426171
Borther Low	SK 19716086
Wolfscote Hill	SK 13705832
Liff's Low	SK 15315766
Hawks Low	SK 17025674
The Lowe	SK 15965560
Sharp Low	SK16135286
Roystone Grange	SK 20355710
Roystone Grange	SK 20355650
Slipper Low	SK 22075699
Round Low	SK 23895490
Hanging bank	SK 09985800
Ecton Hill	SK 09675736
Wetton Hill	SK 10495623
Gratton Hill	SK 13195715

Stanshope Pasture	SK 13855369	Bamford Edge	SK 21348436
Ilam Tops Low	SK 13585269	Dennis Knoll	SK 22828405
Ilam Moor	SK 13595213	Sheepwash Bank	SK 23008418
Mouse Low	SK 08735335	North Lees	SK 23668366
Grub Low	SK 08045254	Big Moor	SK 27557550
Mare Hill	SK 10535259	Big Moor	SK 27137543
Rushley	SK 11985147	Stoke Flat	SK 24927665
Musden Low	SK 11835008	Curbar Edge	SK 25497560
Thorncliff Low	SK 11344951	Birchen Edge	SK 28277357
Dun Low	SK 11944940	Three Men	SK 27147279
Top Low	SK 12964914	Gibbett Moor	SK 28147075
Nettles	SK 13384915	Rod Knoll	SK 30186986
Weaver Hills	SK 09424655	Harland Edge	SK 28916876
Calton Moor	SK 11114867	Beeley Warren	SK 27826849
Hognaston	SK 24445151	Beeley Moor	SK 28576719
Ows Low	SK 23805267	Beeley Warren	SK 28596827
Stand Low	SK 21325086	Raven Tor	SK 27986649
Wigber Low	SK 20425143	Fallinge Edge	SK 27746591
Lady Low	SK 13934983	Offerton Moor	SK 20678062
Calwich	SK 13174389	Highlow Bank	SK 21128025
Three Lows	SK 07524634	Abney Moor	SK 18807920
Kinder Low	SK 07328666	Eyam Edge	SK 20477769
The Lord's seat	SK 11238346	Stanage	SK 21547865
Mam Tor	SK 12688356	Wet Withens	SK 22557904
Coombe Edge	SK 02049189	Eyam Moor	SK 22237856
Cow Low	SK 06537869	Calton Pasture	SK 23386854
Brown Low	SJ 98829092	Stanton Moor	SK 25136331
Ludworth intake	SJ 98989131	Stanton Moor	SK 24686278
Lyme Park	SJ 96468175		
Sponds Hill	SJ 97008024		
Blackrock Farm	SJ 95857662		
Coatestown	SK 06276631		

Caves

The Roaches	SK 00116388	Calling Low Dale	SK 18376541
Booth Low	SK 08786314	Dowel Cave	SK 07566759
Brund Low	SK 10256182	One Ash Shelter	SK 17266559
Hurst Low	SK 07055529	Ravenscliffe Cave	SK 17397356
Grindon Moor	SK 07075518	Thor's Cave	SK 09865496
Crow Chin	SK 22468562	Carsington Pasture Cave	SK 24155368
Higgar Lodge	SK 25208148	Demons Dle Cave	SK 16897045
Winyards Nick	SK 25328127	Elder Bush Cave	SK 09785486
Toads Mouth	SK 25788058	Fox Hole Cave	SK 09986617
Pike Low	SK 18048976	Harborough Cave	SK 24225523
Bamford Moor	SK 21608587	Ossom's crag Cave	SK 09585576
Bamford Moor	SK 21398479	Thor's Fissure Cave	SK 09855496

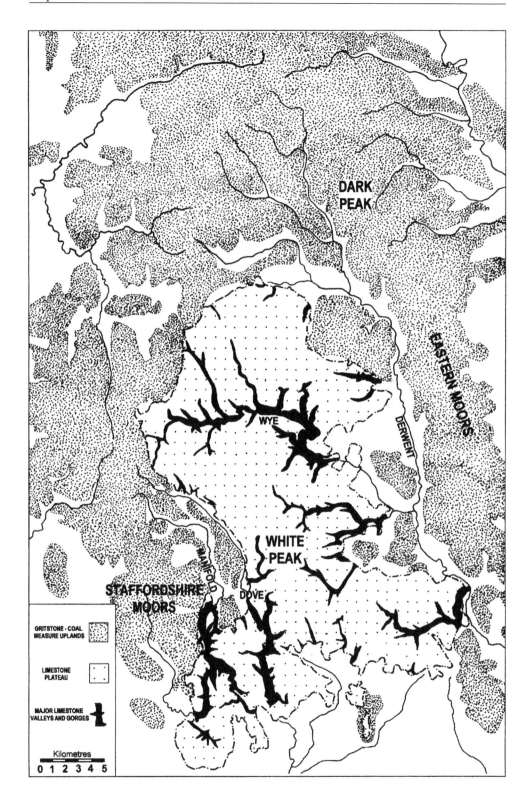

DARK
PEAK

EASTERN MOORS

WYE

DERWENT

WHITE
PEAK

MANIFOLD

STAFFORDSHIRE
MOORS

DOVE

GRITSTONE - COAL
MEASURE UPLANDS

LIMESTONE
PLATEAU

MAJOR LIMESTONE
VALLEYS AND GORGES

Kilometres
0 1 2 3 4 5

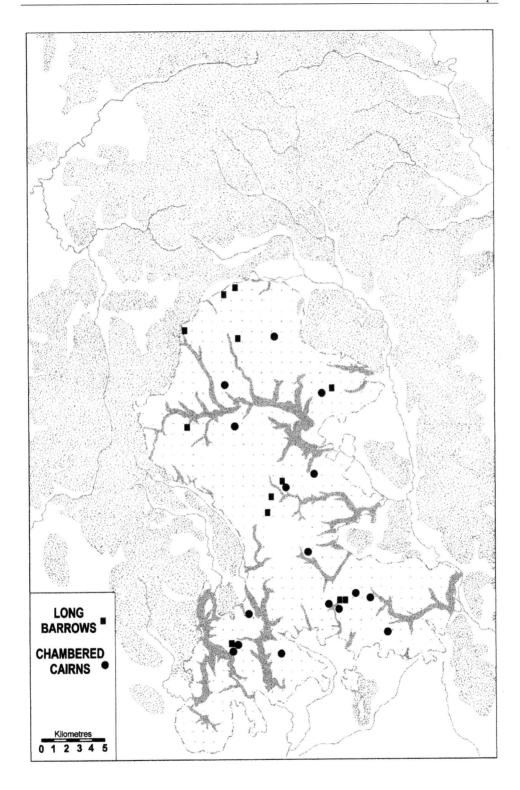

LONG
BARROWS ■

CHAMBERED
CAIRNS ●

Kilometres
0 1 2 3 4 5

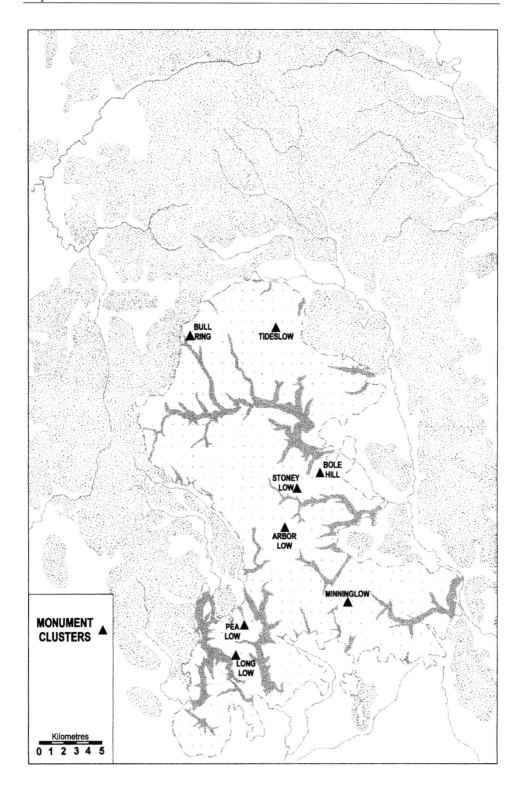

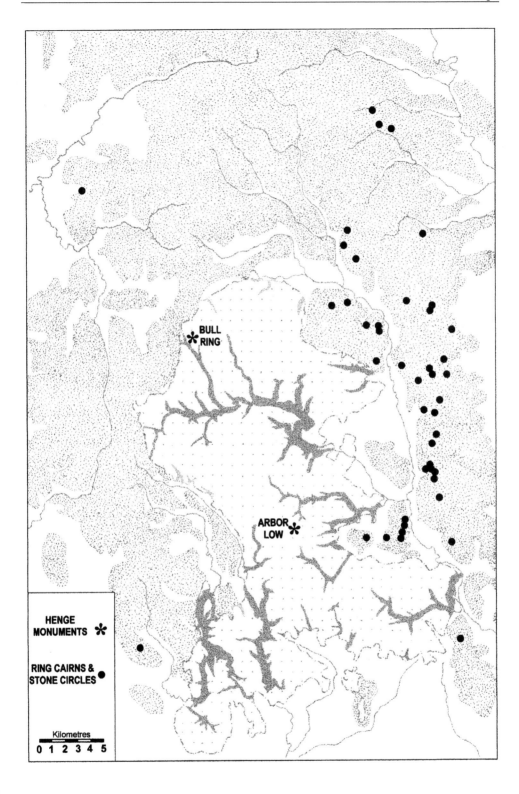

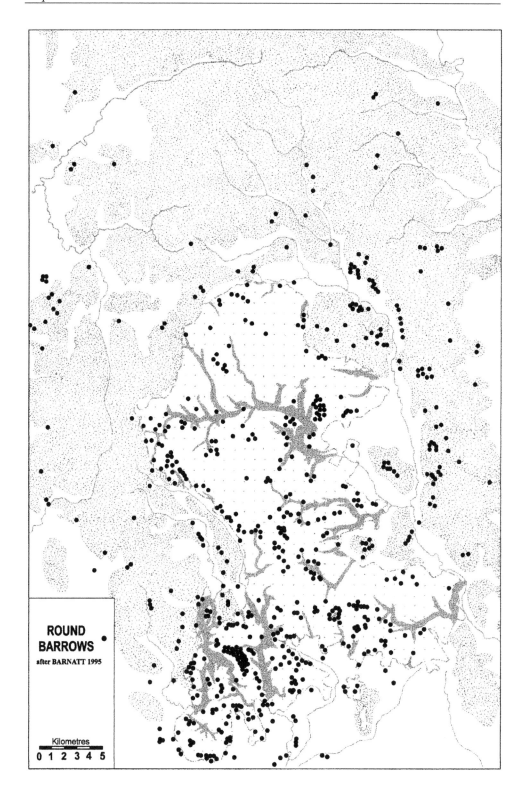

ROUND
BARROWS
after BARNATT 1995

Kilometres
0 1 2 3 4 5

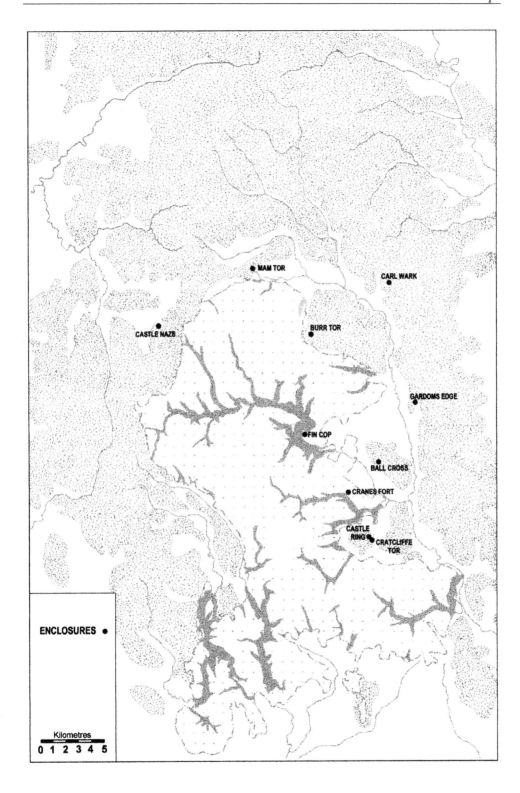

MAM TOR

CARL WARK

CASTLE NAZE

BURR TOR

GARDOMS EDGE

FIN COP

BALL CROSS

CRANES FORT

CASTLE RING

CRATCLIFFE TOR

ENCLOSURES ●

Kilometres
0 1 2 3 4 5

Index

If you are interested in purchasing
other books published by The History Press, or in case you have
difficulty finding any of our books in your local bookshop,
you can also place orders directly through our website

www.thehistorypress.co.uk